While the Children were Sleeping

COMBE, JESSOP & CADDY families

Combe line

Robert (Roy) Nicholson Combe (1878-1941) = Hilda Engelhardt (1880-1973)

Children:
- Robert (Nick) 1907-2002 *had issue*
- Janet 1909-1999
- Elizabeth 1910-1970
- Marion 1912-1990 *had issue*
- **Andrew Combe¹** 1911-1978

Jessop line

Albert Jessop (1885-1932) = Muriel Bull (1879-1936)

Ida (Florence) Jessop 1883-1973 *(had issue)*

Children of Albert & Muriel:
- Rex 1919-1941
- Patrick (Paddy) 1916-1988 = Joan Syrett 1916-1997 *had issue*
- Florence (Torrie) 1920- = Edward Hutchinson (Hutch) 1915-1983 *had issue*
- **Eileen Jessop** 1917-2006

Andrew Combe¹ 1911-1978 = Eileen Jessop 1917-2006

(Eileen =² **Peter Caddy** 1917-1994 *had other issue*)

Children of Andrew & Eileen:

Jennifer 1940- = Peter Hinton
+ Andrew, Georgina

Richard 1941- = Helen Harrod
+ Patricia, Stephen

Suzanne 1942-
¹=Allan Stormont
+ James, Jonathan
²=Grant Fraser

Mary Elizabeth 1947-
¹=Eric Shackleton
+ Garvin, Clive
²=Bruce Bell
+ Heather

Penelope 1951-
¹=Peter George
+ Tammy, Michael, Nicholas, Cathi
²=David Gorrie

Children of Eileen & Peter Caddy:

Christopher 1955- = Judith Burden
+ Timothy, Thalia, Tegan, Travis

Jonathan 1956-
¹=Karen Hood
+ Jason
²=Alison Hunter
+ Caitlin

David 1958- = Kathleen Crisp (Kacie)
+ Arran

WHILE THE CHILDREN WERE SLEEPING

ΦΦΦ

JENNY HINTON

ASTRA
Books

*Dedicated, in gratitude, to our parents,
Andrew and Eileen, who gave us life;
and to my brother Richard and sisters Suzanne,
Mary Liz and Penny, without whom this book
could not have been written.*

First published 2013
Revised edition 2014
Astra Books
Westbury Lodge
Arundel BN18 9RZ

© Jenny Hinton 2013
peter@hinton3.freeserve.co.uk

*The right of Jenny Hinton to be identified as the author of this book
has been asserted by her in accordance with the
Copyright, Designs and Patents Act 1988*

Designed and typeset by John Munro in Palatino 11 on 13.5pt
ISBN 978-0-9575120-1-6
Printed & bound by Berforts Information Press

CONTENTS

	Foreword by Canon Michael Cole	7
	Introduction	9
	Acknowledgements	15
Part I	1. The Bread-and-Dripping Years	19
	2. Challenges Ahead	32
	3. Of Sugar-plums, Cotton Fields & Home Sweet Home	40
	4. The Stage is Set	54
	5. Hoodwinked!	65
	6. Hijacked!	76
	7. The Spider's Parlour	80
	8. Soul-snatchers	87
	9. The Voice, the Choice and a Web of Lies	95
	10. "You'll be Sorry when I'm Gone"	106
	11. A Joyful Return?	119
	12. Divorce, and Life thereafter…	124
Part II	13. The London Years	141
	14. We Meet Again	155
	15. A Year of Travel and Revelation	163
	16. Glorious and Incontrovertible Evidence	179
	17. The Dynamic of Forgiveness	192

Part III	18.	All Change!	206
	19.	A Solitary Journey	220
	20.	Birth of a False Prophet?	230
	21.	A Wolf in Sheep's Clothing	245
	22.	Against Thy Divine Majesty	261
	23.	A Bucketful of Frogs	269
	24.	Fresh Insights	277
Part IV	25.	A Pathway towards Healing	287
	26.	Celebration!	299
	27.	Further Steps along the Path	307
		Poem for Eileen	321
	28.	A Long Summer of Bitter-Sweet Content	322
		Mother of the Daughter	341
	29.	Going Home	342
	30.	Desert Flowers	353
		Notes	364

FOREWORD

'While the Children were Sleeping' is a remarkable and genuine family story that covers four generations, living in different parts of the world.

It is also an account of a family that was attacked by the subtle and powerful influence of people controlled by, and seeking to promote, New Age philosophy; and to extend their influence world-wide through the establishment of the Findhorn Community, based in Scotland from the 1960's. Their world-view has quietly spread around the world, undermining and marginalising the three religions that have Abraham as their patriarch – Judaism, Christianity and Islam – since the New Age is an ideology aiming at a One World religion.

But it is also the story of a family, restored, healed and forgiven through the love of God and through the unchanging truth of their Christian faith that was maintained through regular reading of the Bible. There is much to encourage Christians facing similar spiritual attacks and battles that they can be victorious through the grace and power of God.

It was after church one Sunday morning in Funchal in Madeira in 2002 that my wife and I first met Jenny and Peter, her husband. It is a privilege to be invited to write this foreword and to commend, very warmly, 'While the Children were Sleeping'.

Canon Michael Cole

INTRODUCTION

THIS true family story begins with my parents, and is about how they went their different ways. It tells of their five children who were deeply affected by their parents' choices, and of what held the family together through rough seas. The plot only began to take shape in 1978 after our father's Thanksgiving Service at Hengrave Hall, in Suffolk, when four out of five of his offspring gathered to decide how to distribute his meagre possessions.

Hengrave rises up out of emerald parklands like a jewel in the Suffolk countryside. Built in 1525 by a rich cloth merchant, Sir Thomas Kytson, it has remained unchanged in its Tudor magnificence. By 1976 it was being run as a retreat and conference centre by a Roman Catholic order of nuns. My father was the resident maintenance man for the old building. Both he and the centre were deftly managed by Sister Warden with a handful of sisters, together with a few workers and supporters. These inspirational nuns had created a family-like community out of this varied bunch of individuals. My father's main frustration among many duties there was to keep the huge, antiquated boiler pumping to provide a hot-water system throughout the Hall for its visitors.

Being a practical man, Dad was always up for a challenge, and ready to put his hand to most things. He had retired early from the Royal Air Force as a Group Captain under the Golden Bowler scheme in the nineteen fifties. Since then he had tried his hand at selling encyclopaedias, operated in industry as a Work Study officer, and even served on the forecourt of a garage in the Fens – all such employment geared towards providing for himself and his family of five.

He died in March 1978, and his ashes lie buried in a

field beyond the beautiful little chapel, alongside the graves of several nuns and former members of the community. It was early April and very cold. We four gathered in his icy room in one of the smaller dwellings behind the Hall. There was no will to read and no estate since all had been spent on his children's education.

My younger brother Richard, the only male heir, took charge of all Dad's memorabilia accumulated since his Royal Air Force career and adventures dating from his training at Cranwell College, followed by his world record long-distance flight in 1938.

Among other books and correspondence, two items came to light which I could call my inheritance. Each has played an influential part since, both in understanding my father as a person and the latter part of his life's journey; and as the cornerstone on which to build our family saga.

The first, his King James Bible, was falling apart from constant use, and verses on most pages were underlined in ink. None of my siblings showed an interest in this, so I claimed it. Well-thumbed pages, annotations in the margins and many high-lighted passages revealed much of our father's spiritual pilgrimage and personal struggles to stabilise his volatile character. Daily he had pored over and meditated upon some discovery within the dilapidated covers. Daily he wrestled between his rugged human nature and God's truth. Just a few months before his fifth and final heart attack, he finally hoisted a victory flag.

His children will always be grateful that he pursued the quest for anchorage in those ancient truths. They would become the bed-rock which anchored our lives later, and we harbour profound respect for the persistence and determination which led him to discover a real friendship with Jesus Christ towards the end of his life. It was thus that he found total freedom from a tortured conscience which had kept him shackled to his past.

As part of a tribute to that faith, I have used some of the truths he treasured in this account. But it was not until after my marriage, while living and working in Spain for some years, that some of those eternal truths leapt out at me as they became relevant in my own search for Truth. These would prove to have an important bearing on understanding the second part of my 'inheritance'.

Dad had mentioned to me some recent correspondence between himself and a Benedictine monk, Dom Edmund, and the letters received from that venerable hand now lay hidden in two brown envelopes. I claimed these for later perusal.

The monk's epistles opened a window onto an astonishing field of unknown and as yet little explored material in connection with my mother, who had left us when I was thirteen. They began to throw light on her commitment to a new mind-set, beliefs which had been changed by the new man in her life, Peter Caddy, and by his wife Sheena. This couple had performed a 'spiritual abduction' of our mother in order to turn her into an effective channel to help usher in Sheena's 'god of the new age'.

Their credo appeared diametrically opposed to the Christian grounding of faith instilled by our parents which had brought us through the war years and provided the foundation upon which each of us could mould our own beliefs. In 1956 when my father filed for a divorce, the judge overseeing the case deemed it undesirable that our mother's under-age children should be exposed to those particular ideas and lifestyle, and forbade any access to our mother.

Dom Edmund's research had been prompted some years before by concern triggered by media coverage in what appeared to be influential work pursued by a community established near Findhorn village in northern Scotland. Sometime after her departure from the family, my mother and her then second husband, Peter Caddy, had started this community on a caravan site in Morayshire. Ten years on in 1972, this became known as the Findhorn Foundation. The community developed quickly into a training ground for the burgeoning New Age movement in Britain and enabled its outreach to other countries.

Naturally, our mother's first family was deeply affected by the removal of their best loved family member during those initial manoeuvres by Peter Caddy and his wife Sheena to claim her for their purposes. Since then, both our mother and Peter Caddy have each written autobiographies, giving somewhat differing accounts of these events. The time seems ripe to record the behind-the-scenes drama that the first family played in the action. Hence this attempt to complete the history of our early involvement in Sheena and Peter Caddy's moves to advance their stratagem, and the subsequent repercussions.

I hope my three half-brothers can accept this narrative as seen from the view-point of the eldest of our mother's eight children. It has been like completing a jigsaw, with pieces taken largely from Peter and Eileen's own stories of what happened in the lost years of our relationships, together with extensive research and collective family memories.

In contrast to the Combe family's perspective, I have tried also to explain some of the Caddy parents' philosophies, which in the early fifties aimed to bring about the dawn of a new age (the Age of Aquarius). My Caddy brothers will recognise how, during the past fifty or so years, the Findhorn Foundation has released an extensive shower of ideas which have spread far and wide.

Due to the labyrinth of philosophies abounding, I have drawn on the explorations and statements of other authors and sages better versed in God's wisdom than me, and have trusted them to lead me through this maze. Mainly Christian authors, these pilgrims on a similar road as my own have understood the continuous battle ensuing in spiritual as well as earthly realms. They have been able to discern genuine truth amongst the debris of counterfeit half-truths littering humanity's progress down the centuries. To put it simply, by laying New Age philosophies alongside what Christ called the Spirit of Truth, they have rumbled the emergence of a seemingly all-embracing, tolerant, permissive ideology which—

among its hotchpotch of philosophies—has set its face firmly against inclusion of Christianity, Islam and Judaism.

In this journey of discovery, whenever and wherever the spirit of Truth rang bells in unison with my own inner promptings, interpretation of given facts, or explorations, I have attempted to express those truths in relation to our two families' story. Many may disagree with much of what is written here—for each must choose his own road to travel—but I trust there are a few who can understand something of the eternal struggle for predominance of influences which were beamed into our family circle and which have grown since, to contribute to, and become absorbed into, the bloodstream and confusion of this present age.

In these ever-shifting quicksands of ideas, how vital it is to discern rock from sand, truth from fake, in order to shape sound values of right and wrong. Is not this the pivot for the choices we make? Such wisdom can generate not only an enhanced quality of life in, and survival of, family life; but I believe it will also preserve the future of our planet.

J.A.N.H. November 2013

ACKNOWLEDGEMENTS

MY sincerest thanks go to the many who have walked this path with me: to Dom Edmund Fatt, O.S.B. who began these explorations; and to his superior, the Abbot, Rt Revd Dom Hugh Gilbert, O.S.B., now Catholic Bishop of Aberdeen, for his prayerful understanding and encouragement, together with his community; Drs Richard and Connie Smith for unravelling the truth, and pointing the way forward; to our Vicar Philip Martin for his helpful comments; Dr Philip Boobbyer for his encouragement to share more of my own faith-journey, Mrs Anne Wolrige Gordon for her advice, and Peter Everington for his wisdom; to my mother's sister Torrie for her memories, together with those of my siblings and my Sinclair cousins for their clear recollections; to Leone Exton Beale for her timely and loving hospitality, and constant friendship.

Special thanks to a remarkable team of editors without which this book would not be seen in print: to Valerie Bell in the initial stages; Susan Faber for her insightful comments throughout; Helen Combe for her thoughtful overseeing of facts and omissions; and to John Jenkins who taught me how to write and edited the final version. To our old family friend John Munro, who 'picked up this ball and ran with it' towards the goal of design and production.

Canon Michael Cole, to whom I am indebted for writing the Foreword, was a contributor to *What is the New Age* (published 1993), and has written several other books. He is presently involved with The Nationwide Christian Trust and is the editor of *Living Light*, and also a weekly programme on Premier Christian Radio on Sunday evenings.

Lastly, and most importantly, my profound thanks to my

husband for his patient proof-reading and technical assistance, with valuable technical help from our friend Frank Sims, from start to finish.

Φ

THE writing of this book has been cathartic and has taken many years, during which my attitudes and style have changed and improved over time.

To avoid confusion between the two Peters mentioned in the narrative, I have used Peter Caddy's surname at the beginning of the story, and my husband Peter's Christian name towards the end.

J.A.N.H.

PART I

How the happiness of a family is sabotaged

1

The Bread-and-Dripping Years

I STARED unbelievingly at the postcard in my hand. It had the audacity to describe my mother as 'bewitched' and 'lost deep in her enchantment'. Dumbfounded by these words, I struggled mentally to juggle this outlandish description of someone I still loved deeply, in spite of our long separation. The words 'bewitched' and 'enchantment' belonged to a world of fantasy, imaginary people, fairies, witches and strange creatures. Once upon a time, there lived... So began most of the fairytales we read as children, and read later to our children. Yet here in this twentieth century, I held a postcard, received while my family and I were living in Spain, which had the cheek to use language about my mother which I could not begin to imagine was true.

The hundred-years' sleep of an enchanted Sleeping Beauty, yes; the handsome prince transmuted by a witch into an ugly monster until Beauty's love for the beast broke her evil power, I could handle; the wand of a fairy godmother sending rags-to-riches Cinderella into the arms of Prince Charming, OK; a bewitched prince who became a frog, saved by kindness and a kiss, and now Shrek and Princess Fiona. These well-loved tales always ended 'happily ever after' because good always conquers evil, and love plays the comforting final hand.

Angry and hurt by the message on the postcard, I wrote a stinging reply to the author to say I felt 'blitzed' by her words. I never heard from her again. Only very gradually, over the next few years and through much research, would I begin to understand better what my correspondent had intimated – that a member of my family had, in fact, been 'bewitched', and that the effect of her 'enchantment' had rippled its way far out beyond our family circle.

The words 'enchantment' and 'bewitched' may well have featured on the postcard, but at the time of reading them I was a long way from discovering what was meant by their author, and how they could possibly apply to us.

When this tale began, ours was an ordinary happy family in every way—united parents with five much-loved children who had all we needed. Our secure and contented childhood lay in the hands of parents who loved us, believed in us, and provided for us, despite the deprivations of war.

My parents first met in 1937 while my father, Andrew Combe, was a pilot stationed at RAF Upper Heyford, Oxfordshire. As part of a team, he was involved in pioneering work with the Long Range Development Unit. My mother Eileen and her brother Paddy owned and managed a roadhouse nearby, often frequented by officers and men. Andrew was one of this rumbustious crowd. His heart was quickly captivated by Eileen's merry brown eyes and warm Irish humour, and it was not long before they became secretly engaged. This had to remain a secret because all personnel about to attempt the long-distance flight record were required to be single and uncommitted.

In 1938, my father and his team flew successfully from Ismailia in Egypt to Darwin, Australia in a single-engined Vickers Wellesley, setting up a flight record of 7162 miles, held for eight years. He returned to England early in 1939, after a victory flight tour of Australia, was awarded the Air Force Cross, promoted to Squadron Leader, and was free to announce his engagement to my mother.

They were married in Christ Church, Kensington, on 13th May 1939, and made a handsome pair as they passed under a Guard of Honour at their wedding, my father in Air Force uniform, his hard-won Sword of Honour from the RAF College Cranwell at his side. At twenty-eight, he was a dynamic, good-looking young man, well over six feet tall, sporting the modish handlebar moustache befitting a squadron leader's image of the time. My mother was twenty-one.

They settled in Farnborough, Hampshire, since his first posting was at the Royal Aircraft Establishment. These were probably the happiest years of my father's life. Having won a lovely bride, he was now set fair for a brilliant career in the Air Force. Among his achievements was the reversal of the wind-sock winched out behind a Mosquito for anti-aircraft batteries to practise shooting. The narrow end would then face the plane and reduce drag on the aircraft as the wind passed through the sock.

War had been declared on Germany, and Dad was required to test all types of aircraft for the research and development of various secret weapons and war machines. He became known in RAF circles as 'the man who could fly anything'. By the time he retired from the RAF in 1956, his sister stated he had flown 166 different types of aircraft. My brother Richard claims it was nearer ninety, based on Dad's log books which he later inherited.

I began life at Farnborough in April 1940 when England was already at war. Richard was born eighteen months later. 'A girl and a boy. Now I'm happy,' said my mother. Then by 1951, three more daughters had swelled our ranks.

In July, the Battle of Britain began. The Luftwaffe tried to gain air superiority by attacking RAF Fighter Command in the hopes of weakening British air power as a prelude to invasion. September 7th saw the first real air raid of the London Blitz, which then lasted fifty-seven consecutive nights. Hitler's aim was to destroy British civilian and governmental morale at the outset, but he met head-on with British bulldog determination to hold on to liberty and life, even unto death.

For so many people then, such joys as security, contentment and peace were already luxuries of the past. What was to be Britain's fate - freedom or tyranny? For hundreds of thousands of British, the Second World War would end in death. Our towns were being ravaged by bombs, our once-peaceful shorelines scarred with barbed wire, mines and concrete gun-turrets in preparation for invasion. The fast-dwindling ranks of young men and women fought on doggedly for our freedom, on land, in the air and at sea. For those who remained to look back, this nightmare period in our history had somersaulted the happy-go-lucky society of the Twenties and Thirties into a vague, far-distant dream. The British way of life and thinking would never be the same again.

Soon after the Blitz, my father was posted to the Air Ministry in London. Our mother Eileen decided it was well worth leaving our Farnborough home, *Starbarrow*, to brave the London bombs to be near husband Andrew. He found a large flat for us in a block of flats called Cedar House, in Marloes Road, Kensington.

Throughout the war years, thousands of families like ours grew up under enemy onslaught. The fortunate remained intact, and we among them. By May 1941, more than 21,000 Londoners were dead, and more than one million houses had been destroyed or damaged in London alone. Although destruction lay around us on our doorstep, at no time during the whole of the war did we see the inside of an air-raid shelter or run for safety into one of the eighty underground Tube stations where over 177,000 people sheltered nightly.

For my mother, the sound of the familiar warnings calling all to safety went unheeded. We never tasted fear, because she was fearless. Throughout this time of hardship and an unknown fate, it was to be our mother's faith in God's protection and her tranquillity which shone through for us children in the midst of the horrors of London's gradual devastation.

Most days, when we were taken out for a walk to Kensington Gardens by Nanny Shortland we witnessed another gaping hole in the ground, another half-demolished building, its rooms exposed to the elements where yesterday had lived a secure and happy family like ours. Not once did we imagine this could also be our fate.

Night-times were equally memorable. Heavy blackout curtains would be drawn, with only a candle or torch in use, since every beam of light must be snuffed out from being a visible target for enemy planes. Things would become easier in 1944 when partial "dim-outs" were permitted, even though sirens continued to wail and the drone of engines overhead were still a frequent, well-remembered occurrence.

Richard and I, later joined by baby Suzanne, would sit in bed in semi-darkness, listening to Bible stories read to us in candlelight by our mother. We would live into the bedtime stories, often read from a series by Dorothy Prescott and delightfully illustrated by Marjorie Proctor. My favourite was about the boy Samuel serving in the Temple where he heard the voice of God speaking to him for the first time. Another was Jesus' parable about the men who each built a house, one on rock and the other on sand. Such tales as these, and a Margaret Tarrant painting on the nursery wall depicting Jesus surrounded by children, laid the groundwork of our Christian belief.

Intermingled with these loved stories from the Bible, we revelled in the adventures of J. M. Barrie's Peter Pan and Wendy. Each character played an active role in our early imaginations when television did not exist. Ours was a Peter Pan world. My first theatre visit was to see *Peter Pan*. I had scary memories long afterwards of Tinkerbell and her naughtiness, the terrible Captain Hook, and the ticking crocodile. Also, Pooh Bear, Piglet and Christopher Robin featured as our friends, and rubbed shoulders with elephants King Barbar and Celeste, and the much loved tales and illustrations of *Peter Rabbit* by Beatrix Potter. A strange, lonesome, brown-eyed creature called *Parlicoot* was my introduction to romance when he met a blue-eyed version of himself, and lived happily ever after with her.

Among my earliest memories was kneeling by my bedside saying prayers with my mother. Suddenly, a terrible explosion rocked our block of flats. I stopped in mid-prayer to ask, 'What was that?' and my mother's calm reply was: 'Only a bomb, darling. Carry on.' An echo of King George VI's war-time encouragement to his subjects: 'Keep calm and carry on.' Apart from two memorable breaks, London was our world. We had not known any other way of life, and took war in our stride.

Φ

Meanwhile, when he wasn't away flying, Dad's work in the Air Ministry involved planning war strategy. At one stage, he was based in Gibraltar, and we saw little of him. He was in command of a 'Leigh Light' squadron of Wellington bombers for which he designed the squadron badge – a lantern in front of a harpoon – to signify the searchlights and depth-charges they used. The bombers were fitted with a new 'secret weapon' – a device for hunting and sinking submarines at night. He must have taken command of 179 Squadron there with high hopes.

In the event, his war experiences traumatised him. Years later, my brother recalls him talking of how the German U-boats would surface at night to recharge their batteries, and the squadron would spot them with the aid of powerful searchlights and sink them with depth charges. When the U-boats grew wise to this, they waited for the searchlights, and shot down many of Dad's squadron, resulting in a loss of 60% of his pilots and crews. He never spoke to us of these experiences or of the terrible misfortunes of war, until Richard, the only other male family member, was old enough to appreciate his father's heroism as well as the horrors he had endured during those sorties. Richard was always interested in hearing about his father's escapades.

In spite of tragedy and trauma during the war, flying remained the great love of Dad's life. He never lost his joy and wonder at being airborne, and felt poet-pilot John Magee's poem expressed perfectly that special type of ecstasy with his words:

Oh! I have slipped the surly bonds of Earth
And danced the skies on laughter-silvered wings;
  Sunward I've climbed...
  And, while with silent, lifting mind I've trod
The high untrespassed sanctity of space,
Put out my hand and touched the face of God.

These prophetic words proved to be the young poet's epitaph. Magee was killed in action before the war ended.

Φ

Twice during those five years, the family sought safer havens outside London. The two evacuations provided many happy memories for us children. On the first occasion, Dad decided to transfer his family temporarily to the north coast of Norfolk to be near his mother, away from the London bombing. He had been posted to Gibraltar, and there was another baby on the way. While we were there, our sister Suzanne was born in nearby Sheringham, in December 1942, fourteen months after Richard.

Blakeney had become the home of our paternal grandmother after a move from Bloomsbury Square where my father had been born (within the sound of Bow Bells, so technically he was a Cockney). During our time there, my mother rented the Old School House opposite Blakeney Church. The church was a huge and beautiful grey-flint edifice built by rich wool merchants centuries ago. It stood on the highest point of the coastline, its tower acting as a beacon to guide seafarers when Cley had been a port. Its scenic graveyard overlooking Cley Mill in its fast-dwindling creek, Cley Beach and the unending seascape beyond was the final resting place of our paternal grandfather in 1941, and now holds my grandmother and Aunt Betsy.

To visit Granny from the Old School House, we needed to descend the steep, cobbled High Street, pass the bakery with its delicious smell of fresh-baked bread, pause to watch Mr Holliday cobbling shoes in his window and see his Labrador pups at play in the yard behind his shop; then on down the cobbles towards the widening vista of quayside, moored boats, yachts pulled up on the Hard, and the marshes beyond. We would skirt past several fishermen in their ancient navy Guernseys, sitting on a bench on the corner by the quay whiling away the time waiting for the next tide, exchanging news and comments in their slow, broad Norfolk dialect; then along the front of the Blakeney Hotel and round the corner from Blakeney Quay to The Boat House. In the back garden, there was a pear tree which came to life in Spring with a mass of white blossom. Richard and I went to stay there with our grandmother when Suzanne, our second sister, was born.

Blakeney would become a favourite holiday haunt for years afterwards. The church was a most welcome landmark as we rounded the last corner of the narrow road by car, on our way to visit Granny. As we grew older, we would spend endless hours down on Blakeney Quay, with cockle-meat or bacon on the end of strings, fishing for gillie crabs and racing them along the quayside. At low tide, we could paddle in the Cut, or row a small boat called *Brat* across the inlet to a narrow beach on the other side of the creek where we built sand-castles at low water. There was timelessness and peace here, and a mind-boggling natural world to explore. Gulls, oyster catchers and terns wheeled overhead, grey seals basked on rocks only a boat-ride away on Blakeney Point where terns nested, and the marshes echoed to the curlew's cry.

When we returned to London's noisy streets, constant sirens and dust with the daily uncertainty of turmoil and increasing destruction of war, the wide horizons at Blakeney, the echoing seabirds' cries, the taste of samphire gathered from the marshes, the cockles we dug up from mud which squidged between our toes, were all part of a distant dream. We would always be drawn back gladly by these ever-beckoning memories of sight and sound, ready for a further dose of timeless tranquillity. Blakeney was a haven where we felt at home, loved, free and completely safe.

Our second evacuation was to a Suffolk farm, where friends of my parents invited my mother and her three children to stay in a thatched cottage on their lovely estate. My mother's little terrier, a Brussels Griffon called Glory, came too. *Old Thatches* had been built in the time of the Tudors, probably for, if not by, some of the farm workers. It had low ceilings with blackened beams and crooked, sloping stairs. People in those days must have been smaller, perhaps bowed by hard labour during daylight hours, for the cottage itself seemed cramped in comparison with the spaciousness of our London flat.

Among the rolling fields of sugar-beet, the hedgerows and narrow lanes or tracks, we were to discover the joys of farm-life, love and respect for animals, the smell of rain on freshly-ploughed fields; enormous barns full of hay in which we tumbled and played; and met a huge cart-horse called Blossom. Blossom pulled cart-loads of muddy sugar-beet, and sometimes we were allowed the thrill of being carried astride her broad back. It was to this same farm that my brother was apprenticed some fourteen years later which gave him the practical skills for the career that was to take him to South Africa as a pig-farmer.

Back once more in London, the unruffled surface of our lives continued in a smooth routine. We took our afternoon walks in Kensington Gardens with me trotting beside white-haired Nanny Shortland who pushed the double carriage-pram in which Richard and Suzanne sat opposite one another. When it rained, they wiggled their fingers out between the raised hoods with accompanying giggles. Both had a great sense of fun and got on well.

Nanny would point out yellow and purple crocuses in Hyde Park, poking up their heads round the boles of trees, or comment on the carpets of daffodils stretching across the open parkland. We fed ducks on Round Pond with stale crusts, and fished for tiddlers with nets made from flour-bags tied to the end of sticks, proudly bearing home our catch in a jam-jar with a string handle to show our mother. The Peter Pan statue in Kensington Gardens was a fascination, and our childish hands were among the many small fingers to caress the bronze horns of snails and tiny ears of mice gathered at Peter's feet. A recent visit to this statue revealed that the horns and ears had long since been stroked away by little worshipping hands.

My mother's Celtic up-bringing also encouraged vivid imagination. She told us about her aunt in Ireland who as a child had actually *seen* a leprechaun sitting on a rock. Not surprising then that I believed in fairies by the age of four. On bath-nights, I watched one spiralling down the plug-hole with the bath-water, resplendent in silver and black stripes. On our daily walks, I imagined fairies hiding behind trees in the park, always just out of sight. The first note I ever wrote was addressed to one. I hid the scrap of paper carefully away in a hole in a tree, and next day it had vanished. This was cast-iron proof fairies existed, even though when I returned to the tree several times there was no reply.

We had never known a time when food was not rationed so took frugal menus as the norm. Ration books were an essential part of life. Obesity did not exist, and our teeth never needed dental attention since sweets were strictly rationed. We were fortunate to have a mother who made the best of the few provisions available. A Sunday roast was three ration books' worth for the four or five of us for the week, and provided bones for nourishing stock for soups. Mum always made delicious soups. The dripping from the meat pan was spread on bread or toast as a special treat. More than one memorable picnic took place on the nursery floor, sitting on a large Union flag. We often devoured fingers of toast and dripping, or sometimes for supper she would make us another favourite dish we called 'Goody' – cubed white bread sprinkled with sugar and hot milk. At a tender age of three or four, I remember being allowed to stand on a chair at the stove in our enormous kitchen, learning how to scramble the family's weekly ration of eggs in a saucepan.

The first live pandas had arrived recently in London Zoo, and of course quickly became fashionable as toys. Richard had a large panda companion which lived in the toy-chest. One day, as Richard leaned in to grab his friend, the heavy chest lid crashed down on his thumbs and literally flattened them—a painfully distressing incident. To this day his thumbs are like two spatulas. The only other nasty experience I recall was the taste of Milk of Magnesia curdling on our tongues at bedtimes, until our disgusted protests changed the dose to Syrup of Figs.

Φ

At about the time of the tough posting in Gibraltar, Dad was home on leave for a short time, and happened upon an old 'boozing companion' of his. Wing Commander Edward Howell was a fellow officer and pilot. He told Dad about his amazing recent home-coming as a wounded prisoner of war, when he had been 'inspired' to escape from a prison hospital in Greece. As he recounted his adventures to my father, Dad became more and more intrigued by the way his friend, whose plane had been shot down in Crete, had been guided in his escape from captivity following his imprisoned hospitalization.

Shortly before the war, Edward's brother David, also in the RAF, had met the Oxford Group, a movement gathering momentum through people inspired by the ideas of an American Lutheran minister based in Oxford, Dr Frank Buchman. Buchman's vision in 1938, when there was much talk about disarmament, was to re-arm people morally and spiritually on the basis of Christ's standards given in the Sermon on the Mount. This group soon became known as Moral Re-armament (MRA) and is now called Initiatives of Change.

The transformation in David Howell's life had riveted his brother Edward. He took on board many of the new truths passed on by David. One was his belief that 'when man listens, God speaks; and when man obeys, God acts.' While Edward lay close to dying in the prison hospital in Salonika he had begun to pray, and decided to put the idea of listening for God's voice to the test. Not only was he a POW, but he was weakened by loss of blood from a badly shattered arm. When he asked God for help, he found he was given some clear instructions. With minimal strength and only his life to lose, he set out to obey those commands. He found they led him, step by step in a miraculous escape from a well-guarded hospital, across Greece to Turkey and eventually to repatriation in UK.

The evidence of Edward's bullet-ravaged arm and the change in his character and life-aims captivated my father who decided to try out this way of living for himself. Indeed these ideas were to have a profound influence on both my parents' lives, and started them on a spiritual path from which my father never wavered throughout his life, despite frequent failures, back-slidings and some devastating falls.

Throughout those first five years of our lives, my parents' loyalty to one another was probably their strongest bond, 'for better or worse.' Their siblings, though clearly suspicious of Andrew's new-found principles and desire to be part of a cure in the world, had no doubts that the couple were as happily settled as possible under war-time circumstances. In actual fact, it was this common goal they pursued in harness which held my parents together for fifteen years.

Unreal though our family-world may have been, we believed our house was the one securely built on rock, as in the bible parable. Ours was a contented Christian family with a home which became a staging-post for an enormous variety of new friends of different nationalities passing through London at the time. Despite the stark backdrop of bombers, bombings and uncertain life-expectancy, all was well.

Bread-and-dripping Years

Our young lives continued to bubble along like a meandering and cheerful stream during this happy period. We were learning to adapt speedily to ever-changing circumstances, moving from one location to another, meeting new, interesting people and ideas. We thrived on a diet of excitement and took the next unexpected adventure in our stride. All unknowingly, we were developing resilience against any difficulties which might lie ahead.

2

Challenges Ahead

FOLLOWING Dad's Gibraltar experience of losing a terrifyingly high proportion of his personnel, he spent a short time with Coastal Command at Wick, in Scotland, before returning to work at the Air Ministry. A posting to Strategic Command as a Group Captain took him to SHAFE (Supreme Headquarters Allied Forces, Europe) in Paris later in the war, and on completion of this tour, he had the unusual honour of being awarded the American Bronze Star. 1945 saw him crossing to the States on a two-year military exchange. Fortunately, this was an accompanied posting, and Eileen and his three children were able to join him, as will be recounted later.

Meanwhile, Edward Howell had become a frequent visitor at Cedar House and with him came a breath of wartime reality into our sheltered lives. The new Edward's transformed lifestyle having made such a dramatic impact on my father, changes in our lives were bound to become evident.

It was a shock when Dad poked his head out of the bathroom door one morning, having shaved off his handlebar moustache. He became less distant and more thoughtful of his children, and would bring each a present on his return from foreign parts: for me, a piece of lace from Paris, which my mother made into a collar on my best red velvet dress; another time, a little chalet musical box from Switzerland after my parents had visited there. These were treasured gifts.

I claimed handsome 'uncle' Edward as my first (and only) hero. I sat on his knee asking to see the terrible scars down one arm which had been ripped open by gunfire in Crete before his capture. Years later when I read his book, *Escape to Live*[1] the full story of how those scars had come to be became clear. Often afterwards a bulky envelope would arrive from Uncle Edward, full of stamps from letters received from friends he had made while in Greece. These were kept for me, and later awakened an avid interest in stamp-collecting.

What we children could not have known at the time was how the change in Andrew affected our parents' relationship. We had no idea that this new lifestyle was a result of his adoption of the principles of Moral Rearmament with which my mother concurred enthusiastically, probably with some relief. She must have realised that these ideas highlighted his personal difficulties, because he vowed to overcome them.

Edward and his friends *enjoyed* life. Their sense of freedom from any shackles to the past made their lifestyle attractive.

Looking back, I can understand how he must have nurtured the hope that, together with my mother in pursuit of this new way of living and looking outwards towards helping others, he would surely find healing for his own character traits and troubled past. He not only wanted this freedom for himself, but surely it would have a knock-on effect for the well-being of his family? For many years it did.

The evidence my parents saw in the quality of life and friendship demonstrated by their MRA friends matched my father's idealism. He yearned to possess their infectious faith in God, translated into action. The absolute moral standards of purity, honesty, love and unselfishness they tried to live by were very steep indeed, but as someone pointed out, these values were not only the essence of the Sermon on the Mount Jesus had preached; they were also like the North star, providing pointers to help one navigate through life, even though unattainable.

My parents had found their moral compass: a big enough aim to unite them in a positive, creative and refreshing partnership which carried us all along in its momentum, working smoothly and practically at home as well as out in the community. My mother followed my father's lead without demur, surely hoping subconsciously that their friends could do for my father and their marriage what she had felt powerless to achieve alone.

Φ

While Dad submitted to the rigorous demands of war and long absences from home, Mum was, of course, the permanent fixture in our lives. We did not know then that the pain and tragedy encountered in her earlier life was to have some bearing on the rest of this story. Self-centred as children are, we could not understand how vital we were to her as a source of comfort and the security she had sought in Andrew and marriage. We went some way in compensating for the loss of her parents, both now dead. She admitted much later, in her autobiography, that 'by now, everything else came second' to her children. She had discovered early on in their partnership that her marriage did not match up to her ideals.

Eileen was born in Alexandria, Egypt, where her father, Albert (Bertie) Jessop, was a much-loved personality among British and Egyptians alike, both on the cricket pitch and as manager of the Anglo-Egyptian Bank, a branch of Barclays Bank D.C.O. in Alexandria. At the age of six, her parents sent her and my uncle Paddy, sixteen months older than herself, back to Ireland for their education. Our grandfather's favourite sister, Florence Drury, took them under her wing and raised them in her small flat in Merrion Square, one of Dublin's largest and most elegant Georgian squares.

We children called her 'Auntie from Ireland'. She was a staunch Church of Ireland Protestant, and we and my mother adored and revered her. She was a woman of much character who had married a doctor and been widowed early. She had twinkling brown eyes like our mother's, a rich sense of humour and fun, and long, white hair, which she could sit on but was normally kept hidden in a tight bun at the nape of her neck. Auntie had style. She dressed smartly, even when, many years on, she hardly had two pennies to her name. She would sail down the four flights of wide stairs in the Royal College of Architects from her little attic flat perched at the top of the building, as though she owned the huge house. As often as not, she wore a large hat with feathers to go out to coffee with her friends, or to church, or the Abbey Theatre. No one would have guessed how poor she was. She earned a living until well into her eighties by teaching piano. To us children she represented an adored grandmother-figure since our maternal grandmother had died before we were born.

I believe it was from Aunt Florence that young Eileen gleaned the rudiments of her Christian faith. She loved being in church with Auntie, putting her penny in the collection plate on Sundays, and she hated being separated from her when she was expected to go to Sunday school. My grandmother, Muriel Jessop (née Bull), had adopted her sister's and brother-in-law's beliefs and become a Christian Scientist. Christian Science was to have a profound effect on the life of Eileen's younger brother Rex, who from the age of eight, suffered from epileptic fits brought on by a swimming accident. The fits worsened as he grew, and finally rendered him an invalid. Apparently, my grandmother steadfastly refused to seek medical help in the firm belief that Christian Science methods would heal him. So Rex began to remain with his parents and younger sister Torrie in Alexandria, while his older siblings ventured unaccompanied to Ireland each summer for their year's education.

When Eileen was fourteen, she was in England at school at Leigh-on-Sea where Torrie had joined her by then. At this time, further tragedy struck the family in Egypt. A telegram to their headmistress bore the shocking news that on December 12th 1932 their beloved father had died suddenly of peritonitis. My heart-broken mother explained later in her autobiography how she fought both mentally and emotionally to come to terms with, and overcome, this untimely wrench from the father she loved. 'I felt he had gone to some distant shore and I knew I would see him again one day. It was just a matter of time. I felt a tremendous flow of love towards him as if he were physically present next to me.' His 'presence' was a comfort and would remain with her all her life as a source of strength.

She and Torrie left that school in the spring of 1933, to return to Egypt: Mum to care for her mother and younger brother Rex, and my aunt to continue her education at the Scottish School in Alexandria. The needs at home seemed far more critical than education at the time.

Eventually, in 1936, my grandmother decided to move from Egypt back to England, prompted chiefly by Rex's condition. 'Mummy wanted us all to be together,' recalled my mother, so the family found a small cottage called Woodlands, in a Berkshire village. Paddy reluctantly took up training in banking, walking in his father's footsteps, while young Torrie continued her schooling in Slough. Because of their travels from an early age Eileen had been used to taking responsibility, and she now kept house for her mother.

Within a year of their arrival, my grandmother fell ill with meningitis. Weakened by continuing grief at the loss of my grandfather as much as by the illness, she died two weeks later, on August 2nd, 1936. In the space of little over two years, the family had lost both parents.

Meanwhile, brother Rex's unpredictable black-outs became more frequent and violent. More than once, when visiting in the village, he was brought home recumbent in the post van. He was sent to reside in a nearby mental institution where he was miserable. Rex had grown very close to and dependent upon his mother and missed her unbearably. Her death, and then being sent away from his family, must surely have broken his heart. He transferred to a happier home in Salisbury, where he died five years later in 1941, aged twenty-two. My aunt Torrie was the only family member able to attend the short funeral service in Salisbury Cathedral.

Eileen was nearly eighteen when she enrolled in a domestic science college. Always practical, she enjoyed the cookery course and housekeeping, but admitted she struggled with the theory. She soon found a job as cook in a school, and had at least one suitor on a string by then. Only a short time afterwards, she and her brother Paddy used some of their inheritance to buy a roadside inn, Hopcrofts Holt, in Oxfordshire. The pub was frequented by members of the RAF working at Upper Heyford. There she met a tall good-looker named Andrew who was about to attempt a long-distance flight record. One thing led to another, and they became secretly betrothed. As previously recounted, the rest is history.

By the time my parents met, Eileen ached to find love and security to soothe her soul's grief arising from the sad demise of both parents. In her own words, she had 'longed to meet a man who would marry me and take care of me forever.... I was tired of being on my own, struggling through life, so I accepted Andrew's proposal of marriage'. In the exhilaration and thrill of romance, she thought she had found It: the solution to her inner void. Perhaps marriage would provide all she craved. This hero-pilot, so handsome in his Air Force blue, and an officer with a string of successes to his credit, seemed a fine catch for any girl.

Andrew had been a top student at the RAF College, Cranwell, and was preparing to achieve a long-distance flight record. His successes at the time overlaid his well-guarded frailties. What he sorely needed was a wife who could understand and cope with his ebullient, untameable and complex character. He found a sympathetic, if bewildered response to these needs in Eileen.

Only during their honeymoon had Andrew begun to fill in some of the details of his past. He had not known much happiness while growing up. His mother was a matriarch who ruled her five children, largely single-handedly, with an iron hand. His father, a struggling barrister with a fine mind, possessed a generous disposition that never insisted on payment by clients in financial straits. Whether this latter was the reason they eventually moved to England from their beautiful home in Donacloney, Northern Ireland, or whether it was for his children's education, remains a mystery. What I do know is that he suffered the early onset of what my grandmother called 'melancholia' and was dispatched to an institution. His eldest daughter Janet, recalled that he became quite violent and 'tried to jump out of a window'. He apparently knew of my birth before he died in 1941, aged 62.

Although his work and subsequent illness had prevented him playing much of an active role in his teenage sons' lives, my grandfather had enabled them to attend a preparatory school, followed by a good education at Rugby School.

Andrew's school years were a time of great turbulence for him. He was quick, intelligent and, much like other boys, lazy. He lived in the shadow of his brilliant and charming older brother, Nick, who rowed for his Cambridge College, took a law degree, became a solicitor and finally High Court Judge in Brunei. My father once admitted how, in his desperation to win attention, he set fire to a wing of Rugby School! History does not record the result of the damage, or the consequences to himself of these pyrotechnics.

The old fagging system at public schools – where an older student chose a younger pupil to be his fag and do his chores for him – often led to abuse. Starved of natural affection as my father was, and placed in an all-male environment where hero-worship relationships were frequent, emotional and physical involvement proved inevitable.

My brother wisely explained to me that 'most men have encounters with homosexuality in their young lives: it is part of the maturing process. The majority grow through it to become heterosexual. Others, perhaps more sensitive, remain emotionally stultified in this phase.' The most vulnerable could be doomed to suffer consequential damage from such relationships: inner conflict, confusion and guilt, as in my father's case.

He confided to my brother that the boys at his

preparatory school had been encouraged by the masters to skinny-dip, and that this environment had cultivated an initial sexual interest between small boys. This fact, together with 'the distortion of parental role models, which is the single major cause in disrupting a child's heterosexual orientation', were prime factors in moulding his sexual behaviour. My father averred strongly that this was *learned* behaviour from his school days, and not genetic. 'Yes,' agreed my mother when I read her this paragraph, years later. Naïve as she had been on their honeymoon, I doubt whether she had much idea at the time about what my father was trying to explain to her.

Back in the earliest days of their wartime marriage, my mother began to realise she had not wed the ideal husband, hero, or paragon of her dreams. The challenge facing her then was way beyond her limited and somewhat sheltered experience. How was she going to handle this larger-than-life character whom she had vowed to 'love and to cherish'? Their marriage vows, taken in all solemnity '... till death us do part' now loomed frighteningly in an eternity of their future together.

Eileen did her utmost to cope with a husband, highly charged as he was with both physical and emotional energy, and totally absorbed in the war and his career. He seemed unable to give her the understanding and comfort she sought, so her creative energies and love were poured out for her children, who adored her. She quickly accepted that her role as wife must be as a 100% giver.

Despite the dramatic changes in their lives wrought by the introduction of new ideas introduced by Edward Howell and many subsequent friends, which became the cement holding them together, no one could have foreseen at the time that the parabolic house built on sand, learned about at our mother's knee, would prove eventually to be the fabric on which our family's foundations were built. When cracks began to appear, and the storm burst, our parents' last-ditch battles proved no protection against its final collapse.

3

Of Sugar-plums, Cotton-fields, and Home Sweet Home

... The children were nestled all snug in their beds,
While visions of sugar-plums danced in their heads...
A Visit from St. Nicholas - *by Clement C. Moore*

THE last V-2 bomb had fallen; the Japanese had surrendered, and victory had been secured. The end of the war marked a new posting for Andrew, to America. He was assigned to lecture to the U.S. Air Force on war strategy at Fort Leavenworth, Kansas. My mother was to follow later with their three children.

In September 1945 we set sail aboard the *Queen Elizabeth*, together with hundreds of Canadian and American troops returning home after the war. For us children the journey was another exciting adventure, as we tripped up the gangplank at Southampton dock in gathering darkness. As the ship steamed out of the docks, we peered, wide-eyed, over the stern into dark waters glowing with phosphorescent scales of a million fish dancing in the depths.

Our mother succumbed to sea-sickness, and retired to her bunk for much of the trip, leaving us in the care of a watchful stewardess. We wandered the corridors, stepping over the ever-present soldiers who slept there each night as accommodation was scarce. These men would have been aching with anticipation at being re-united with their families on the far-distant shores of home; one or two were glad to keep us children amused. We were well supervised by both stewardesses and these kind men, and able to roam the long decks fearlessly, attempt deck quoits or spend happy hours in the sunny playroom.

Whenever our mother could face the ordeal of sitting through a meal, we dined in the grand restaurant. The rich food was sheer luxury compared with our frugal fare throughout the war, and fried 'white fish' (probably whitebait) became a favourite.

Apart from all the fun we had, one vivid recollection towards the end of the voyage was the view looking out of our cabin porthole at the Statue of Liberty. Her raised torch as we sailed into New York Harbour marked the triumphal homecoming for the thousands of patriots aboard who had fought long and hard to retain that symbol of freedom, not only for North America but for our small island and much of the world. Cheers resounded from deck to deck: the rejoicing shouts from those men and women who had survived the ravages of war in Europe to return safely to their homeland.

It was early morning when we docked. From the moment we set foot on American soil, we met instants of delight along the way. We were welcomed by friends of our parents, to their smart New York apartment. First things came first, and we were lined up to be plunged into a hot bath. Richard (probably the grubbiest), was first in, but the water was too hot and burned his foot. The ensuing pandemonium was quickly tempered by a breakfast of Cheerios, another food revelation! Thus began two happy years in this Land of Plenty which had remained unscarred by the deprivations of war in Europe and the Far East.

In Fort Leavenworth our serious education began. We studied incubation and had a live broody hen sitting on her eggs in the classroom! We visited a nearby farm to watch eggs being hatched out in huge incubators. This was a far cry indeed from the smart, rather dreary Kensington kindergarten in London where I had started my schooling. There I remember the daily misery of struggling into an impossible criss-cross pinafore and wrestling with the intricate art of lacing-up pink satin ballet shoes. In the States, learning was not only different but enjoyable.

Kansas must be one of the coldest places on God's earth. It could give you frost bite and take your ears off.

The heavy snows of our first American winter saw us tobogganing down the steep slope behind our married quarter in the coldest temperatures we had yet known. To climb from bottom to top of the hill again, we had to slither and slide up a long flight of icy steps—a challenge that caused more than a few tears. Our first Kansas Christmas was magical: Santa had made it across the Atlantic, with a range of toys we had not imagined even existed—for me, a little push-chair for my dolls. Each stocking had a red-and-white aniseed-flavoured candy-stick poking out on top of its goodies, to greet us when we awoke far too early on Christmas morning.

Holidays were memorable too. We would take off in the large DeSoto with Dad singing at the wheel, and covered hundreds of miles either south from Kansas to Florida, or north across the border to Canada. Often we drove through the night, and we three children took turns to stretch out on the back-seat or floor. At the end of one long night's drive down to Florida, where we were to spend our second rather warmer Christmas, we ran short of fuel at dawn, and drew into a filling station. We children awoke, wondering where we were and why we were stationary. 'We're out of gas and waiting for the station to open,' Dad explained. So we whiled away the time by singing Yankee Doodle until a bleary-eyed petrol attendant stuck his head out of the bedroom window above and shouted, 'I'll be right down to fill you up!'

Fort Myers Beach, Florida, was idyllic with its azure sea and white beaches edged with coconut palms. These sheltered the beach cabins and one palm drooped over the verandah of our cabin. I still remember the taste of fresh coconut and its milk when Dad cracked one open between two stones on the decking. Every evening the darkening sea threw up a wide, gloriously painted sky streaked with a gold, orange and vermillion fan as the sun sank below its horizon. By day, we wandered the balmy shoreline to beach-comb, collecting pocketfuls of delicate pink and white shells from the bleached sand. It all seemed like a beautiful dreamland.

Christmas Eve arrived, and a huge bonfire was lit on the beach. Out of the darkness from the sea appeared a leaky canoe with Santa Claus paddling towards the fiery beacon on the beach, ready to greet his landing. He swept us all merrily up to the beach hotel, and distributed gifts to everyone. As children, we were ecstatically happy with this novel way of spending a warm Christmas. As we gathered around Santa's knees, I thought I recognised a familiar voice. Only later that evening, when I noticed my father's wet socks, did it dawn on me who had played that wondrous role. My faith in Father Christmas was gone forever.

In the summer of 1946, we visited a beautiful little island set like an emerald in the sapphire waters of Lake Michigan. Mackinac Island had no motor cars. Horses, ponies and carts were used for transport; an old fort stood high above the landing stage where boats docked; and we met real Native American Indians in real tepees, displaying their intricate and colourful beaded crafts, and tiny canoes carved from birch bark. This island had been chosen as an international conference centre by Dr Frank Buchman, initiator of the work of Moral Re-armament. We were to stay there with him and his large team of people during that summer, in a white hotel called Island House overlooking the lakeside.

Everyone was included in the practicalities of running the conference, even the children. I was on the 'trash' team which involved doing a daily round of all the bedrooms and emptying the wastepaper baskets into bin-bags. I was six, happy and proud to be deemed old enough to be part of a team with a responsible task.

The children always had a programme of activities, and never felt excluded from all that was going on in the conference. One never-to-be-forgotten day we learned how to pack up a bed-roll each and then rode out on a little ice-breaker called *Beaver*, to Round Island nearby. There we set up camp, and spent a night under the stars in a pine forest. Another time, we put on a children's musical called *The Bungle in the Jungle*, staged in a large converted barn-theatre. Dressed as animals, we enacted a play about a moody black animal called a Bungle which had become a bad influence in the jungle. Eventually he was bundled away in a barrel by a snowy white polar bear who sang the final song which gave away the secret of his radiant white fur. Right living was what had overcome the Bungle's mischief. As we sang the chorus, we were learning about good triumphing over evil.

Another event was being one of many flower-girls at a wedding; then there was the fun of riding in a pony-and-trap round the island, with Rainbow—Uncle Frank's pony--between the shafts; and one hot sunny day we walked through fragrant pine woods to Arch Rock, to swim in the sparkling blue lake. Whatever we did was new and exciting, always surrounded by friends, and safe.

For the adults the aim of that memorable summer was to learn more of what my father had been experimenting with: the mechanics of how lives could be transformed through putting faith into action, so people could become free to take part in God's amazing plan for His world. A beautiful song written by composer George Fraser for the delegates that summer, described Mackinac and the old fort. It ended with the words: *But where men united so that wrongs were righted, stories of Mackinac will tell.* And evidence that they did has been captured on film since, telling stories of genuine reconciliation.

Our second major move in the States was to Maxwell Fields, Alabama, where sister number three was born, in 1947. She arrived home from hospital on the day Alabama had elected a new governor. Dad always wanted us to experience the full flavour of any historical event. This one, almost on our doorstop, was not to be missed. We had gone to participate in the celebrations which I viewed across the heads of an ecstatic crowd from my tall father's shoulders. But I fidgeted impatiently throughout, not at all interested in seeing the inauguration of a new governor. All I wanted to do was get home to see our new baby. When we returned from this outing, I ran straight upstairs and peered eagerly over the edge of the wicker cradle. I was enchanted by our new baby sister, and thought her the most beautiful thing I had ever seen. I can still recall the thrill of joy I felt. In true Southern States tradition she was given two names, Mary Elizabeth – thereafter shortened to Lizzie, or just plain Liz.

We had a delightful African American cook, Sarah, who was the blackest person I'd ever seen. She produced delicious breakfasts of waffles with bacon and maple syrup, served up from a new waffle machine. Sarah stays in my memory for two reasons: the first being the day she spilled boiling water down her leg. The burn turned septic and poor Sarah had to stay at home, unable to walk or come to work. It was Easter time, so my mother and I made up an Easter basket filled with coloured boiled eggs, and took them to distribute to Sarah and her family. We found her little tin-roofed house in a kind of township (much like those I saw later in South Africa), the family living in two small rooms, so different from our comfortable married quarter. I was shocked. It felt strange and uncomfortable. When Sarah unravelled the bandages on her scalded leg I recoiled in horror at the sight and putrid smell of pus. I wanted to get out of the house quickly and run all the way home. Fortunately Sarah did get better in time, and her waffles continued to be the best ever.

Our cook was my introduction to the story of sadness evoked by beginning to see first-hand the tail-end of slavery's history there in the Deep South, with all its aching tragedy. Even at the age of six, through listening to spirituals I had become aware of the incredible faith and grace of the African American people. Their patience and suffering shone through their sadness. The tortured spirit of their struggle through slavery struck a poignant chord in my young heart, and found full expression for me in the song, *Poor Old Joe*. I had learned to pick out the tune on the piano, and the words brought tears to my eyes when I sang them:

Gone are the days when my heart was young and gay,
Gone are my friends from the cotton fields away.
Gone far away, to a better land I know,
I hear their distant voices calling 'Poor old Joe.'
I'm coming, I'm coming, for my head is bending low,
I hear their distant voices calling, 'Poor old Joe.'

In Alabama State, years later, the Reverend Martin Luther King Jr. launched the civil rights movement in the town of Montgomery, near our home. It all began when the African American Rosa Parks refused to give up her seat to a white woman on a bus one day. She made the point that black people were also citizens who had rights.

Through 'a sophisticated strategy of war fought with grace not gunpowder,' ... and in countering 'violence with non-violence, and hatred with love,' Dr King's inspired policy of rising again and again 'to the majestic heights of meeting physical force with soul force,' eventually won for African Americans their full recognition and acceptance as a people: true liberation, at last, from the slave-bonds of racism and discrimination. I am truly content that the colour-bar evil is fast fading into the past, and they can live to enjoy a new climate of freedom in which their first black President, Barack Obama, has been elected.

If I missed the school bus, I could take off on roller-skates to school quite close by. Again I enjoyed school and learned to read fluently. At home in the backyard, Red Cardinals were as plentiful as blackbirds are in England. From the kitchen doorstep one day, I witnessed our neighbour's son swinging a cat round his head by the tail. A surge of unspeakable anger and distress at this horrifying sight created hatred for that boy from that day forward. I still shudder at cruelty to animals.

During the torrential summer rains, when tortoises crawled out onto the streaming roads, we children would also splash about in the road in our bathing suits with other kids in the neighbourhood.

This happy and stimulating phase of our lives came

to an end when we sailed on the SS *Aquitania* (scrapped later that same year) back to England in 1947. Dad had been posted as commanding officer of RAF Station Hemswell, in Lincolnshire. Mum carried a babe-in-arms, accompanied by we three older children who had acquired broad American accents and boasted a doubtful and competitive proficiency at blowing large bubbles of bubblegum. Such American ways seemed to shock our paternal grandmother when we met her again, but we heard her later recounting to her closer friends, with much amusement, how Richard had told her one day in her car: 'Listen, Granny, I can talk American!'

In Hemswell, we lived in a horseshoe of married quarters, set in open flatlands over which merciless winds direct from the North Pole swept unimpeded. We had suffered these same Arctic blasts before on the north coast of Norfolk, but after the more tropical climes of the southern States, this wintry 'welcome' back to our native England seemed cold and bleak.

We soon acclimatised, and spent a merry time there on the whole. Hemswell stands out in my mind on several counts – my brother and I graduated from riding the Family Tricycle to wobbling on bicycles; we often had to walk, though, to the tiny village school of Glentworth, which seemed miles away but was probably not more than one. We took packed lunches to school, with favourite marmite sandwiches. I worked hard at learning different embroidery stitches on a sampler, later to become a hanky holder; and we were initiated into the beautiful tales of *Little Grey Rabbit* by Alison Uttley, and her hilarious tale *Hare Joins the Home Guard* read aloud to us.

While in the States, I learned early about dating. Aged seven by then, I saw it as a priority to acquire a boy friend. Paul Hart sat next to me in class and became my first love. We had all been transferred by then to the RAF school on the base. As we walked home one day across the green in front of our quarters, I asked Paul what he was going to be when he grew up. 'A sailor,' said he. I told him, then and there, that I would marry a sailor one day. Twenty-five years later, I did.

We moved schools a third time, and were bussed daily back and forth into Gainsborough to what seemed like a huge school spilling over with children. After a short time there, we changed once more, back to the RAF school at the camp. The reason for these quick changes of school was never clear, but I suspect transportation and availability of teachers must have played a part.

Three schools and a Sunday school later, Dad was posted back to the Air Ministry in London, and we moved down to Surrey. We rented temporarily a small, dark apartment in Grange Road, Sutton, while our parents house-hunted. Just before Christmas 1949, they bought our first home down the road in Cheam, at the cost of £4000, a lot of money back then. This mansion was slightly battle-scarred from the fall nearby of a wartime bomb. Where a conservatory had stood was now a pile of rubble and glass. The name on the wide green gate was *Kingstackley*.

Our new home appeared enormous to us. It boasted seven bedrooms and two bathrooms on three floors, with a large basement in the cellar. The cellar became Dad's workshop. A hole knocked in a foundational wall down there opened up a dark labyrinth underneath the floor boards which became our den and secret base for planning and playing war games.

Kingstackley was our home for two years. We had moved in December, and our first Christmas was magical. On Christmas Day the sitting-room door was flung open to reveal the biggest Christmas tree we'd ever seen, every branch draped in silver icicles glinting in sunlight. At its foot nestled a beautiful nativity scene. New neighbours and nearby friends were invited to gather round the tree to sing carols, while one friend accompanied us on our fine Steinway grand piano. We knelt or sat on the floor and one musical visitor not much older than myself, taught me how to sing the descant of *Silent Night*. The atmosphere of warmth, friendship, and of great pleasure at being able to entertain in our own home still pervades my memories of that first *Kingstackley* Christmas, when I was nine.

I appreciate now what a privileged childhood we had. To have a home of our own was a novelty, and the two years there were happy and secure. Our fourth sister, Penelope Jane, was born in a maternity home in Sutton in 1951. I hoped she would arrive as a birthday present, but she only came at the end of April, two weeks after my eleventh birthday. We adored our small blonde newcomer with her big blue eyes and infectious chuckle, and nicknamed her Poppet because we all agreed she *was* one.

With first four, and then five children to rear almost single-handedly, our mother sought help. A succession of foreign au pairs began to troop through our lives. My father's aim was that they would teach us French. Some were more successful than others. The most popular was an artist from Paris, who was full of *joie de vivre* and humour. She came to us on two occasions and became a life-long friend. Successor to Chantal was the rather solemn Swiss Suzette who tried hard to teach us the rudiments of French. Sadly her most memorable quality was the store of delicious Swiss chocolate she kept in the bottom drawer in her room. Then came Loos, a Dutch girl in the throes of a whirling romance. Her mind seemed much preoccupied with her fiancé, Vim (pronounced Wim) whenever he came to visit. We thought this romance exciting, and hid behind the lounge-hall curtains to spy on their cuddling and kissing. It was somewhat of a relief to my mother when Loos returned to Holland to marry her Vim. The house settled back to its normal chaotic routine once more.

On two different occasions, we had whole families living with us. We lived communally together quite peaceably. This international pageant of strangers consisted mostly of friends whom our parents had made during their work with, and continued interest in, MRA: the men and women to whom Edward Howell had introduced my father during the war years. (*See Ch. 1*)

From one good-looking young Dane we learned the 'on guard' and 'lunge' positions in fencing; another friend wrote us a pantomime which we performed in the garden to our parents. The action broke down when the pantomime horse, made out of brown paper, came apart in mid scene, and both horse (Richard and I) and audience collapsed in helpless laughter. We enjoyed play-acting, and the lounge-hall, with its thick brown velvet curtains, proved a perfect theatre. The entrance hall became the stage, and the audience sat in the lounge part, subjected to whatever small sketches or pantomime we had written ourselves. In *Cinderella*, Richard's talent for comedy so surpassed itself that the panto finale became impossible to perform, such was the merriment all round!

Another of our parents' friends told us spooky ghost stories, and gave me a book he had written called *The Princess and the Goblin*; another was a botanist who decided to improve my education by taking me for long bicycle rides up hill and down dale on chalky Banstead Downs. He taught me how to look for and identify wild flowers. Inevitably, our young lives were enriched by all we learned from these informative people.

Φ

My mother's efficiency and warm-heartedness often eased Dad's way with other people, though at home his performance did not always match up to his idealism. Mum often stood between his frequent sternness with us and quick temper. She tried to shield us from his disciplinary ideas of child-rearing—attitudes gleaned, no doubt, from his own unhappy childhood memories of 'how things ought to be done'.

On Sundays, for instance, we would vacate the cosiness of the family kitchen-cum-breakfast room, with its big AGA cooker, and were permitted to enter the formality of the dining room for lunch. We regarded this as an inner sanctum. Not only was it our father's study, with a roll-top desk sitting in the bow window, but it had a snow-white carpet and tall orange velvet drapes which did little to relieve the unwelcome cold of the north-facing room. My father would preside at the head of the table, facing the Sunday roast. He loathed carving. It made him irritable. When we had all been served, we were required only to discuss matters of General Interest – a request bound to plunge us into total silence! If any food was left on the side of a plate, he would thunder at us reasons for 'not wasting food'. More than once Suzanne was relegated to the scullery because she refused, point blank, to eat gristle. A tense silence would ensue, and sometimes tears, which did nothing to relieve his mood or ours.

We did not enjoy Sundays. They often began by trooping to church, which was boring except when the vicar lost his temper and thumped the pulpit in an effort to make a point. Then lunches were invariably followed by being marshalled into the car and heading towards the Downs for an obligatory walk.

About this time, I began to develop a keen sympathy for the underdog. Not only did I seethe at what I saw as the injustice of Suzanne's punishments for her obstinacy, but I remember discovering Richard and Suzanne one day teasing and bullying our younger sister, Liz, causing her obvious distress. Consciously and furiously I chose to take her part from then on as her protector.

At the same time, such incidents as I've already described fanned in me a growing criticism of my father. He seldom relaxed and played with us, or laughed and joked, romped or even played football with his son. In his own way he really tried to be a father, but lacked a role model from his own youth. Once he constructed a wooden fort in the corner of two fences at the end of the garden, with a ladder up to a trapdoor only big enough for children to enter. He cut holes in the lawn, inserted flower-pots in each, and proceeded to tell us the rules of clock golf. This rather interfered with our frequent French Cricket matches as we had to avoid the pot-holes.

As youngsters we never quite managed to understand or connect with Dad. More often than not, of course, he was in London working or away travelling, so we were left to make up our own games and amusements and would always be in bed by the time he arrived home by train at night. As I grew older though, desperation sometimes drove me to beseech his help with my maths homework. I would stand beside his big desk trying to grasp his method as he explained how he moved from A to B to C to reach the solution, and would leave him afterwards feeling more confused than ever. His approach was different from that which my fiery-headed, quick-tempered Miss Taylor was trying to knock into my thick head at grammar school.

We were altogether freer and rowdier when he wasn't around, and never missed his company. A child doesn't know how a father ought to behave unless he is there to show them. He remained a distant figure whom we regarded with some awe and not a little apprehension whenever he was in evidence. On any occasion he returned from abroad, we gladly accepted the gifts he brought us. There is no doubt that Dad loved and cared about us, though we only realised this fully years later. He just never hit on how best to express that love in ways we could all connect.

Our mother was a person to whom we easily related. She created a bubble of love which bore us along, radiating light and happiness into each day of our young lives, so we were not aware of our father's absences or inadequacies. We grew up as normal children, squabbling, falling off our bicycles, scraping knees and elbows, losing rabbits or mice because a careless or over-attentive brother or sister left the cage door open, and playing hard at cowboys and indians, or inevitably, war games with our school friends. We were fortunate indeed to be well buffered against the world's problems by this parental vigilance and love.

Perhaps almost tangible was the unreality which cushioned us effectively against the harsh suffering and disasters of war. Our trip to the States, immediately after the war, had shielded us from the desperate struggle going on in our nation as it staggered to its feet and began to gather up the debris of cities, and rebuild the remnants of torn lives, homes, communities and industries. Therefore, by the time I turned eleven, those few short years in our lives had remained sublime.

Bubbles are beautiful, radiating rainbow colours and bringing joy to those who behold them. But, of course, they cannot last. When they burst, they evaporate into the air. The time was fast creeping upon us when our fragile life-bubble would burst: when the mainstays of our childhood years—security, peace of mind, happiness and love would be kicked from under us and vanish in the fall -out of rapidly changing circumstances.

In 1951 Dad was given an overseas posting to the Middle East, and we were about to enter yet another new phase in our family history. But this time, our seven lives would never be the same again.

4

The Stage is Set

All the world's a stage, and all the men and women merely players. They have their exits and their entrances...
As You Like It, Act 2 - *Shakespeare*

IN the autumn of 1951, Andrew was due to take up his new appointment as Wing Commander (Admin.) on the RAF Station, Habbaniya, in Iraq. Although this meant being down-graded a rank for the job, he accepted with alacrity for two good reasons: first, the posting was accompanied—he could take his family with him; and second, he already knew Iraq from the time when he had spent many happy months as a young man piloting flying boats, mainly in Basra and the Persian Gulf, before he married. The hum-drum of commuting daily from Cheam in Surrey by train to the Air Ministry in London hardly challenged his innate thirst for adventure and dynamism. This new posting rang with the echo of those far-off halcyon days spent in Iraq in the 1930s. It was just too good an opportunity to miss.

At the time, we had living with us in Kingstackley a family of five, friends of ours who were house-hunting in the area. Their three children comprised a blond, sensitive boy called Peter about Mary Liz's age, and his baby twin sisters, the same age as Poppet. She and the twins often spent noisy, happy hours together in the confines of the same play-pen.

When the Iraq posting was confirmed, the move seemed an ideal solution to the Foss family's immediate need for accommodation for the next two years. We were then free to leave our home safely in the care of friends.

Dad flew out first, followed by the rest of us some weeks later. With mounting excitement, we five children set forth with our mother from RAF Lyneham on our maiden flight. The old Hastings bomber transporting us had few of the comforts of modern air travel — no air-conditioning or adjustable seats to lie back and sleep; the seats had steel frames, the engine noise was interminable, and the pockets in front of us bulged with 'sick bags' instead of shiny in-flight magazines. This was inappropriately called an 'indulgence flight'. Thus was the lot of RAF men and their families, but we knew nothing to the contrary and were too excited about the Great Unknown ahead and two whole years living in a large oasis in the Iraqi desert. Visions of waving palm trees around a well rising out of an endless yellow desert full of shimmering mirages lay ahead.

The flight took two days, with a night in Tripoli for refuelling. The journey seemed to last for ever, flying over hundreds upon hundreds of miles of dun-coloured hills and plateaux, broken only by a few thin, silver snaking rivers thousands of feet below. This aerial map was our introduction to the timeless desert-world of the ancient Mesopotamian Bible lands that were to become our home.

When we reached Habbaniya, we stepped out of the plane into an Arabian enchantment. The warm night-air was balmy under a black-velvet, star-besprinkled sky. We walked down the flight steps into a changed world filled with exotic scents and sounds, date-palm silhouettes and ringing with the ceaseless singing of cicadas. Our married quarter, home for the next two years, was a tin-roofed bungalow in Palm Grove, cradled among gently rustling palms outside the screened windows and wide, covered verandah. Not so far distant, the eerie howling of jackals prowling along the banks of the River Euphrates wafted on the breeze.

To us suburbanites, this was as different as the moon is from the sun. This was paradise. Early on, we learned that the Garden of Eden is thought to have been sited at the confluence of the Tigris and Euphrates. Be that as it may, I fell in love with this ageless historical land which embraced us with its eastern charm.

The "oasis" turned out, in fact, to be a busy RAF base 52 miles west of Baghdad. It consisted of an aerodrome, a high-fenced civil cantonment to house the indigenous staff, a vast area of military barracks and married quarters, shops, including the NAAFI, a school and a man-made canal running along its borders—all this, sitting in the middle of a desert.

Never one to miss an opportunity to enlarge his children's experience of a country, father took us on a tour of some of the ancient sites. We gazed in awe at the four-thousand year-old water wheel at Hit on the Euphrates River, turning with the river-flow, spilling its clay water-pots into irrigation channels which carried its life-force into the vast fields of grain and vegetables along its banks, as it had done from time immemorial.

We went on to see the tall remains of what is thought to be the original Tower of Babel near Nineveh, and then moved on to the ruins of the once proud and beautiful Hanging Gardens of Babylon, built by King Nebuchadnezzar for his queen, Amytis. Only the liveliest imagination could conjure up from those dusty walls a picture of the wealth and power of King Nebuchadnezzar, 'the king of kings' as the prophet Daniel had called him, and ruler of all the then known civilized world. Nothing remained of the splendorous capital except excavations where numerous archaeologists had laid bare parts of its decorated walls. Pieces of broken cuneiform-script tablets, and even part of a blue glazed tile (found by Richard) – perhaps the records or libraries of the rich – scattered the dust-floor below the ground-level of the desert. It only needed a few vultures wheeling overhead to complete the shimmering air of desolation where once had throbbed the strength, cruelty and power emanating throughout Babylonia.

Saddam Hussein, during his reign of terror, began to reconstruct this ancient seat of power for himself.

We launched into this new and fascinating lifestyle with youthful enthusiasm. We admired young Arabs who shinned up tall palms in the grove behind our house to gather dates for their lunch. They ate these with chapattis made from a mixture of rough-ground brown flour mixed with water, patted into flat cakes and slapped round the sides of a little hole dug in the hard earth with a fire lit in the middle of it. They may have been Bedouins, or were reverting to their nomadic Bedouin traditions. The age-old system of irrigation flooded our lawns with river-water every week, bringing life to the pink and white Oleanders and lush green to the lawns and foliage in the camp. Daily along the dusty roadside near our house, we saw black-clad women in purdah riding donkeys side-saddle, as they hugged the shade of towering Eucalyptus trees. Bare-footed men, astride these overladen beasts of burden, would goad the patient animals in the flank with a large stick or cruel-looking nail. Just up the road from Palm Grove, the station cookhouse vented a pervasive smell of hot grease from its high windows, and several transistor radios at once would blare forth warbling tones of Arab songs or eastern pipe music.

Our bungalow was identical to all the others in the Palm Grove officers' quarters, with a corrugated iron roof, and walls made of sun-baked bricks plastered with a mixture of mud and straw called 'mutti'. The interior was modern, and every room had a large ceiling fan, while all doors and windows were fitted with a metal screen of mosquito netting. The red-tiled floors, highly polished by our cook/bearer Dinkah, helped preserve a cooler temperature during the day when every window was shuttered against the sun's blistering heat. Sometimes, without warning, a fierce sandstorm swept in from the desert and layers of fine dust blew through every crack in window or door in the house. At such times, Dinkah taught us to tie handkerchiefs round our faces to filter out the choking dust. After the storm had abated, he would spend hours cleaning and polishing the dust-laden surfaces on furniture and floors. The smell of dust remained on our bed linen.

Dinkah Dawid Ishoo was a cheerful Kurd from northern Iraq, who lived in the civil cantonment on camp with his family. His lean, handsome features with hooked nose and mischievous grin attracted us all, and we often gravitated to the kitchen quarters where he would hum or sing his native Kurdish songs while preparing some meal or other. He would supply us with endless jugs of Jungle Juice, powdered lemonade mixed with water. His culinary specialities were Ladies' Fingers (Okra), boiled and covered with vinegar; he also tossed the lightest pancakes, served with lemon juice and sugar, devoured hungrily by us children as they left the pan. He distinguished himself in our eyes by demonstrating how to smoke his pungent Turkish cigarettes. Richard asked Dinkah to buy some for him and his friends, which they duly smoked hiding behind the bushes. From Dinkah we also learned rudimentary Arabic which included the odd naughty phrase which he forbade us to use within earshot of the Sahib or Memsahib.

We had a second servant called Laya, the large-bosomed Assyrian mother of many. Laya washed our laundry in the wash-house beside the kitchen, reluctantly shared the housework with Dinkah, and looked after our sister Poppet in the afternoons like one of her own. I can see her round, happy face now, her head bound in a scarf, carrying Poppet who had one hand plunged deep inside the front of Laya's ample clothing! She was as delighted as we were when our youngest sister took her first careering steps on the front lawn. I can only surmise that Laya's own children were already grown up or able to take care of themselves, and that they too must have lived in the civil cantonment, or CC as we called it.

With this help in the house, mother, used to running a large household at home in England raising five children, now found herself a lady of leisure. She played tennis, knitted and crocheted to her heart's content, made clothes for us, including the minutest bikinis for little Poppet, and spent many hours each day basking beside the officers' swimming pool across the road from our quarter, talking with other wives. She soon grew accustomed to the relaxed lifestyle, and became dark-tanned and befreckled. Her Egyptian childhood had inured her to high temperatures, and she revelled in warmth and sunshine throughout her life.

Φ

Meanwhile, we four older children attended the RAF School (now my eighth) which began each day at 7.30 a.m. We would walk there in the cool of the morning, sometimes followed by our young donkey Frisky, which our father had bought as a pet in order for us to learn to ride. Father had a donkey-size saddle and bridle made for this purpose, but had overlooked the fact that he would need breaking in. Richard was the only one who dared ride him, as Frisky's sole aim, it seemed, was to land any potential rider in the nearest irrigation ditch. He was a small bucking bronco, and even though I was riding by then, I never dared risk trying my luck. Frisky remained tied to a verandah post outside the bungalow where his loud braying, day and night, became a local nuisance-feature. He discovered he could bite through his rope and break loose, especially when he felt he was missing some fun with the children. This invariably happened when we were about to go out, and we had to do a rapid search for him; or when we were walking to school, Frisky would come trotting up behind us, eager to join in the action. This raised disapproving comments among the teachers at school about time wasted taking him home again, but the fun of the furore amongst the pupils was well worth it.

In summer, we would go home at 1.30 by bus or army 'gharry' (truck) for lunch and a compulsory rest during the hottest part of the day, after which we spent most of our free time swimming, playing tennis or, in my case, often riding at the local stables. In the cooler days of winter, there was afternoon school, so more bussing back and forth, singing songs such as 'There were buns, buns, bullets for the guns... in the quarter-master's stores.'

Like many a teenage girl, horses claimed my passion at the time, and up at the stables there was a dappled grey hunter called Quicksilver. He was twenty-two years old with an awkward and uncomfortable gait, but had truly earned his name by his amazing speed. I learned how to groom him, feed him, and I loved him dearly. On frequent rides outside the boundaries of our camp oasis, I always rode Quickie, serenading him on my mouth-organ.

The desert with its light and shadows at dawn and dusk, its ever-changing moods in heat and cold, was so different from what I had imagined. Instead of sand, it was a fine light-brown dust, anchored sparsely by prickly tumbleweed similar to dried gorse. The beige contours of undulating hills or plateaux shimmered in the blazing sun. On some days, strong winds would sweep over it, whipping up clouds of suffocating dust, mouthfuls of grit, and then clumps of tumbleweed rolled haphazardly across the desert, their shallow roots ripped out by the force of the storm. The dusty hills glistened with layers of flaky gypsum and mica, and were peppered with dark cave-mouths, shadowed gullies and wadis where erosion by heavy, infrequent rainfall and strong winds moulded and re-moulded the desertscape in their timeless task.

When the weather allowed, we rode through the hills, with a picnic and swimming gear packed in a saddle-bag, making for the four-mile-long reservoir of Lake Habbaniya. We would start early in the cool of the day, and ride out past straggling encampments of black tents where nomadic Bedouins dwelt, surrounded by half-wild, lean pie-dogs (as we called them) and goats, having settled near the canal surrounding part of the air force base. As we crossed the canal bridge, we would stop to watch the shadowy forms of large terrapins meandering ponderously beneath in the murky waters.

A frequent sight was a Muslim at worship, pausing in his travels or work, reverently bowed towards Mecca praying to Allah, during one of the five daily prayer-times. The Arabs' all-time-all-weather ankle-length garments of undyed cotton with chequered head-dresses crowned with black rings of twisted goat-hair, seemed stiflingly hot for such sweltering temperatures.

Mustapha, our stable-boy companion, explained that these were ideal for a desert dweller, protecting him against the merciless glare of the sun's scorching heat: his body heat thermostatically controlled, and the ample material on head and neck swathing the face against both sun and dust-storms. Equally, these weathered nomads must have wondered at our thin cotton shirts, hats, arms bare to the sun, and cotton (though in my case, woollen) jodhpurs, as we rode past.

Lake Habbaniya was a basic holiday resort, with a Rest-and-Leave Centre run by the Air Force for British troops on the camp. The vast expanse of water was frequented every weekend by swimmers and members of the sailing club. When our riding school arrived there, we swam on horseback in its cool waters. The rocks and cliffs round the lake were natural diving-boards. After a day out swimming and picnicking, we returned to the camp in the evening, with Mustapha always in close attendance, and the young airmen who also rode with us.

My father's one relaxation and enjoyment was sailing on Lake Habbaniya in his Airborne dinghy. He won the Coronation Regatta, largely due (he assured us) to the large quantities of Mansion furniture polish with which we children polished the bottom of the boat. We often sailed with him. (After the British ceded all their responsibilities to the Iraqis in 1956, the camp and the lake were later developed by Saddam Hussein into a grand sports and leisure complex, probably for his own use since it was fairly accessible to the capital Baghdad.)

My father learned Arabic, and was soon able to converse with the locals and read an Arabic newspaper (from right to left). His administrative position included playing host to frequent visitors to the camp, giving and attending cocktail parties, and appearing at any social occasions laid on as entertainment at the station officers' and airmen's messes in the evenings. Isolated in the desert as the camp was, the residents made their own amusements, and always welcomed new faces.

Inevitably, ennui set in among the wives, and there is nothing like boredom to disseminate the latest gossip and create rumours, especially while lazing round a swimming-pool.

My parents' rather wider life-view than suntan and pleasure prompted them to introduce a weekly Bible-study evening in our home. This gave support and fellowship to some of the Christian servicemen and officers on the station, and aimed to raise morale. The RAF chaplain and his family became friends. On one occasion, we entertained for lunch the visiting Bishop in Jerusalem, whom I regarded with awe. As he departed to his waiting Bentley, I chased across the lawn to ask for his autograph in my Bible. I remember, too, the Bishop's encouragement to my parents to visit him in Jerusalem to see something of the Holy Land. I was captivated by the idea of such a visit, and begged them to let us go. When sometime later it became necessary to seek respite from the intense summer heat during our final summer holiday in Habbaniya, we should have heeded the Bishop's invitation. Had we done so, events might have turned out very differently...

Instead, it was decided that our mother should travel north with us children to a camp in the Kurdish mountains which had been set up for servicemen and their families. Ser Armadia was on the Iraqi/Turkish border, far from the blistering heat of the dusty plains. On arrival in buses at the foothills, we transferred to sure-footed mules which carried us up and ever upwards on an incredibly narrow rocky track, towards the cool, craggy heights and trickling mountain streams, where we found the khaki army tents which were to be our holiday home. Richard had arrived at the camp three weeks ahead of us, with the Scouts.

Away up on the Iraqi border, we could see mountains in both Turkey and Iran from this eyrie as well as enjoying the beautiful natural theatre of snow-capped Kurdish mountains with their dramatic changes of scene, climate and colours, and the violence of sudden electric storms such as we had never yet experienced. We were mesmerised by lightning flashes below us and thunderous rumblings overhead as we sheltered between the double coverings of our tents.

Unbeknown to us, storm clouds of a different nature were gathering. I was enjoying myself so much that it only gradually impinged that all was not well. My mother was unhappy. She would lie for hours on her camp bed in our family tent, showing little interest in any of our exploits. Back at the airbase I had been aware for some time of the growing tension in my parents' relationship. My mother had confided to me some of the issues on her mind. But I did not want to think about anything uncomfortable and unpleasant while away in our mountain eyrie, even though I felt uneasy seeing her unusual state of inertia. Aged thirteen and developing fast in a hot climate, I was discovering an attraction to men. Also out from Habbaniya, and holidaying there, was an army engineer, almost twice my age. The gentle art of flirtation developed out of an exciting and flattering disScovery of male interest and quickly became a novel pursuit. I became infatuated, and certainly had no time to be of any comfort to my mother.

In that idyllic amphitheatre of majestic peaks and grassy valleys we had been somewhat lulled by the hot days of summer into a trance-like forgetfulness of reality. Who would have imagined that our imminent return to the air base at the beginning of August was to be the end of an almost perfect childhood?

My father was caught completely off guard. In his

wildest nightmares, he could not have envisioned the forthcoming chaotic scenario. Only our mother perhaps, wrestling her way through her confusion of thoughts and loyalties on her camp bed in the mountains, would have had any inkling of impending disaster. She sensed danger, and intimated as much to Dad once in the ensuing few days back at the base, as we prepared hurriedly to leave Habbaniya to return to the United Kingdom, but he was not inclined to listen. His denial was to cost him dear.

Shortly, the scheming, invisible snake of Misfortune would slither from the wings. Twice he had pursued his prey in other families, and now he awaited a third chance to flick out a forked tongue to strike at ours.

Our paternal grandparents Hilda & Roy Combe

Grandfather Roy and family: Janet, Andrew, Nick, Marion and Betsy

'Sir John Salmond presenting the sword of honour to Cadet-under-officer A.N.Combe at the passing-out inspection of flight cadets at RAF College, Cranwell.' (caption from newspaper)

Record-breaking Vickers Wellesleys    *Andrew with the crew of his Wellesley*

The Long Range Development Unit arrives in Darwin, Australia

Dad, Andrew Combe

Eileen Jessop's engagement photo

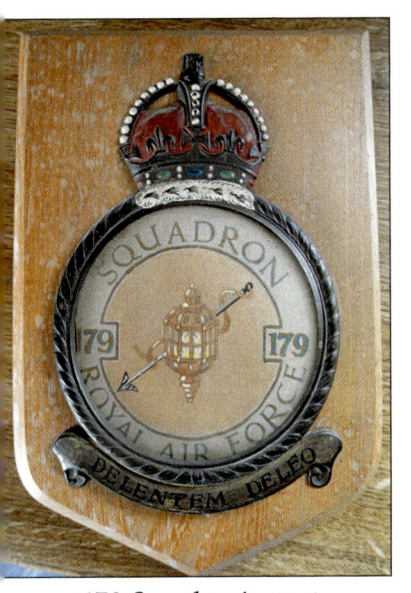

179 Squadron's crest designed by Andrew

Wing Commander Edward Howell (Dad's boozing chum)

Andrew Combe and Eileen Jessop
13th May 1939

Eileen's father,
Albert William Jessop

Our maternal Grand-parents

Eileen's mother,
Muriel Clutten (Bull) Jessop

L to R Rex, Eileen, Torrie & Paddy
sailing from Alexandria to Ireland

Eileen and sister Torrie
in their teens

*Great Auntie
Florence Drury*

*Granny
(Hilda)
Combe*

*Richard & Jenny
at the Old School
House, Blakeney,
during evacuation*

*Blakeney,
Norfolk,
home of
Granny
Combe*

*Richard,
Suzanne &
Jenny
paddling in
Blakeney
Cut*

Richard, Jenny, & Suzanne in
Kensington Gardens during WW2

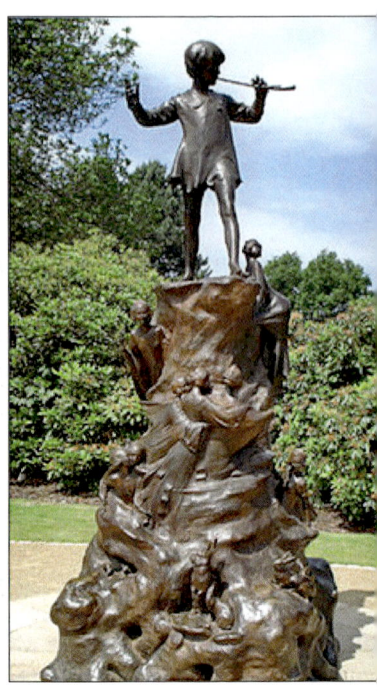

Peter Pan in Kensington Gardens
sculpture by Sir George Frampton

Peter & Doë Howard, with their
children: Philip, Anthony & Anne
at Hill Farm, Lavenham, Suffolk
(below) scene of our second
evacuation in WW2

5

Hoodwinked!

The owl looked up to the stars above
And sang to a sweet guitar,
'Oh lovely pussy, O pussy my love,
What a beautiful pussy you are…'
The Owl and the Pussycat – Edward Lear

THE threat to our Utopian existence crept up on us unseen, and the gradual awareness of it is hard to pin-point. We certainly never questioned the appearance in our midst of a fellow officer called Squadron Leader Peter Caddy. He was one more person in our lives. My parents knew little about him other than that he had met friends of theirs at a house-party in Kenya. On one of Caddy's visits to that hospitable Kenyan home (where I gather he sometimes read love-poems to the assembled company) my father's name had been mentioned as an RAF officer serving in Habbaniya. Ours was one of the many Air Force bases in the Middle East for which Sqn Ldr Caddy had overall charge of the catering.

My father had read an article on leadership written by him, and was interested to meet him. Reports conflict as to how they first met. My father's job was administrative, and catering was one of his fields of supervision. They soon discovered they shared a common interest in the work of Moral Re-armament (later to be renamed Initiatives of Change) which doubtless would have been a strong reason for my parents extending friendship towards him.

My first recollection of Caddy was at a Bible-study evening my parents had initiated in our home. He was tall, athletic, sun-bronzed, super-confident and good-looking. Assuming him to be a friend of our parents, we called him Uncle Peter. Not long after Peter's arrival on the scene, my parents were invited to a fancy dress ball at the RAF officers' mess. At home, Dinkah hovered in the background as baby-sitter, and Poppet was already in bed. It was a hot night, and the doors into the sitting-room from the verandah were wide open to encourage a breeze. We chose to play pirates before bed-time, and up-turned all the drawing room furniture so we could leap from one piece to the next without setting foot on the floor (the sea). In the midst of this mini-mayhem, a loud shout came from outside and a knock on the fly-screen door. We pirates froze. Tentatively, I pushed open the screen door and peered into darkness to see who was there. It was an old tramp. He asked to see our parents. I was quite frightened, until I recognised the voice as Uncle Peter's. He was off to the fancy-dress party. We told him our parents had already left, so he went on alone. Being a newcomer to the social scene, Peter had hoped to be included as a guest of my parents, but for some reason they had not invited him. We heard next day that he had gate-crashed the party and that my father was furious. Trouble was brewing.

This seemingly unimportant incident triggered off both a dislike and distrust for Caddy which persisted for years, probably partly due to my father's reaction about the party. From then on, he was a 'tramp in the dark', and I never quite lost my initial sense of fear - perhaps only a 'gut-reaction' at the time. A child can quickly detect the motivation behind an adult's doubtful intentions. At the time, I had little idea of the tension his presence was prompting between my parents. Years later I learned something of my father's feelings around that time, expressed in a letter he wrote to a friend...

(Peter) Caddy came - and talked - and was clearly setting his cap at my wife. I got uneasy, and more so when I found a book by her bedside which Caddy had given her to read called 'The Gospel of Thomas' or something like that, published in New York. It emasculated the gospel of Christ and presented

Jesus as a non-Divine do-gooder - or so I thought. But Eileen was clearly attracted to Caddy...

Whatever my father may have noticed going on, he did not voice his growing fears. However, the change in my parents' relationship began to be noticeable: raised voices over money-matters, accusations about my mother spending too much; an argument about the make-up she was now wearing, and the odd drink she was taking. (This was a reversal of my parents' lifestyle in which they neither served alcohol in our home nor drank it socially. And my mother had never worn make-up, from as far back as I could remember.)

One evening, before my parents were due to attend a function, Mum popped her head round my bedroom door. She looked quite beautiful in a green, white and black evening dress we had chosen together before we left England, and I noticed her red lips then, for the first time. In her book, she tells how my father told her to 'go and wash that muck off!'

Change was in the air, and not for the better, I felt. Why were these things happening more often now, or was I growing up and seeing things I had not been aware of previously? My mother began confiding in me about her distress. We became extremely close friends during that time when she could not confide in anyone else for fear of station gossip.

A sense of dread began to take root, and I found myself now and then taking my mother's part in sympathy against my father. Sometimes I dared speak up in open conflict, fuelled by fury at seeing her tears, and the person I loved most being wrongfully hurt by him. That was how I perceived her situation from her viewpoint. As a growing child, I had taken for granted the love I felt for our mother, but when I saw her unhappy, I felt threatened with her. The common front with which we faced my father at that time, must have been a formidable force, and would have added to my father's anger and growing jealousy. This would have made my mother's position even more untenable. Rows escalated between the three of us, but were shielded from the rest of the family.

On one occasion as I stood at the wash-basin in the bathroom trying to swallow the obligatory salt tablets (prescribed to all air force personnel to replace salt lost in perspiration in the hot climate), my mother came into the bathroom crying. She had just come from a fearful shindig with my father, and blurted out, 'I wonder how all this will end?' Both her tears and her remark made the cold hand of dread clutch tighter in my stomach. 'An end to this situation' was a thought I had never entertained before: things would surely soon settle back to normal. The unpleasantness was only a passing phase, and would vanish as things improved. It did not click then that Peter Caddy had become the X-factor in the troubled equation.

It should be explained here that I had felt contempt for my father for some time. Something in me had rebelled at being 'put on show' (as I felt we often were) with the rest of the family whenever we had visitors. Whether this was because I had sensed we were acting out a 'happy family' charade, or whether I recoiled at his blatant display of parental pride, I cannot say. Probably both. I only know I hated being dragged from my room and my books by his command each time we were to be presented. Added to this, whenever he put a hand on my shoulder or pushed me in the direction of some request he asked me to carry out, I made a point of squirming out from under his hand, openly defiant.

Contempt flared into open rebellion because of the unhappiness he was inflicting on my mother. I was twelve by then, and old enough to grasp that when father shouted at mother and mother was in tears, my ideal world was falling apart. As my father's jealousy and over-protectiveness of her increased, so did her reaction against his authoritarianism.

No one else in the family circle or outside it was aware of the ominous rumblings of this emotional volcano. As I did not have the courage to admit even in my own thoughts what my fears might be, they remained unconfided to anyone. My brother Richard and sisters Suzanne and Mary Liz remained blissfully ignorant of any ructions.

Then illness struck. I spent my thirteenth birthday in bed. My parents thought I had 'flu, accustomed as they had been to my frequent ear troubles from babyhood. This time, however, I went stone deaf, and the doctor put this down to an excessive amount of swimming and diving which had ruptured both eardrums. I was confined to bed for a week, and had just begun to get up for meals when matters took a turn for the worse. A meteoric rise in temperature caused a somewhat dramatic departure to the hospital in a jeep-ambulance. Though semi-delirious, I was vaguely aware of a dust-storm raging which had borne with it a swarm of locusts. The latter reduced the entire local flora to desolation.

Not surprisingly, the doctors thought I had contracted sandfly fever which was rife at the time. To be certain, however, they decided to take a lumbar puncture, for by now I was paralysed. The pain of this injection into my lower spine was excruciating, but my retching and groans went unheeded. The diagnosis: poliomyelitis. My mother did not tell me I had polio. I lay paralysed from the neck downwards for six weeks, unable to move any part of my body, being fed like a baby from a teapot-shaped feeding cup. All I craved was lettuce and potato crisps. I felt embarrassed and humiliated at being bed-bathed and turned over many times daily like a pig on a spit, and swabbed with surgical spirit to prevent bedsores.

Every afternoon Mum would visit me and sit chatting by my bedside, embroidering a tablecloth which she nearly completed in the eight weeks I remained in the RAF hospital. One day I asked her what was wrong with me. 'You've had polio,' she said quietly. I was horrified, and found it hard to believe I had become victim to the very disease I had most feared, ever since a boy from our class in Cheam, England, had disappeared one day with polio. We heard he had nearly died. I learned from my mother that there were three other polio victims on the camp. One was the fair, curly-headed two-year-old Janet Radcliffe, in a cot nearby, who reminded me of Poppet. She would never be able to walk again without callipers. The other two were airmen one of whom was in an iron-lung in a Baghdad hospital by then, and another who died. None of us knew each other. It was later thought that the polio virus had been transmitted by irrigation water used for locally-grown water melons - a reasonable theory in my case, given my penchant for water melon.

Total paralysis can have its frightening moments. One of these occurred when I was moved from isolation in an end ward to another single ward, within shouting distance of the nurses should I need them. By day, I gazed out of the window at a laden fig-tree. One particularly warm night, the mesh window had been left open, and dozens of small black beetles flew in, attracted to the light above the bed. Each one pinged against the glass light-shade and dive-bombed onto the bed, temporarily stunned. I watched, horrified, as they gained consciousness and began crawling all over me. Unable to move to escape, I let out a scream which brought the night nurse running.

After this incident, six weeks of inertia led to boredom. I was determined to get well and became a little stronger each day. When I could sit up, and work my arms again, the kindly nurses put me in a wheel chair so I could accompany them on their rounds and visit the other patients. I learned how to take a temperature and make gauze swabs, and how to fold a neat hospital corner when making up the beds. I played endless solitary games of clock patience, and did jigsaw puzzles. One day, a nurse brought me a brand new puzzle, and I was delighted to find a small Gideon New Testament Bible in the box among the pieces as I opened it.

Finally, the doctor gave me an ultimatum: I must be able to kiss my knees before I could get out of bed to walk. I practised every day until I could lean and reach my knees. Unsupervised, I eased my lifeless legs over the edge of the bed, and dropped my feet to the floor. As they took my body-weight, my feet and legs were shot through with pain like a million needles piercing every sinew and atrophied muscle. Teeth clenched and sweating, I was determined to reach the door handle of the big swing-doors which stood open only centimetres away from the high bed. At first, my spindly legs crumpled like rotten sticks as I lurched forward and clung to the doorhandle. I crawled back to the bed, hauled myself up on to it to re-group so I could try again. Determined, I launched the weight of my skinny body on those two aching pins again, and yet again, until I could walk a few steps.

Some months previously, I had watched Poppet take her first halting and unsteady steps before she collapsed in giggles. We had been so proud of her, and so excited as she careered round in circles, learning to become fully mobile. I little dreamed I would feel the same sense of pride and achievement a short time later when I took those first few steps recovering from polio.

The road to full strength did not take long once determination set in. I was discharged after two months, and swam every day, on doctor's orders. Before long I managed fifty-two lengths of the officers' pool non-stop, which amounted to one mile. My mother watched me, amazed. Thanks to the swimming and the week's rest I had had before the paralysis developed, I suffer no ill effects - unlike my little golden-haired friend, Janet.

Mum told me that the earache before the polio had saved my life, and my parents talked of my recovery as a miracle. They told me that I had been prayed for at church. The kind congregation's prayers had certainly been heard and answered, but it was some time before I understood how fortunate I had been. People seemed interested in my recovery, and I began to feel somewhat of a celebrity.

I had not known the extent of my parents' anxiety over my illness. Months afterwards I learned that each of them had thought independently that, as they put it, God was 'calling me for His own.' They concluded naturally enough that my illness was terminal, and had prepared themselves mentally for that outcome. When they told me about my close brush with death, I was more than glad and relieved that I had been spared. I loved life, and was by no means ready to die.

One of the bright memories during the convalescent months was of the Coronation of Her Majesty Queen Elizabeth II. At school that day, we were presented with Coronation mugs and a certificate. As head girl, I had to make my first public speech of thanks. That afternoon, I lay on my bed on a sweltering June afternoon, with the huge fan on the ceiling whirring at high speed, and tuned in to the BBC World Service. I pictured every glittering, romantic moment of the occasion through the rich tapestry of commentary, as if I had actually been among the London crowds, or sitting in Westminster Abbey watching our new monarch being crowned in state. I was proud of my Queen and proud to be British, even if we were several thousand miles away, sitting in a hot desert.

Soon afterwards, I was sent back into hospital with an ulcerated throat, but was out again after two days as my mother succumbed to the same, but more virulent, virus. She needed me at home to help with the rest of the family. 'Look after the family, darling,' she bade me, as we passed on the lawn outside the house exchanging places and roles, I heading for the house, and she for the waiting jeep-ambulance which had just delivered me home. Her words proved somewhat prophetic. My mother had just handed me a baton, as in a relay race. All at once I felt both honoured and very grown-up at her words, conscious for the first time of being the eldest and, in my mind, the most responsible for my siblings. In the mêlée of memories of that time, this stands out as a pre-vision of what was to come.

However, as I entered the house, the deep-seated sense of dread returned. It was so different without Mum there. Her absence cast a cloud over the household. I wanted to escape from under its dark shadow, and found the easy way out was into the world of books. I began to shut myself away in my room to read, listen to old opera records, tried to write a children's novel, and set up a lending library of my book collection. The routines of each day happened anyway, with Laya looking after Poppet and the laundry, and our meals provided by Dinkah; school in the morning and swimming in the pool across the road in the hot afternoons after a rest. Morning dressing, and bed- and bath-times were my only real responsibilities. That is when the bossy big sister took over, but it was a great relief when Mum returned from hospital.

At this point, the merciless summer heat took us up to northern Iraq into the mountains, I suspect as much to provide a temporary breather from the mounting tensions between my parents as for a pleasant holiday. When we arrived back in camp at Habbaniya at the beginning of August, it was to find that arrangements had been made for my mother to take the five of us back to England, ostensibly to find schools for the three eldest before the new academic year started in September. My father's posting was due to finish in October.

Our departure from Habbaniya was so abrupt that we hardly had a chance to say goodbye properly to all our friends. I could not understand the hurry and bustle of leaving so fast. I packed up my bedroom sadly, with its wardrobe full of books from the lending library, and wrote a 'goodbye' note, which I hung behind the mirror for the next occupant. It was upsetting to be wrenched unceremoniously from our paradise with no warning, and worst of all, I felt angry at being parted from the slowly developing relationship I had with my man-friend from Ser Armadia. I had flexed my teenage wings and tasted the excitement of a new interest - in men. In those circumstances, our departure could not be anything but an unhappy one, the least happy and most apprehensive person being my mother. She revealed years later in her autobiography:

(Andrew) fixed a date for us to travel, and when Peter heard about it he said he would try to get a seat on the plane at Tripoli so he could help me with the children. I had an ominous feeling that if I got on that plane something awful would happen. I could not put my finger on what that might be, but I felt strongly enough to try to persuade Andrew to change the date. I couldn't tell him of my premonition, as it sounded foolish, and he brushed my request aside. The night before we left I lay awake with a sinking feeling in my stomach.[1]

In her confused state, Mum managed to over-dose us children with travel-sickness pills for the flight, which left us reeling like under-age drunkards on the airfield. My riding friends from the stables turned up on horseback on the landing strip to wave farewell and I was asked to hold Rafai, one of the horses, while a young airman dismounted. The animal proceeded to lie down and roll in the sand, saddle and all, and I stood there stupidly watching it, too doped up and dizzy to prevent it. I knew perfectly well we were never allowed to let our horses roll.

After tearful goodbyes, we climbed aboard the aircraft, and my sister Suzanne sat beside me. A short while after take-off, Sue's sense of humour recovered enough for her to start singing Arab songs, mimicking Dinkah and Arab pipe music and singing into a sick-bag as we bumped our way through the hot air thermals over the desert on the long flight towards Africa. She kept me in a state of giggles. I look back on this bit of comic relief with gratitude, as it dispelled some of the misery caused by the untimely wrench from friends and that lovely land.

Our departure had been rapid, but someone was already at work with swifter plans. As our Hastings bomber lumbered down onto the airfield at Tripoli for overnight refuelling, who should we see waiting there to meet us but Peter Caddy. My mother had suspected he would be there, of course, but the rest of us had no idea then of his intention to be there to greet us. On the face of it, this was a thoughtful gesture: a friendly face smiling as we came down the steps. So what was there about him being there that gave me an uncomfortable sense of distrust? Well, it would not be long before the reason would become all too clear.

6

Hijacked!

*...a puppet in the power of great forces that cared
nothing for family or class or creed, but moved
machine-like, with dread processes to inscrutable ends.*
The Forsyte Saga – *by John Galsworthy*

PRIOR to leaving Habbaniya, there had been some talk about my mother taking a crocodile-skin handbag back to England for Peter Caddy who said he wanted to give it as a present to his wife, Sheena. This may have been a customs evasion, but when we found Caddy waiting in Tripoli, I convinced myself that his presence there had something to do with the precious handbag.

Although it seemed strange that he had arrived at the airbase in Tripoli at the same time as us, it did not occur to me that he was really there to get to know my mother better. Nor did I realise until later, when I saw my mother with the crocodile bag at home, that in all probability the handbag had been a present for her and not for his wife.

That evening in Tripoli, Caddy took Eileen out to see the town by night while we slept off the effects of the flight. Emotional exhaustion had taken its toll after the sadness of leaving our friends in Habbaniya.

The following day, Peter was there on the tarmac ready to usher us on board for the final stage of the flight to RAF Lyneham. Then to my amazement, he climbed on board to accompany us. My mother recalls:

Although he had been told that the plane was already 2000 lbs overloaded, he was determined to get on it. It was my first experience of the power of Peter's positive thinking. He arrived at the airport next morning to discover there was one seat left, which happened to be next to me... [1]

When we landed and stepped off the plane at

Lyneham, the lush green trees and grass of England's 'green and pleasant land' was startling, after the arid desert wastes we had left behind. As wind blew drizzle into our faces, we knew we were truly back in England.

Events moved fast after that. Sheena (Peter's second wife) met us at the airfield in Caddy's sleek black Lagonda, and drove us to Cheam. They lived in London, so we did not see Sheena again for a while. Peter, however, became a regular visitor, though we were hardly aware of this during all the excitement of those early days of our homecoming. Little by little he impinged on our consciousness, as he regaled us at meal-times with stories of his exploits. One in particular was of an expedition he had led on foot into Tibet. He talked of his prowess as an athlete, and in particular as a long-distance runner.

He tried especially hard to make friends with us, and gave each one of us children an expensive present. As he was due to return to Habbaniya shortly, my special request was for a swish (to keep flies at bay when riding in a hot climate) of Quicksilver's tail. My old friend had been put down after we left - a parting which added to the great wrench of leaving Habbaniya. I had asked for Quickie's long silver tail in memory of him, and Caddy promised he would try to get this for me. This wish never materialised. In the end I had to be content with a bone-handled riding crop instead, and some rare Tibetan stamps, as he had discovered my interest in stamp-collecting.

He gave no explanation as to what had happened to Quicksilver, which might have softened the edge of my disappointment. I remember, too, the embarrassment of having to thank him for something I did not want and his insistence that I keep it. The pressure made the gesture feel he was bribing me to like him. Bribery was a practice we had learned about in Habbaniya when my father, in his administrative capacity, often received beautiful gifts from traders hopeful of his doing some favour for them in return. All gifts were quickly returned to their owners.

Caddy's presence in our home did not seem unusual. We had been used to having people being part of our family life. However, I had come to dislike and distrust the man, not only because of his boastful demeanour. Worse than this, he was monopolising mother's time and attention. One day I walked unannounced into our drawing-room in Kingstackley, and found him with his arm around my mother on the sofa, close together, and studying photos.

Deeply embarrassed, I closed the door quickly, conscious that I had interrupted something special. I flared up in angry jealousy on my side of the door. How *dare* he put his arm round *my* mother? I was dumb-struck that she had seemed quite unconcerned at my interruption, and had showed no discomfiture. Clearly she was caught up in her interest in the photographs, and just continued talking to him normally. I stole away, full of foreboding.

The mental image of their togetherness shocked and haunted me. Surely what I had seen could not be real? My mother had never behaved like that before. I was sure there must be a reasonable explanation and that she would tell me all about it later.

She must have realised that she was being wooed, but probably did not know that she was also being cleverly manipulated by the Caddys. Peter knew, but Eileen did not, that the physical and spiritual director of this charade was his wife. Sheena lurked in the wings watching every move, carefully choreographing her cast of two adults and five children.

In hindsight, I see her as a spider enticing her prey from the safety of a nearby branch into the hopeless entanglement of her web. Shamelessly using her husband as the lure, they wove a web of intrigue around the unsuspecting prisoner. The spider crouched for the moment to pounce upon the trapped victim.

My mother was certainly infatuated by Peter's debonair charm. But although she was playing a dangerous game, would she listen to the warning bells sounding in her conscience? As the web-strands grew tighter, her conscience's exertions against the combined Caddy-force became feebler.

By this time, she may have found the allure and magnetism of a man who (as she wrote years later) made her feel 'truly loved for the first time' in her life too difficult to resist, compared with enduring the pains of an empty and volatile marriage, not to mention the restraints of rearing her five children who, it must be said, adored her.

It did not occur to Eileen to give any thought to Peter's past: to question his track record of two wives and two children already in his wake. She saw only his successes and charm.

It was the middle of August 1953, and the Caddy partnership needed to work fast if their dark scheme was to reach fruition before my father's return from Iraq in October. Sheena applied herself assiduously to dispel each difficulty standing in the way of full capitulation.

Dazzled by this new explosion of feelings, Eileen could not yet see that her destiny was being mapped out for her. Agonizingly, she found herself caught between her family life and her new love for Peter. At this point, my father played right into the schemers' hands. He returned home early, and slammed the door of our family home in mother's face, which pitched her effortlessly into the Caddys' web. There was no longer a choice to be made.

Finally, she was trapped, and found herself hovering on the brink of a terrifying discovery.

7

The Spider's Parlour

'Will you walk into my parlour?'
Said the spider to the fly;...
'The way into my parlour is up a winding stair;
And I have many curious things to show you when you're there...'
Mary Howitt (1799–1888)

MY mother and I had been invited to a private preview of a technicolour film called *Jotham Valley* by some friends in London's West End. I was excited at the prospect, since we had been starved of any culture, television, and films for two years, except for one Indian melodrama at a drive-in cinema. Mother said we could combine this outing with a visit to the Caddys since they lived nearby in Victoria. Unbeknown to me, this was part of the Caddys' plan.

The film was a colourful musical set on a deep-southern farm in the States, almost Oklahoma-style, but the beautiful songs held a message of hope, as the story was about the hatred of two brothers who became reconciled. Their re-union affected the whole valley and town, and the audience. It was both uplifting and enjoyable.

Then we took a bus to Lupus Street, and climbed some dark stairs to the first-floor flat belonging to the Caddys. The room seemed only a little brighter than the stairway, and as we entered the gloom, we saw Sheena sitting in an armchair. I became aware of her as a personality for the first time. She was thin and pale, a delicate-looking woman with large, dark eyes and dark curly hair. Immediately behind her armchair, were display cupboards filled with rows of silver cups, trophies and shields. There were more still along the tops of the cupboards. Following my gaze, she explained that these represented Peter's triumphs as an athlete.

As far as I remember, we were only there a few minutes before Caddy suggested he would take me off on my own to eat at a West End restaurant, while my mother and his wife had an opportunity to talk. I was glad to get out of the dark, claustrophobic apartment, yet uneasy at this turn of events. But I was whisked off firmly by Caddy who, in spite of efforts to make me feel self-important, failed to dispel the unease about being separated from my mother.

To this day I do not remember which restaurant it was, except it had a familiar name. I had never before been in such sumptuous surroundings, and felt quite out of my depth when confronted with the lavish menu, so ordered egg and chips. I could not relax and do justice to this expensive treat. It seemed irrational to want to get back to make sure my mother was all right, and I was relieved when we returned and found her happy and at ease.

The following day, I had retired to read in my bedroom on the third floor. Thoughts still whirled in my mind about the previous day's events. I had my nose in Shakespeare's *Two Gentlemen of Verona* when my mother sat down by the bedside to talk. She wanted to tell me about the conversation between her and Mrs Caddy the night before. She had realised, during their exchanges, that she had fallen in love with Peter. Gently seduced into such a confession, she found only encouragement on the part of Sheena, and had ended up discussing the implications of their new relationship.

Mum paused, while I took in this momentous information. I could not believe what I was hearing. I was embarrassed and bewildered, and stunned. She told me that Sheena had convinced her she was 'doing the right thing', (though what action was proposed she did not divulge). This could hardly have been an easy task, and quite how Sheena had succeeded in banishing my mother's scruples, I never knew. She had just walked into a carefully laid trap. It was little wonder that on the previous day I had sensed things were not right.

Love is often blind, but this situation struck me, even then, as simply ludicrous. It was also way beyond what I could handle from the perspective of my teenage experience. The values with which we had been brought up and heard talked about from childhood: integrity, purity, loyalty, the single-unit and happy family, hurtled around in my head like pieces of a crazy jigsaw, with the key piece—our father—still missing.

I did not know what to say to my mother. Somehow, I knew that her happiness was at stake, but the future she had hinted at seemed to demand too high a price for us all. I could not believe that she would act so out of character. She adored us children, I was sure about that. Surely this was only a confession of guilt—we had grown so close through her difficulties with Dad, and now she was unloading herself on me as the only friend in whom she could confide at such a crucial time. The old dread was back again, gnawing in my stomach.

With polio, I had experienced physical paralysis, but now I was beginning to feel a different kind of paralysis—helplessness, powerlessness to do anything to prevent our world from crumbling around us. I wanted to hibernate until this horrible season of turmoil was over.

Much later, I asked myself questions over and over again: What could I have done to stop my mother falling for Peter? Why didn't I kick up one hell of a fuss at what I saw happening in the drawing-room? Why didn't I go to my brother and sisters, tell them what was going on, and combine together with them to devise some kind of a children's protest plan?

But in the face of this apparent fait accompli, I did nothing.

Unconsciously, I chose to go into a state of trauma - my feelings did a nose-dive into a deep-freeze where I turned a key on the sense of misery and locked it away for ever. I was left in confusion with an overwhelming sense of falling apart and impotence. I stood by and let it all happen. The result was deep-seated guilt which haunted me for more than thirty years.

The combined Caddy-force must have been exultant. The last stumbling block, my mother's conscience, was about to be eliminated from their path, and all could be plain sailing. August 26th marked my mother's thirty-fifth birthday, and she was invited by the Caddys to a London show in celebration. When my mother arrived at the flat in Lupus Street, however, she found a note from Sheena saying she had a migraine, and would Eileen mind if Peter took her alone to the theatre? She had little choice but to accept the 'diplomatic headache'. Afterwards, it was simple for Peter to offer to drive Eileen back to our home in Cheam, and then to take my father's place in her bed.

For my mother, that night sealed a contract. For her, the last qualm of uncertainty had been removed. She knew she had crossed the threshold into adultery. Head-over-heels in love, she wrote at once to my father requesting a divorce as the natural consequence of her actions. In her own words, (worth repeating here) she argues,

It didn't seem possible that I, a married woman, had fallen in love with a married man. But at the same time it felt as though it was meant to be. I knew without a doubt that I was to be with this man, and now I knew, too, what he had meant by us being two halves of the one whole.[1]

There could be no turning back.

One might question, at this point, the motivation behind Caddy's enigmatic wife's role in all this. Why had she magnanimously given her blessing for her husband to go off with someone else's wife? Well, my mother wrote afterwards in her autobiography, 'Peter was strangely unconcerned about Sheena,' and had told her (Eileen) that he and Sheena had not lived together as man and wife for some time. 'I've kept her fully informed about everything, and she has confirmed that you are my other half,'[2] he reassured her.

Other half? Did my mother fully understand what he was talking about? It is easy to be wise in hindsight, but had I been in my mother's shoes at that moment, I might have been in some trepidation, if not openly suspicious or even jealous, about such a close liaison as Peter kept with his wife. It was clear that Sheena wielded some kind of power over him.

As it was, the emotional high on which my mother was riding blinded her to everything else but her love for him and his apparent love for her. She was like a helpless puppet in the manipulative hands of another. She was no longer in control of her own life. 'I was reeling with the intensity of my love for Peter and I *had* to be with him.' [3] She had made her choice. Her love for Peter must override her conscience, maternal instincts, ingrained beliefs and values - all now subjugated to a stronger force at work.

In so doing, however, my mother was allowing someone else to shape her destiny, someone she loved utterly and therefore trusted. But it was not Caddy who was pulling the strings in their lives at that time, as he would have been the first to admit. Beyond his control and overshadowing them both stood Sheena, the puppeteer, directing her marionettes' actions and even their emotions. The full import of these machinations, however, was by no means clear.

At the end of August, Sheena moved down to Cheam to be in our home, unquestioned by any of us at the time. By then, no effort appeared to have been made to find schools for us. With my father still away, the road was clear for what was to be the final phase of my mother's entanglement in Sheena Caddy's web. However, that *coup de grâce* did not go quite according to plan. The idea was that Sheena would take charge of us children in order to enable Peter and Eileen to go off 'for a holiday' together (as Sheena explained to me later). Nothing more was said. Their departure was planned to take place at night, after we were all asleep.

Hastily, our mother had gathered a few things together in a suitcase. (When I moved into her room after she had gone, I found most of her belongings still neatly folded in the chest-of-drawers). She was completely unaware of the ugly twist that events were about to take, or how devastating, both to herself and to the rest of her family, this next move was to be.

Or did she, perhaps, have some premonition, some sense of foreboding, such as she had feared — and voiced — quite definitely before leaving on the airplane from Habbaniya? Years later in her autobiography, she recounted what happened. As she and Peter reached our front door on the night in question, Penny (Poppet) awoke upstairs, and started to wail 'Mummy!' Eileen's maternal instinct aroused, her first thought was to run up and calm her child. 'That's my baby!' she cried.

It is easy to imagine Sheena, like an overstrung violin by this time, being terrified my mother would change her mind and ruin her whole Plan. Somehow she managed to keep cool and make soothing noises of reassurance to Eileen, as she ushered her and her own husband quickly out of the door into the darkness. As Sheena closed and bolted the front door, she would without doubt have breathed a huge sigh of relief. Now there *was* no going back. Then she would make her way upstairs to tend the crying child. The rest of us children were still sleeping.

As the big front door of Kingstackley closed behind our mother, and she stepped into the Lagonda, she could not have grasped the finality of her actions. She had, in fact, stepped out of our lives, and out of her practical role as our mother for the rest of our lives. The big car quietly slid down the driveway in the darkness, with her future happiness in the hands of the man behind the steering wheel.

It was now September 8th, and she and Caddy were northward bound to tell her siblings of the choice she had made, and the steps she thought she would be taking. She probably had no idea the fate decreed for her by the

Caddys had just been sealed. It would take some time, as shock followed horrifying shock, for the truth to dawn. Far from the joy of a new life she had been lured to believe in as she pursued her overwhelming passion for Peter, she quickly began to experience unbearable pain in the circumstances now facing her. Embroiled as she was in such emotional turmoil, she failed utterly to realise the insidious deception with which she had been led by the nose out of her known, God-protected world.

Near the end of her days, when she and I were talking about this phase of her life, I tentatively broached my own perspective of how I saw she had been hoodwinked by the Caddys, and her only comment was, 'Oh dear!' followed by a long silence. I wondered if she had ever given any thought to how it all came about, before that moment.

8

Soul-Snatchers

*Oh, what a tangled web we weave
When we practise to deceive.*

From *Marmion* — Sir Walter Scott (1771-1832)

SINCE we children were neither privy to the plot, nor what happened to mother after she left us, I have relied on my mother's autobiographical accounts of how her life became inextricably entwined with the Caddys during the next two-and-a-half years.

Sheena took great pains to make her plan work. But what exactly was she up to, and for what reason had she devised such a scheme? At that time no one but herself – and perhaps Peter partially — would have been able to answer these questions. However, some months later, and then only little by little, my father discovered Sheena was being motivated by some unseen power-source driving her to create the situation destined to affect more than just herself, Peter and Eileen, and ourselves.

Peter had lived with Sheena for five years, worked closely with and been trained by her, so he knew the way her mind operated. He had divorced his first wife Nora, leaving her to bring up their two children alone, to marry Sheena: a deeply passionate union further enhanced by their mutual beliefs and ambitions. He followed her direction because he trusted her, and had played his seductive part without any compunction.

As far as Sheena was concerned, the main characters in her drama were now in position to bring her scheme to fruition. But not all her puppets were so ready to fall in with her plan, and we children proved to be difficult. She soon realised this when she decided to look after five unknown, confused children who were now beginning to miss their parents. Undaunted, however, she drafted in her friend, Dorothy Maclean, to help her.

Having got her two main actors in place, she set to work to win the confidence and support of Mum's family. Since I was the eldest, she worked on me first. She discovered my interests in poetry and music, and used her own gifts in these arts to try to win me over. As an accomplished pianist, she could play any of my requests on our beautiful grand piano (now moved to the lounge-hall). I was delighted she could play Sinding's 'Rustle of Spring' which I had often heard played by my great aunt (Auntie in Ireland). Sheena's rendering of 'Greensleeves' will for ever remind me of her. She professed similar catholic tastes to my own in poets and poetry - Shelley, Keats, the Brownings, and Tennyson.

One afternoon, she took me to see the film *Hans Christian Andersen* in Reigate, leaving the rest of the family in the care of her helper. Afterwards, we visited a family she knew nearby. This turned out to be that of an Air Force officer who had been in Habbaniya at the same time as us. Sheena encouraged me to befriend his daughter, Fay, as we were about the same age. As Fay and I wandered out in their garden, I learned from her that her parents had separated and that she was most unhappy—a story with which I was beginning to identify. More discomfiting than this, though, was the fact that I had recognised her father, Wing Commander Davies, as an officer from Habbaniya, and remembered that I had once overheard him saying some unkind things about my father. He had been sitting around in a group of people having drinks under a marquee at the Rest-and-Leave Centre on the shores of Lake Habbaniya, and Caddy was one of the same group. As I walked past, I heard my father's name mentioned in a derogatory way, and someone said, 'Ssh! That's his daughter.' I pretended not to hear, and continued up the slope towards the centre, feeling mortified that my father had become the butt of unkind remarks.

It seemed a small incident maybe, but when I found

myself standing in the Davies' garden in Reigate, it came back to me, and I wondered how Sheena could possibly know this same man that had been out in Iraq? Was it coincidence? Or perhaps she had been introduced to him through Peter? So were he and Peter partners in some sort of smear campaign drummed up against my father to prepare the ground for why my mother should eventually leave him? And why was Sheena here with Davies now? I dared not ask her. But I found the relationship between Davies and Sheena too startling to be mere coincidence. They spent a long time in conversation while Fay and I dallied in the garden, and I became increasingly suspicious of Sheena's motives for this visit. Something quite outside my ken was afoot, and whatever it was our family was becoming involved.

The most vivid memory from those confused days, however, was a walk I took with Sheena in Nonsuch Park, Cheam, one afternoon. Nonsuch Park had been King Henry VIII's hunting grounds where he had once built a fine hunting lodge, or mansion, in which Anne Boleyn could reside. This abode had been burnt down in the last century, and later rebuilt as a rather plain, grey-stone building called Nonsuch House. The gardens, however, were beautiful and well tended, and probably much as when Anne Boleyn had looked out upon them. Four hundred years later, the same lawns rolled and dipped, shaded by giant mature oaks and yews, and herbaceous borders which splashed a riot of colour and cheer with the freedom of an artist's palette, decorating the rather dull house and its sweeping lawns.

Beneath the wide spread of an ancient yew tree was a bench, and Sheena sat me down to talk. She told me my mother was on a holiday with Peter, but I could not believe she had gone off without a word to any of us. Somehow, it felt all wrong and I sensed that Sheena was not giving me the whole picture. I listened dumbly to unfamiliar words: to her theory of free love – about how two planets had met in the universe, called Peter and Eileen, and had recognised one another as 'soul-mates'. These two stars were now indivisible and would always stay together as two halves of the same whole. But surely *she* was Peter Caddy's 'other half'?

Such words fell strangely on my young ears. In my mind, I was busy processing them, and actively rejecting them. In spite of my inexperience and naiveté, it slowly dawned that not only was this woman confirming the changes which my mother had told me about, but was giving me reasons why *she* saw fit to change her partner and hand him on to my mother, whether we liked it (or him) or not. She was oblivious to anything we might feel about this cold-blooded removal from our midst of the person around whom our little universe had revolved and whom we children loved most in the world.

I was like a stunned rabbit, and still unable to take in fully what my numbed ears were hearing. I cannot remember anything more that took place after that. I suppose we walked back to the car in silence. Gullible as I was normally, I could not swallow these ideas. They did not make sense. I had already decided I would not give her an easy time.

Sheena no doubt thought she had told me enough to explain the import of her next moves, and clearly had been confident I would understand. But she failed to grasp the strength of the mother-daughter bond, or the hatred seething inside me as I realised what was happening. I never told a soul. After the talk in the park, I knew for certain that this woman's intentions were evil and that I could not trust her. At thirteen, I was ill-equipped to know how to wrestle with Sheena's weird beliefs. I was powerless to dare question her about them. My mother was away, so I could not discuss my conversation with her, as I might have done had she been around. I knew my brother and sisters could not possibly understand. They had not been privy to the confidences of my mother or seen anything of the Caddy intrigues in the last weeks.

For the first time in my life, I felt utterly alone. What

was worse, I blamed myself for the moral cowardice which had prevented me from acting in any way in my mother's defence, in spite of my fierce love for her. I remembered then how mother had often warned us, whenever we children made life unpleasant by our persistent bickering and squabbling, 'You'll be sorry when I'm gone!' This phrase came back to me as a sickening prophecy of the present truth. Now she really *had* gone, and not even I knew for how long or exactly where she was.

It seemed an age before father would return. In the meantime, we had to suffer Sheena and Dorothy's bungling ways, and either allow the temporary frustration and impotence to erupt in open warfare; or push everything down to some secret corner of the human soul where a door could be closed, locked and sealed.

I decided on the second option - in an effort to blot out any pain. I did not know at the time that this is an age-old ruse of the psyche to anaesthetise suffering – a chance to buy time for wound-licking and healing. This second choice resulted in a comforting grey cloud of unfeeling which settled over me, and blanketed the rest of my teenage years. Many years later, when I asked an American psychiatrist what this 'grey cloud' might have been, I learned it was known as Clinical Depression.

While we were beginning to rebel against the unwelcome attentions of Mrs Caddy, her husband had taken mother to visit Eileen's brother near Reading, and her sister in Nottingham, and their families. Eileen wanted to explain in person exactly what was taking place in her life and ours, hoping to gain their sympathy and support before Andrew returned from abroad in October. She was riding high on the crest of a tidal wave of the love she felt for Peter, about which she wrote later: 'For the first time in my life I felt utterly complete. I was committed to whatever life with Peter Caddy had in store for me, without considering for a moment what that might mean. I was helpless to resist this love that engulfed me.'[1]

The first blow came when she and Peter came face to

face with blank unbelief on the faces of her relatives, quickly followed by shock, horror and open disgust, as they listened to their story. Quite understandably (from our view-point anyway), our relations were left dumbfounded, angered and upset by this imminent family split. Their feelings of condemnation and unforgiveness were so strenuously expressed that Eileen found herself shocked, and isolated from any support. Her sister and brother-in-law refused to speak to her. Their wrath and disbelief would hound her for many years.

As for Auntie (in Ireland), Eileen had been so dear to her, and now her beloved Eileen had left her own flesh and blood for a virtual stranger. After hearing the terrible news, I can only imagine how she must have grieved. In Dublin, she went faithfully to St Anne's Church down the road from Merrion Square every Sunday, and must have carried her sadness there to ask for help to bring her through the shock, and for Eileen to change her mind.

This was but a foretaste for Mum of what was to follow. My father, who was still abroad, takes up the story of this unhappy time in a letter written a long while afterwards.

In Iraq, I was having nightmares and forebodings of terrible danger for my family, and felt anguished but unable to share my concern with anyone. Then came a letter saying that when she (Eileen) had gone to London, Sheena had sent a note excusing herself and she'd spent the evening with Peter Caddy and fallen in love with him, and would I divorce her? (Later I found a note from Sheena to Eileen encouraging her to associate with Peter...we were still in Iraq then; Eileen had never shown me this note.)

Forty-eight hours later, I entered the front door of my house in Cheam to find Sheena in possession and looking after my children while her husband and my wife had gone off on a motor tour together. She was collected within the hour by two women in a car who took her to the Caddys' flat in Lupus Street.

History does not record what happened during that

first and last encounter between my father and Sheena, but before he demanded she leave, he ascertained from her the whereabouts of the absent soul-mates, and rang my aunt in Nottingham as soon as Sheena had gone. Understandably, he was beside himself with wounded pride, grief and fury, and it is no wonder that he told Eileen on the telephone that she was 'never to set foot in his house again', and that she was 'unfit to be the children's mother.'

Those terrible words were to ring in my mother's ears for years to come. She had never anticipated such anger, was completely unprepared for it and did not know how to handle the ugly situation. Nor could she have imagined that her letter to him would have had the electrifying effect of bringing him straight home to England on compassionate leave. That phone call to Nottingham, combined with the opposition of her relatives, had splintered the dream-world into which she had been seduced. She suddenly awoke to the stark truth of her position, and wrote in her autobiography much later of her 'devastation' at Andrew's reaction and of how she 'didn't know where to turn.' Knowing him as she did after fifteen years of marriage, had she honestly imagined he would quietly acquiesce with her demand for a divorce?

In the whirlpool of her emotions, and deeply disturbed by now, the only solid fact remaining to her was her compulsive love for Peter. But...would this be enough to carry her through all the difficulties ahead? With every close member of her family now alienated, where could she go to escape? Was her love for Peter strong enough to counter the pain of enforced separation from her children? Wasn't this all more than she had ever bargained for, and certainly more than she could possibly bear? She was, first and foremost, a mother. (Her role as Andrew's wife had long since taken second place.) Yet... with Andrew's forceful words, she had been cut off from all her dependants. Her former life had been severed with the swift death-blow of a guillotine. Thus, despite all her natural mother-instincts, she could not go back. Surely her children would one day be with her again. But this battle would need to be fought later.

At the moment, the emotional leap she had taken left her with a horrifying price. She found herself with no other option but to face the pain. The one thing all too clear to her was that she could not retrace her steps. Her husband had made quite sure of that, while her lover and her lover's wife must have been secretly rejoicing at the success of their plan so far. Eileen was hemmed in on every side. It had all happened too quickly for her to evaluate the full impact of her actions.

So instead of her expected return from Nottingham to Kingstackley to the bosom of her family, Eileen found herself having to accompany Peter to rejoin Sheena in the dark confines of the spider's parlour in Lupus Street. They had her to themselves at last!

To distract my mother the Caddys took Eileen to visit one of their favourite haunts, a power-centre for spiritual pilgrims over many centuries. Perhaps this fresh ambience and the spiritual tranquillity of the place would be beneficial in helping Eileen sort out her problems. So, *à trois*, they turned the Lagonda towards the West Country, and drove down to Glastonbury, in Somerset.

9

The Voice, the Choice and a Web of Lies

*The heart is deceitful above all things and
beyond cure. Who can understand it?*
Jeremiah 17:9

FOR many centuries, Glastonbury on the Isle of Avalon in Somerset has been a place of pilgrimage for pagans and Christians alike. 'An incomparable mystique pervades Glastonbury and its countryside, where history blends with legend. Its origins are as clouded as the mists which at times enshroud the flat pastures towards the Bristol Channel at Bridgwater Bay.' [1]

The present-day ruins of the tenth century abbey by the River Brue, dominated by Glastonbury Tor, had once been a great centre of learning under the scholarly administration of St Dunstan, and long before that St Patrick had become a monk and then abbot at Glastonbury, and was buried there. Even further back still, one legend tells how in about A.D. 60, the Apostle Philip sent Joseph of Arimathea to preach the gospel in Britain. When Joseph disembarked at Glastonbury, he thrust his staff into the ground and it took root, flowered as a thorn tree and has blossomed twice a year since, in Spring and at Christmas, and can still be seen in the abbey grounds.

Another legend was established by medieval theologians who claimed that Joseph of Arimathea was Jesus' uncle and a rich merchant who 'was engaged in trade between the Levant and the West...fled to Britain during the persecution of the Christians...arrived in Somerset with twelve companions...was given a grant of land to settle on by the local King Arviragus' and this was Glastonbury. He is said to have brought with him 'several valuable relics from Palestine' including the cup, or chalice, from which the wine was drunk at the Last Supper. This was called the Holy Grail. 'Glastonbury Abbey held that the Grail was lost in early times, was found at the time of King Arthur, and subsequently lost again. Its rediscovery will herald the dawn of an age of peace and enlightenment.'[2] The remains of that same semi-legendary King Arthur and his Queen Guinevere are supposedly buried seven feet beneath the abbey grounds.

Yet another story is that Joseph of Arimathea, as uncle and guardian of the child Jesus, brought him several times to Somerset on his travels. On one occasion Jesus had built himself a small hut of wattles, which became known as the Old Church.

With all these tales woven into the fabric of its history, it is little wonder that pilgrims have trodden a well-worn path to Glastonbury in search of the Holy Grail, or simply seeking solace for their souls. In modern times, it is perhaps the promise of 'a new age of peace and enlightenment' to be found there that draws searchers for spirituality. It has become a market-place for the spiritual wares of all religions, for New Age festivals and occultic activities, raves and rock festivals.

Before it became popularised in this way, however, the Caddys had sought out Glastonbury as a 'centre of spiritual power', and took Eileen there hoping she would discover its mystique and tranquillity. The 'power' she was to encounter in that place was to change her life.

In September 1953, while they were staying there they visited Tudor Pole's 'Upper Room' at the Chalice Well - a small sanctuary set aside for prayer and meditation. Eileen, troubled in mind and spirit, felt calmed by the atmosphere. She turned to prayer, her heart crying out for help from God. She had never experienced such confusion.

An answer came in a voice which said: 'Be still, and know that I am God.' In her own account, she says the voice was so clear that she turned to see who had spoken, but only Peter and Sheena were in the room. She thought she must be going crazy. The voice was in her head, and she sat very still, 'rigid with fear, my eyes tight shut,' she recalls. The voice continued: *'You have taken a very big step in your life. But if you follow my voice all will be well. I have brought you and Peter together for a very special purpose, to do a specific work for me. You will work as one, and you will realise this more fully as time goes on. There are few who have been brought together in this way. Don't be afraid, for I am with you.'* [3]

Eileen recounts how she wrote down this message, and immediately recognised those first words from the Bible. She was deeply troubled by them. Indeed, the whole experience shook her to the core of her being. As she left the sanctuary, she told Peter and Sheena what had happened. To her amazement, far from telling her she was insane, they listened with avid interest. Sheena's immediate response was, 'This is marvellous, Eileen. It confirms everything. Now I'm certain that God brought you and Peter together.'

In my mother's words: *'I was appalled. To me there was nothing to be excited about. They asked me to repeat the words I had heard, and were convinced that I had heard God's own voice. I wasn't at all sure, and yet if I accepted what I heard, it must be the voice of God.'* [4]

Eileen continued to be assailed by inner doubts. She thought of the Ten Commandments, and was plagued by the word 'adultery' and the fact that she knew she was 'living in sin' with Caddy. How, therefore, could the voice she had heard be right?

Now the all-persuasive voices of the Caddys spoke even louder and spurred her forward. She found herself trapped between doubts and misery, and the steady beckoning of this voice within her. In this dilemma, she could see no other way to turn than to allow herself to be led onwards by the voice. There could be no going back to her old life now, she believed. My father had barred the door to her, dashing any hope of returning to her former family-life.

Once again, in her own words, '... *I had nowhere else to go. So with only my love for Peter to nourish me, and this strange voice whispering in my head, I stepped into the most frightening time of my life.*' 5

Had the choice been made for her, by Peter, Sheena and the Voice, by the powerful spiritual forces gathered around her in that little room in Glastonbury? Had Eileen made that choice because she saw no other way out since my father had also played his part in forcing her hand? Was this voice her subconscious mind throwing up rational reasons for her chosen course of action at this point? The Caddys, however, thought the voice was divinely inspired, and recognised in my mother a spiritual sensitivity which was a vital component necessary towards achieving their Plan.

After the Glastonbury visit, Peter Caddy had to return to his posting in the Middle East as catering officer, leaving Eileen in the Lupus Street flat with Sheena, feeling utterly abandoned. His last instructions were that she must accept Sheena as her teacher, as he himself had done, and learn all she could from her. He had handed out not even the tiniest crumb of comfort to the love-lorn woman whom he claimed to adore. Eileen suddenly saw herself in the pitiable position of being totally dependent, both economically and spiritually, upon Sheena — a woman who had already made it obvious she did not even *like* her.

Eileen goes on to relate, matter-of-factly, that she adored Peter even though she found it impossible to interpret his extraordinary behaviour; that she was fast learning to hate Sheena; and that she had been left no choice — or so it seemed to her at the time — but to submit to Sheena's power over her. Alone she was no match for the combined Caddy-force.

The charisma surrounding Sheena Govan-Caddy seemed to begin with Peter himself, or perhaps it had begun earlier with her friend Dorothy Maclean. Be that as it may, Caddy made no secret of his worship of Sheena and that he believed in her totally. But this aura of love never included or attracted my mother, or drew her into Sheena's orbit. Between the two women there would remain an invisible barrier - possibly generated by jealousy on Sheena's part, and certainly due to the fear, distrust and open dislike of her by my mother. In spite of all the sweetness and light spoken about Sheena, mainly by Peter Caddy, my mother could not, in her heart of hearts, change her attitude towards her 'mentor', (perhaps better termed 'tor-mentor'). Years passed before the memories of Sheena could be healed to the point of feeling pity for Sheena as a person.

I draw freely from my mother's own account in her autobiography. The story is the way she saw it. She remarks that her all-consuming love for Peter was the only thing left to her. And ever overshadowing this was... Sheena.

Sheena claimed to the end, in her own words, that she 'always operated within a Christian framework, striving to give birth to the New Age.' The constant allusion to God in Sheena's religious phraseology was the second of the two reasons why my mother was able to swallow the unsavoury diet of loveless tyranny fed her by Sheena, upon which she must survive over the next months during Peter's absence.

There followed for Eileen, in those early days of her relationship with the Caddys, a dark period of agonising spiritual and mental conflict—between her heart and conscience which were in rebellion against, and at total odds with, Sheena's demands for discipline and obedience. Her heart ached for her children, but this source of comfort had been denied her. The act of adultery had violated her moral code, and by doing so, had cut her off from all her former friends.

So with Peter as the lure, Eileen was exposed to an indoctrination process as thorough and diabolical as Solzhenitsyn describes his compatriots undergoing in the camps of *The Gulag Archipelago*. She herself admits that, for all she knew, the vivid visions she began to see 'may have been the work of the devil or caused by emotional distress.' The pressure to which she was subjected by both Caddys, mentally, physically, psychologically and emotionally, impacted heavily on her character and changed the direction of her life.

She confessed that... 'The only reason I was there was Peter.' It would have taken super-human strength at this stage, to come to her senses and strike out on her own. Even had she braved Andrew's fury to seek forgiveness, she would have to admit it was really only in order to claim access to her children and not him. What, she wondered, would have been the response anyway? She felt damaged and vulnerable; and strongest of all she felt the power of the Caddys ranged against her. So 'with only the voice' to lead her on, she could do nothing now but hang on and wait for Caddy's return.

But Eileen did not take everything lying down. Inwardly, she set up 'terrific resistance' to Sheena, who treated her as a despised and lowly servant — there only to fetch and carry for her, look after her through her illnesses, and prepare her meals. Sheena exacted the highest standards of perfection, night and day, and used every unpleasant incident or reproof as a lesson to teach Eileen that she must learn 'from God'. There was an internal telephone between Sheena and Eileen's rooms, and she was expected to be on call, night and day.

Eileen's main duty was to be trained. She was to pray and listen for her inner voice three times a day, and then relay all she heard to Sheena. She was permitted to spend the early morning session, at 6 a.m., on her own, but wrote down every message and gave it to Sheena when she awoke. Sheena made sure Eileen recorded whatever came to her in those sessions, whether it be a vision, a dream, or words. She trained my mother to listen 'for the very first voice' she had heard at Glastonbury, so that... 'there won't be the slightest shadow of a doubt which voice is the voice of God, and you will follow no other.'[6]

The Voice, the Choice and a web of Lies

When my mother was late for anything, Sheena would accuse her of being 'late for her appointment with God'. She drove Eileen to see that nothing in her life mattered more than these times she spent 'with God'. That priority in my mother's life remained unchanged until near the end of her days.

At this time Sheena stopped receiving any messages of her own, and openly relied on my mother's spiritual contact. There were others working with them in the same vein. One of these was Sheena's Canadian friend Dorothy Maclean with whom she had worked in Intelligence during the Second World War in the United States. Dorothy often visited Sheena on her way home from work, and spent long hours with her, closeted in Sheena's room for meals while my mother ate alone.

Never once during those tortuous months did Sheena show any sort of understanding of, or feeling for, my mother's plight, it seems. Her own friends and followers adored and worshipped her quite openly. Peter himself told Eileen that Sheena was the most loving person he had ever met. 'I trust her totally and you should too. In the five years I lived with her I always found that she knew everything I was thinking and feeling and that she was always right.'

Sheena had once experienced similar torture and heartache as my mother was now undergoing, when she had given up her only son for adoption in Canada in 1938. If *she* could make that sacrifice, then my mother could also give up *her* family! That had been Sheena's decision at the time, but in my mother's case, the decision had been made for her. Sheena professed to love the world and to being a 'redeemer of mankind', but she acted like one totally desensitized to my mother's feeling, so what quality and depth of 'love' or sympathy could she present to the rest of the world?

Puppeteer Sheena had been manipulating her marionettes in an extraordinarily successful drama, the outcome of which was by no means obvious to puppet

Eileen. I would guess that the Peter-puppet knew more or less what was happening and where he was going. He was still taking all his instructions from Sheena, and was always her most attentive disciple. Hence his 'perfect trust' in her as handler, teacher and guide.

Peter's intentions, however, were also motivated by a basic 'lust for the woman' (Eileen) — as one of my mentors put it years later. This, of course, lay concealed beneath his enthusiastic pursuit of things 'spiritual'. I have little doubt that, from the first he would have been deeply attracted to my mother — though he stressed on several occasions later that he was not. Yet he had no compunction about allowing Sheena to hone Eileen into just the right tool for 'the work' he and Sheena dreamed would emerge from this ill-assorted trio. Caddy's track record with two wives already had proved his disloyalty and self-seeking, and after twenty-seven years with Eileen, he went on to form other liaisons. By the end of his life, he had worked his way through five wives in all.

After some months, the last of Eileen's fighting Irish spirit, together with the self to which she had tried to be true, finally lay dying at Sheena's feet. All former values, ideals and what faith in God she had known, had been unpicked by Sheena, removed or warped, and then re-woven into new, powerful strands which bound her into the Caddys' life-sapping web of deception and her own self-deceiving lies, once and for all. How could all this marry up with Sheena's vision of 'enlightenment, leading to the dawning of a new age' to which she believed they would eventually aspire?

My mother wrote of this time: 'I gave Sheena complete power over me.'[7] That was all Sheena needed. At last, Eileen's conscience—so recently overloaded with fear and guilt—was moribund. No longer did she harbour any sense of wrong-doing, any sin. She had been 'liberated'. She had learned from Sheena and Peter that everything which happened to her served one end—the accomplishment of The Plan. To them, good and evil were one and the same, light and dark painted on the same canvas. It was, after all, easier to talk of 'working out one's karma' in another life, Hindu-style. By so doing, the need for forgiveness, redemption and any saving Grace could be eradicated for ever.

Mother had visited my aunt and uncle with Caddy after she had left our house. Torrie, my mother's younger sister, told me years later that when they *first* visited them, my mother devoted much of her time to copying out passages from the Bible. Was this exercise supposed to act as balm to a tortured soul, or as a stabiliser (though I rather doubt Sheena's care for my mother went thus far)? Or was it already part of the subtle re-programming, newly set up by Sheena?

Whatever its purpose, Eileen's former understanding of the scriptures and God's eternal truths must, in such circumstances, have already become somewhat distorted by the pressure of emotional blackmail being thrust upon her by the Caddys.

Out of the ashes of Eileen's Christian beliefs there arose a virtual reality which quickly formed itself into concrete conviction: that she had stumbled upon what 'God's plan' really was for her life — so long as she could also have Peter to love her through it. To listen to the 'voice' was her destiny, and obedience to that voice would lead straight to the purpose (the work) which the voice had promised in Glastonbury. She had indeed come to worship at the feet of The Lie.

However deceived she may have been, I believe that had she not clung to this concept of a future together with Caddy, she must surely have gone insane. She admits herself that the force driving her towards this re-formation in her character was the overwhelming fear 'that Sheena could separate me from Peter whenever she felt like it.'[8] Sheena sensed this dependency, and cut through it with words and action: 'You are not putting first things first. You and Peter are putting your relationship before God and I cannot allow you to do that. You had better not see each other for a while...' ⁹

In Eileen's final attempt to hang on to her sanity, every last grain of truth must be subjugated and blotted out. Her desperate bid to secure her love for Peter meant relinquishing her true self (the self she knew) and her soul. He became her one refuge and solace when all else had been taken from her. Eileen's conscience gave one last death-gasp when she found she had fallen pregnant with Peter's child. The fact horrified her since she still considered it a social stigma for any child to be born out of wedlock, and she had not yet been able to procure permission for a divorce from my father. This would take another three years.

During this fraught period, Peter re-appeared, and took her once more to Glastonbury. While they were there, 'the voice' spoke again to Eileen, and decreed that the new child's name would be Christopher Michael. (Sheena wanted to add John, when she heard of this later, but lost out to the 'voice's' authority.) I must add a note of scepticism of my own here, about the authority of the voice, as I well remember my mother, three years earlier, wanting to call our youngest sister Penny by these two names, had she been born a boy!

Six weeks' after the birth of Christopher, in March 1955, Sheena abducted him. She saw their baby as her own - the replacement for the miscarriage she had while married to Caddy, and maybe even for the son she had given over to adoption. Christopher was her 'spiritual' child, and she was determined to keep him with her at all costs, on the pretext that my mother was 'not fit to be a mother' (echoing my father's damning words), and 'had not yet learned to put God first in her life.' ¹⁰

By this time my mother had moved from Sheena's to Dorothy Maclean's flat in London, while Caddy, who had resigned from the Air Force, was away in Ireland at Sheena's suggestion. He had found a job in a small hotel as an assistant chef. He had already made it clear to Eileen that he did not mind Sheena's possession of

Christopher. 'She won't keep him for ever. There's no need to worry about him; Sheena feels she has a deep spiritual link with him and he'll be quite safe with her,' she was told.[11]

The arrival of Christopher began to look as if it may well be part of their plan. Sheena was bent on making a strong bid to exert her love and influence over this new babe and imbue him with her spiritual power.

The unconcerned father, however, grossly underestimated the natural mother's fierce protectiveness. When Eileen realised she would get no support from Peter and must fight to regain their child on her own, she became frantic. All efforts to retrieve her baby proved fruitless. The door to Sheena's flat remained closed to her whenever she hammered on it, and if she telephoned to talk to Sheena, the receiver was replaced.

In the end, this mental cruelty, the physical separation from her baby and her frantic frustration goaded Eileen to the brink of despair. Trapped once more, she saw no other recourse but to end it all. Finding herself alone one day in Dorothy's flat, she armed herself with a bottle of sleeping pills, drew the curtains across the windows, and put a pillow in the gas oven.

The front door bell rang, and rang again. Reluctantly, Eileen decided to open the door, and found standing outside her brother, Paddy. He had come up to London for a friend's wedding, and had called round to see how she was.

Eileen burst into hysterical tears, and poured out all her pent-up misery and grief to her brother. She told him she could not go on and was about to end her life. In his downright way, Paddy told her not to be such a fool. She 'would do no such thing', and was to collect her things and he would take her home at once with him. (He worked and lived on his brother-in-law's farm outside Reading.) She went with him, gladly. It had been a very close call but this unwitting angel of mercy, in the shape of my uncle, had just saved his sister's life.

10

'You'll be sorry when I'm gone.'

*Rivers of water run down from my eyes,
because Men do not keep Your law.*
Psalm 119:136 (NKJV)

WHILE my mother was undergoing her Glastonbury experience, my father was wrestling with shock and fury at the news in her telegram and of her departure from Kingstackley during his absence in Iraq. His tour there had been due to finish in October. However, the crisis erupting from Eileen's request for a divorce demanded immediate action. He took compassionate leave, and returned home without having time to hand over properly to his successor in Habbaniya.

Back at home, none of us was aware of the gravity of the situation. Sheena and Dorothy Maclean kept the home running smoothly, and we believed our mother had simply gone for a holiday. We did not even question how this situation had arisen. My father's arrival was unexpected as he pitched headlong into his family's midst, to find we were being minded by two strangers.

There had been no great row or ugly scene created, as far as we knew, over the hurried departure of Sheena with Dorothy after Dad's surprising appearance. He told me later that he had 'booted her out', which conveyed all I needed to know about his feelings for Sheena. At least we could identify with him in the fact that we disliked 'that woman' too. That would be his only meeting with Sheena.

The next question was: How on earth was he going to tell the children what is going on?

It was the second week of September 1953, and the warm morning sunshine streamed through the tall kitchen windows of Kingstackley. The six remaining members of the family sat round the breakfast table. Change was in the air. Sheena had vanished without even a goodbye. Something must be seriously wrong. Dad's distress was all too apparent in his face. His temper was to be feared, and we recognised its presence whenever his eyebrows went up in two inverted 'v's. He clutched little two-year old Penny tensely on his knee at the head of the table and cleared his throat to make an announcement. He kept it brief:

'Children, I want to tell you that you must be prepared never to see Mummy again. She's gone away with Peter Caddy, and *she's not coming back.*'

We sat frozen, stunned. No one spoke. The finality of Dad's tone, the pronouncement of doom, this fait accompli, left each of us wrestling with the thunderclap in our own way. The warmth of our mother's love and our happiness had just evaporated. Mummy had gone. The decision was final. As swift as the fall of a guillotine's knife, she had been cut from our lives. Our untroubled childhood had been axed for ever. What could the future hold without our Mum?

Six-year-old Mary Liz, always a sensitive little girl, began to sob as if her heart would break. Penny, unable to grasp anything except her older sister's sorrow, wept with her. My distraught father tried to comfort the younger ones. Suzanne, then ten, looked round the table and consciously vowed she would not shed a tear. She told me later that she did not cry for two years after our mother went. She was always the tough, resilient one.

Richard too, by now nearly twelve, tried wordlessly, stoically, to be brave. And I, better prepared for this dreadful debacle than the others, felt tears coursing down my cheeks. I had gone cold inside. The world had collapsed and the distress I felt then was as much triggered from seeing and hearing my youngest sisters crying as at finally being forced to face the awful truth which had caused their overwhelming sadness.

I gradually began to realise that, as the eldest, I had a responsibility towards my siblings. I had felt it once in Iraq when Mum went into hospital, and now, for the second time, this maternal protectiveness came to the fore. With no mother to nurture us, there would be a practical role with many duties to perform. This would mean I must leave school, of course, and look after the family full-time. Someone needed to take our mother's place, and give them love and comfort through this crisis.

My destiny was mapped out before me. This was my mission in life, my raison d'être – the reason I had been saved when I might have died of polio.

I blurted out my decision to the family and it hit a blank wall. My father was way ahead of me, and did not see things my way at all. He was adamant that he was going to find schools for us all, at once; that I was much too young to stay at home and play mother to my brother and sisters; that he would not contemplate such a thing and wanted to hear no more of it.

So that was that! At its very birth, my self-appointed role lay dashed. I feared my father too much to argue, but I nursed a feeling of humiliation and hurt pride which further widened the gap between us. Since those last months in Iraq, a chasm of loathing and mistrust had opened up and separated us already. Quite consciously, my heart clamped shut against him. I never gave a single thought to *his* difficulties, or felt the slightest bit of sympathy for him after that. If he could not see how I wanted to help, then why should I co-operate with him? Instead, I made him the buttress against which I could hurl all blame for our mother's sudden departure, which was grossly unfair, since he was only partially to blame for the present nightmare.

Looked at objectively years later, my father's situation at that moment was less than enviable. He found himself alone with five children to clothe, feed and educate. By his refusal to allow our mother back home, he had condemned himself to single parenthood. The entire fabric of his supportive home-life had been pulled out from under his feet, and he was reeling from shock. He had just been conned by his wife and her scheming boyfriend. In spite of the full passion of his fury, sense of shame, resentment and towering rage against Caddy and Eileen, all this must now take second place to the urgent practicalities of looking after his children, continue his career, and remain sane.

For the Caddys, Dad's prompt return must have posed considerable difficulties. They had miscalculated, and their plan was in disarray. Caddy had been logging all that went on at the time, 'to keep Sheena fully informed'. In his autobiography, he mentions that he had set off with our mother on September 8th, to visit Mum's sister in Leicester where she was staying with her cousin, Dr John Drury, before Torrie returned back home to Nottingham. When father arrived back next day, he found the lovebirds had flown. Caddy continues:

Andrew turned up on 9th September, having received Eileen's letter and flown back from Iraq on compassionate leave. He evicted Sheena and Dorothy as accomplices in the drama that was taking place and sent Eileen a telegram demanding she return. She had not expected him to fly to England so soon and had been hoping to have the children with her before he arrived in the country. (In her account: 'I told the children I would only be gone two or three days.') *Now he had the children. With tremendous courage, Eileen replied to Andrew's telegram with a letter saying that she would not go back to him. He responded by forbidding her to see the children, which upset her very deeply... A week after her letter to Andrew, Eileen was missing the children so badly that she wrote again, this time begging to be allowed to come and look after them; he refused.* That was Peter Caddy's slant on the situation.[1]

Dad had told us nothing of this emotional wrestling match, of course, so it is no wonder he had looked grim at that breakfast time when he had delivered the awful news.

For him, the continuity of daily living and sheer

survival must take priority. A saintly elderly couple called Riley who were friends, responded promptly to my father's SOS, and agreed to move in to our home to help carry some of the domestic and practical details, thus leaving my father free to return to his new posting at the Air Ministry in London. By this time, Dad had found good schools for us three older children. My brother and I went to local grammar schools in Sutton and Cheam respectively, and Suzanne went to the nearby church school of St. Dunstan's. Mary Liz returned to Northlace School, which we had attended before going to Iraq.

During this brief period, the Rileys undoubtedly had an horrendous time with us, struggling as we were to come to terms with the unhappy change in our lifestyle. Patiently they tried their best. Their relationship with my father must have been particularly abrasive, he being the strong character he was.

Frances Riley was a woman of both faith and fortitude however. During their stay, she helped me face up to two important relationships: the rebellious one with my father, and my relationship with God. Signs of open defiance towards Dad must have been obvious, and only served to increase the tensions within the family circle. Frances suggested I might try being honest with Dad about how I really felt about him. This was a tough assignment which I balked at for some time. Finally I saw sense in at least attempting to put things right.

One night, when we were all sitting round the fire in the big drawing-room, my father asked if any of us would like to express our thoughts about the situation. I mustered the courage nervously to voice my feelings. Out tumbled the fact that I couldn't bear my father to touch me, that I did not love him, but that I was sorry for being difficult. I was acutely embarrassed and uncomfortable. As hard as I had found it to utter those words, they were only part of all I could have said about the depth of mistrust I now had of my Dad, based on secret suspicions which I could not fully understand, or feared even to express to myself. Therefore, the breach between us would not be healed for many years to come, because I had not been able to give him the full picture of the truth, but it was a beginning. The exercise had been humbling, and had eased some of the rebellion in my heart and tension between us for a time. Needless to say, my confession must have hurt my father sorely when he was feeling particularly raw at being rejected by his wife.

The shock of losing mother, together with my feelings towards Dad had the illusory effect of cutting me off from both my parents at once. I became zealously overprotective towards my siblings which in turn often resulted in a power-struggle between my father and myself. Although his duty had been to provide for all our material needs, I saw myself as their moral guardian. I was sure that their real happiness and love were now my place to encourage, and wrongly assumed these assets could not come from him.

Tension sometimes erupted in conflict, however, and persisted all through my teenage years. This added appreciably to my father's difficulties in raising us all. I behaved badly. Puffed up as I felt myself to be with moral arrogance, I tried to put my father down at every opportunity. Fortunately, I did not succeed.

Frances Riley also encouraged me to turn to God and tell Him all I was feeling. Being rather a private child, I had been able to talk only to my mother, who was my best friend and confidante. Now she had gone, I felt withdrawn and utterly bereft of Mum's comfort and love. I was so mixed up emotionally that I could not talk to myself, let alone God. Yet there was Frances, suggesting the seemingly impossible notion that I might allow God to fill the vacuum left by my mother.

My mother had left by her bedside a copy of *Daily Light*, full of wisdom of the saints. I began reading this each day with another little book, given me by a friend, called *The Imitation of Christ* by Thomas á Kempis. As I took those first faltering steps, I began to see how others, who understood God better than I did, viewed and loved Him. The words on those small pages helped open a window in my understanding. Through them shone their experience of the faith which I hoped would draw me closer to knowing Him myself. Gradually, those early morning times of reading, listening and waiting, became a habit and a necessity for each day. I wrote down my thoughts. I soon found that this new discipline not only brought some comfort, but was leading me onwards towards someone in whom, perhaps, I *could* put my trust. This was the dawning of a lifelong walk Godwards: the Anchor perhaps we needed as a family, as we faced the future.

Meanwhile, although the Rileys were made of sterling stuff, even they found the difficulties of caring for a young, grieving but energetic family proved more than they could handle, and they decided to return once more to the peacefulness of their own home.

In the wake of the Rileys, there followed a succession of paid housekeepers and carers. First, there was Ellen — a merry, Irish girl whose real name was Eileen, but we had to call her Ellen as my father wouldn't allow his wife's name to be breathed under his roof. We liked Ellen tremendously, and her sister Mary — a mature student at London University, who visited her often. Ellen brought a breath of fresh air into our home, with her sense of fun, warmth and laughter, and her spontaneous love for us all. She lightened the atmosphere even if she could only partly fill the gaping hole left by mother. Perhaps she was *too* successful, or my father felt his position in some way threatened by her, for after a few short months, she also left us. We never knew why.

Next came Mr and Mrs Adams who answered my father's frantic advertisement for Housekeeper and Gardener. The Adams lived on the top floor of the house where our bedrooms had been, and brought their pregnant black cat with them, which promptly produced kittens. Mrs Adams was a tall, thin, austere, Dickensian-type woman with grey hair scraped back in a tight bun.

We longed to see the new kittens, but she would not allow us near them 'in case the mother ate them'. Mr Adams was hunched, looked ill and miserable and had warts on his nose. I don't remember him ever saying a word to any of us. He would slide through the kitchen at meal-times, and disappear into the garden, or keep to his room upstairs. I don't know where they ate their meals. They brought gloom with them, and it wasn't long before the Adams resigned.

The Adams and their cats were followed by kind, quiet, pretty Mrs Ibbotson, who had been widowed quite recently and had her own home in a nearby town. We visited her a couple of times on her days off. But once again, she did not stay long.

Finally, the strain of strangers taking care of us, in our large house, with a grieving, irascible father, proved totally unworkable. Dad's distress, his work, combined with all our emotional problems as well, were more than he could bear or manage practically. He came one night to sit at my bedside in the large bedroom which we four girls shared. The others were already asleep, but I was crying myself to sleep. His whispered words of comfort could not get through to me. I wanted him to go away, and shut him out. How he must have felt acutely the helpless desolation of parental failure as he left me.

Something had to be done. He had tried two options in his attempt to keep the family together: getting the help of willing friends; and failing that, having resident staff. Neither solution had proved satisfactory. Other than marrying again, which he would not contemplate as he still loved Eileen, what other arrangement was there for holding his home intact, since he had refused my offer to become a full-time carer? As I was only fifteen, he would not accept that option. The painful fact remained, for him and us, that no one could replace his wife, our mother.

As the last resort, he decided to sell Kingstackley, and board us all out among his family and any kind friends who might be glad of some financial help. He had done his utmost to keep us all together, but the effort had stretched him beyond endurance.

A Mrs Jacobson bought Kingstackley and proved to be a ruthless businesswoman. She took full advantage of a distressed sale, drove a hard bargain with my father and bought the house with much of its furniture and contents, at far too low a price, to convert it into flats.

I can only guess at my father's tormented frame of mind by the way in which he disposed of the family treasures which had been my mother's pride and joy — the Steinway grand piano, and her prized blue and white Royal Worcester dinner service which she had collected piece by piece as they had been able to afford it. I remember asking about this particularly, and realised that by selling it with the house, Dad did not want to keep the china or anything else that reminded him of Mum.

Much of the family linen which I packed up in a large trunk on the top landing had been wedding presents to our parents; but all their glassware, kitchen equipment, their books and her belongings disappeared, as did many of ours: books, toys and treasures from our childhood, lovingly carted from place to place till now, vanished. Did municipal dumps exist in those days? For him, the memory of my mother's departure was so raw a wound that he was unable to envisage life much beyond the house-sale and an uncertain future. The sale of our home was not only expedient, but appeared to be an attempt to purge all memories of the past with Mum. Much of our memorabilia went out with the purge.

Of course, he never succeeded in banishing her from his thoughts. He would always love her. But the reality remained: that with our house sold, any normal continuity of home-life from then on had gone. We were faced with an insecure and uncertain way forward. He had made contingency plans for each of us: his children were life itself to him and mattered more than anything else.

Richard, who was already attending Sutton County Grammar School, went to live nearby in Belmont with a kind family, Philip and Catherine Marsh, who were friends. They had a son and daughter much his own age, and I visited him there often. Suzanne boarded with other friends by the name of Challis who lived in Cheam and had two smaller boys. Sue seemed the most resilient of us all, and always seemed positive and happy in her attitude towards life. She continued her schooling at St Dunstan's Church School in Cheam where she learned to excel in bad language, which did not reflect too kindly the standards of the school.

Our two youngest sisters, Mary Liz and Penny, went up to Norfolk to stay briefly with our paternal uncle, a classics' master at Beeston School. From there they moved on to live with my Godmother, Dad's youngest sister Marion, in Letheringsett, for nearly a year. The Sinclairs had two boys who looked forward eagerly to having these two new cousins as playmates, but my cousin told me recently how disappointed he had been to discover what sad little girls they turned out to be.

Both our youngest sisters attended St Joseph's R.C. School in Sheringham (Penny went to its Pre-School), but it quickly became evident that eight-year old Mary Liz was still in a state of shock. She was deeply traumatised by the loss of mother and separation from the rest of the family, and her teacher noted she had severe difficulty in concentrating and learning. She became withdrawn, and later recalled that dark time in her life when she 'shut down - frightened, lonely and confused.'

My new home was just around the corner from Kingstackley, in the small rented flat of a widowed friend, Helen Bostel, and one of her two daughters, Jane. This family had once made their home with us in happier times. Helen was now working as secretary to the headmistress of a nearby school in Cheam. I lived with them for two years. Money was scarce. It was cheaper for the three of us to be vegetarians. Every Friday night we would shop, come home, wash and prepare all the vegetables and salads for the week. These were stored in jars in the little refrigerator. Each night, we would make up a plate of Edam cheese, raw vegetables and parsley, which was our standard diet, and have our evening meal on trays on our laps, listening to The Archers. Even on this healthy regimen, I began to put on puppy fat, and became what my brother rudely called 'plump and matronly', to my chagrin.

Jane Bostel was a little older than me and a boisterous extrovert. Unbeknown to her mother, she tried to lead me many a merry dance at the local youth club, but I was in no mood to join in with her chasing of boys. Since life had taken such a serious turn, I was withdrawn, and not much fun as a companion. Fortunately, we attended different girls' schools, and I would cycle off daily to Nonsuch Grammar School in Cheam, while she went in the opposite direction to Sutton High, our rivals and chief opponents on the hockey field.

Over the next two years, during the school holidays of the year, my father made sure we all spent time together. This must have been quite a feat of organisation on his part, but was well worth the happy times we enjoyed in one another's company, probably appreciating each other more particularly because of our separation during the school terms. Suzanne and I did our best as cooks, our combined knowledge being from the basic lessons given us by our mother on Saturday mornings in Kingstackley's large kitchen: how to make rock cakes and a white sauce. Somehow during the move from Kingstackley, we had managed to salvage Mum's copy of the original *Mrs Beeton* who advised us to 'take 12 eggs, etc...' This was our only recipe book. Sue developed an adventurous flair for cooking, if rather messy, while I followed a recipe to the letter and never produced such a tasty result.

Sometimes we went to stay in our grandmother's lovely home at The Orchard, Blakeney, in Norfolk, or in North End Cottage next door. Once we rented a flat on top of Mariner's Hill, overlooking Blakeney Quay and the wide marshes and creeks we had grown to love in the war years. One summer we camped in Farmer Williams' orchard nearby, among windfall apples... and armies of wasps. We lived largely on the former, and the latter we trapped successfully in jam-jars of marmalade and water, with paper tops with a hole over each jar.

Mary Liz and Penny had moved to Reading, where our maternal uncle, Paddy Jessop and his wife Joan lived with our four girl cousins. The walls of their tiny Tudor cottage on Bulmershe Court Farm, now the site of Reading University, already bulged, but fortunately their hearts were much larger than their home. This hospitable and welcoming family was destined to play an important role in the early upbringing of our two youngest sisters. In their midst, they would discover fun and laughter once more, and grow up free to be themselves.

The Jessops also accepted my father as part of their family so he could be near our sisters. They understood the importance Dad felt to remain closely linked with his two youngest children, both physically and geographically. So he lived either in a rented caravan just outside their front gate, or at one time was based in one of the empty, neglected farm buildings called Tower Cottage. As we often fetched up there for our holidays together, they and Dad provided us older three with a certain amount of stability and continuity during those fragmented years.

My Irish uncle Paddy was the only man on our mother's side of the family. He treated my brother Richard like a son, and imparted much wisdom and down-to-earth common sense to him during his unsettled teenage years. Looking back at those times, our family voted unanimously that the Jessops brought the most fun and happiness into what would otherwise have been bleak years.

Another family called Nicolls, who lived at Banstead in Surrey, rather nearer to the Sutton/Cheam bases where we three older ones were, also opened their home and hearts to us. Jack Nicolls, a widower, was a good friend to my father, and he and his two grown-up daughters did what they could to lighten our lives. We spent two happy

Christmases with them, and many enjoyable hours playing Racing Demon round their dining room table, taking breaks to eat peanut butter and tomato sandwiches for tea. I learned from Jackie and Jane how to iron clothes properly, despite my reluctance and slowness to learn. At my father's request, Jack Nicolls became our legal guardian as a precaution, should anything ever happen to him.

Throughout this time, no word whatsoever had been allowed to filter through from our mother. So final had been the break with her, that she might have been dead. Every letter she sent, every birthday card and gift from her, any pathetic appeal she made to show she still loved us, was fielded by my father and returned unopened, unanswered. If, by chance, a gift arrived in the post and we saw it before he could censor it, we became angry and argumentative. We could see no reason why he would not allow us to accept these small tokens from her, or to reciprocate in any way.

Later, when it became a court ruling that our mother was to have no access to her children, we had no choice but to comply with the judge's policy. I suppose this clause was to protect us from what he may have deemed a form of bribery to win back our affections. What we did not realise at the time, was that it was also to guard against our becoming drawn into her questionable lifestyle. How heart-rending it must have been for mother to be robbed of knowing that our love for her had in no way been dimmed by either time or our ever-changing circumstances.

11

A Joyful Return?

TOWARDS the end of the summer term in 1955, my landlady and friend Helen Bostel, reported that my mother had arrived on our uncle's farm in Reading, and was talking about 'coming back' to us. At first I could not believe it. My joy knew no bounds. I bought a white cotton dress dotted all over with little red hearts, especially for our first meeting. Relishing the amazing news which sounded almost too good to be true, I managed to endure till the end of the term, entertaining the wonderful thought that all our troubles were over at last.

What a joyous reunion it was! From our various homes, we three older children converged on the little thatched cottage at Bulmershe Court Farm. Two difficult years of separation rolled away with her joyful hugs. She looked just the same—our beloved Mum. Now life would resume something of its once normal flow.

To this day, I do not know how the old Tudor walls of Rose Cottage were able to accommodate three extra young people, on top of six Jessops, my mother and my two younger sisters! I do remember that the largest bedroom in the cottage became a dormitory with several of us sleeping on the floor. We were packed in so tightly that it was like the song we used to sing in which there were 'eight in the bed and the little one said, Roll over!' Dad kept his own space in the caravan outside the gate.

How did our aunt and uncle cope with all those mouths to feed? It was just as well that Uncle Paddy had a most productive vegetable garden, and his Webb's Wonderful lettuces were second to none in quality and size. Together with his home-grown vegetables, and my aunt's canny housekeeping and excellent cooking (she had learned to live on a slender salary ever since my uncle had chosen to farm, over his banking career soon after they first married), we all thrived through a hot and happy, salad-filled summer together.

We never gave a thought as to why or how our mother had reappeared so amazingly. It was sufficient that we were all together once more; that she had not abandoned us and did still love us. In fact, all past silent prayers, tears, and heartfelt pleas to our father, and the two-year wall of silence between her and her children, had been forgotten by the reality of her very presence. I had known all along that she had continued to love us, just as we had loved her. Nothing ever altered those bonds.

We did not know then about our mother's timely rescue from the gas oven by our uncle, or of how he had brought her straight down to the farm for safe-keeping, away from the Caddy orbit. Nor do I know how my father received her on arrival. My uncle and aunt waited till Mum was calmer before suggesting she sought Dad's permission to see us all, which he gave gladly. From the picture she gave of her suicide attempt, he must have imagined she had grown tired of Caddy, and that my parents would now be free to make a new start together so we could all 'live happily ever after' – the past nightmare separation and relationship forgiven and forgotten.

My mother, pulling out of her depression and confusion, must have played along with his hope as at least a possibility, because she and my father even went house-hunting together. At the same time, she was still trying to gain her balance of mind and emotions after the effects of Sheena's regime of brain-washing and her abduction of Mum's sixth child.

Although for the nine cousins the hot summer of sunny days was care-free and happy, in the adult world many questions were being posed, and unsettling discussions in progress between my parents. My father had endured long enough without Eileen to know how much he regretted his hasty action in cutting all ties with her.

He was ready to forgive the past, and longed to be reunited with her again. However, he underestimated (and possibly could not even begin to understand) her mental and emotional turmoil, her yearning for baby Christopher, and the depths of the utter despair which had driven her to the point of deciding to end her life. She now found herself torn between her love for her children, yet still in love with Peter although disillusioned with him, but unable to reverse her feelings for Dad. In actual fact, she was by no means ready to start life all over again with him, and it turned out, had very little, if any, intention of doing so.

September and the start of a new school term arrived all too soon. My father returned to work, commuting from Reading daily to the Air Ministry, while we three older children returned most reluctantly to our temporary foster homes and schools in Sutton and Cheam. No decision had been voiced about our family's future. Mary Liz and Penny stayed on with the Jessop cousins, and walked along the track through fields with them each day to the nearby village school of St Peter's, in Earley.

Whatever we may have hoped or envisaged, none of us was prepared for what happened next. Some days later, Helen broke the sad news that soon after our departure from Reading, Peter Caddy had come with Sheena from London to collect mother. Apparently, when he heard from Sheena that Eileen had returned to her former family, he had rushed back to London from the Middle East. Unbeknown to my uncle and aunt, or Dad, Mum had been able to slip away to a phone box in the village, with some excuse of going shopping, and had kept contact with Caddy in London.

In a letter to a friend, written some time later, my father recounted what transpired:

Eileen promised to have no further contact with Caddy, but as soon as I ended my short emergency leave, she phoned him every day and he, Sheena and Dorothy Maclean all came down to Reading and forced their way into my brother-in-law's house.

After a dreadful night of clarifying the choice, with the children (Mary Liz and Penny) weeping audibly upstairs, Eileen was taken away by the Caddys ...

Thus, with her distressing departure, our glorious summer ended. It had indeed all been 'too good to be true'. Dashed were all high-flying hopes and dreams of normal family-life again.

Up to this moment father had always hoped that Caddy would cast Eileen aside, as he had done with Nora, his first wife, and then Sheena, before he met Eileen. His dream was that she would then feel free to return to us. Tantalisingly, this had *almost* become a reality. But Peter had discovered he could not live without Eileen, and she had decided likewise. Dad's somewhat unrealistic hope lay shattered, and he found himself condemned once more to single parenthood, and to living an unsettled, peripatetic way of life while holding down a job to provide maintenance for us all. His own caravan could be moved to any convenient site, but he chose to stay on at the farm in Reading to be near our sisters, and from where it was convenient to travel from Earley station to London. Whenever possible, he would visit each of us in our respective homes.

This nomadic lifestyle was far from easy for him. He confided on several occasions that during long solitary hours of sleeplessness, he would reach a state of near-madness thinking about Caddy and all that had occurred since the last meeting with Eileen. His consuming rage against the man after my mother's second departure led him to fantasise about confrontations with Caddy which inevitably ended in Caddy's murder. Yet Dad never attempted to pursue his wife to make a last bid for her. Perhaps this was not so strange knowing he could not trust his reactions should he meet Peter Caddy face to face.

Nobody can know what my father suffered during those lonely years. His need to provide for his children kept him focused if not always sane. The only real warmth of home-life and acceptance came from his in-laws Paddy and Joan, and he built up strong emotional bonds with his two youngest daughters who were, after all, dependent upon him. As their only parent, he was their security, and they in turn rewarded him with their total love and trust till his dying day.

At this point, the convoluted circumstances forced him to take a long look at the reality of his own position in relation to Eileen's, and at what might be best for their children. He did not believe in divorce, so it was only with extreme reluctance that he decided he could no longer defer the dreaded divorce proceedings his friends and siblings had advised — so long awaited by Eileen and Caddy. The painful reality meant the death of his hopes and was almost more than he could endure. He still loved Eileen, but now must contemplate the ultimate humiliation of giving her over, once and for all, to another. Two-and-a-half years after my mother's first impassioned request, our parents finally faced each other across the divorce court.

12

Divorce, and Life thereafter...

OUR parents were divorced on my sixteenth birthday. We children had been left at our Easter holiday flat on Mariner's Hill, Blakeney, while Dad travelled up to London for the hearing. I remember nothing of that day except waiting on tenterhooks until that evening for his return. I longed to hear what he had to tell us, but he was too drained to say anything other than, 'It was sordid.' It came out with such disgust that I did not dare pursue my questioning.

The material laid before the judge for the divorce proceedings had taken a full weekend to sift through and evaluate. This amounted to more than a straightforward matter of adultery and desertion.

There was never any doubt in my father's mind that Sheena's past had been steeped in the arcane secrets of the occult. A brief résumé of her included how she had strayed from her Christian roots into involvement with the Rosicrucians, adoption of the ancient heresy of Gnosticism, spiritualism and even witchcraft. Whatever the influences had been, she now claimed to be a divine channel, a visionary, and a mystic. She had a number of young divorced women 'orbiting around her' (as my father wrote later to a friend) and he 'suspected lesbianism', but this was not substantiated as far as I could discover.

However, he told me about a vivid description given to him by two of Sheena's ex-followers, who visited him soon after our mother's initial departure. Both women had been present at strange rituals around Sheena's bedside. At one of these, Sheena had manifested frogs on her tongue while she sat in bed, surrounded by her disciples.

Hence my father's suspicion of the practice of witchcraft. He must have submitted this evidence at court along with much else he never divulged to his children.

Unfortunately, an attempt to trace the records of the actual divorce proceedings was abortive, as they must have been shredded long since. At the time mother had come back to us in 1955, it had been evident to my father that a hotchpotch of ideas and beliefs had been drummed into Eileen already, as part of the 'training' under Sheena's tuition. He saw she had changed, though we were unaware of any difference in her. She was simply our loving Mum.

The judge decided that all the factors of the case made it clear that, because mother had been exposed to a series of 'harmful influences' by which she seemed to have become bewitched, her children should not be exposed to them. *'Proceedings culminated...with a decree nisi,'* wrote my father later, *'in which I was given custody and Eileen was denied access. The judge directed that any future application for access should be referred personally to himself.'* This ruling was to remain effective until each child became eighteen. Meanwhile, my brother and three sisters were to remain wards of court and in my father's sole care. Because I had reached sixteen on the due date of the divorce, and therefore the legal age of consent, I was told I was exempt from the court's protection. I realised, on reflection, that any visit I might wish to make to see my mother under these circumstances would be disruptive and unfair to the rest of the family, and unfair on them.

I hid behind this position because, truth to tell, I found myself completely at a loss by then to know how I would handle such a visit to her. I was still hurting deeply after the disappointment of her abrupt second departure the previous year. Fourteen long years of growing up were to pass before I saw her again.

The judge's decision had now legalized the position already imposed by father. Legal or not, mother remained undeterred in her desperate attempts to make contact with us. Letters, cards and gifts for our birthdays kept coming, and sometimes found us when father was not around. By this time my father had taken early retirement from the RAF under the Golden Bowler scheme.

The Hole-in-the-Wall as we called it, or Wall Cottage, was entered through a flint archway from the main street in Cheam. This was the home of another older friend called Margaret Dewey. She had a hut on the inside of the wall in which she gave craft lessons, and her lovely garden climbed up a slope to the cottage. Two other maiden ladies lived at Wall Cottage with her: a retired missionary called Win, who was always kind and jolly, and a rather formidable nurse named Nell. My father had asked Margaret if there would be room for the three of us to live there as it was near my school and that of Mary Liz and Penny. Bravely, she agreed to take us all on, so I moved from the Bostels, and Dad arranged for Mary Liz and Penny to leave the Jessops at Reading so we could be together in Cheam, and I could help look after them.

We spent a not unhappy year or more there, they at Ambleside School where Helen Bostel worked, while I continued at Nonsuch County Grammar for Girls, took my GCE, and launched into the first year of A Level studies. I enjoyed being a surrogate parent, and read to them every night from A.A.Milne's *Winnie the Pooh*. At eighteen, I began to appreciate his writings with new eyes, and enjoyed his tongue-in-cheek humour. We ended up with bear-hugs every night before my sisters were tucked up, ready for sleep.

While Mary Liz, Penny and I were living at Wall Cottage a last-ditch bid was made by Caddy and my mother to unite the two children of his first marriage to Nora with the five of us and their own two boys (by now we had a second half-brother, Jonathan). This crazy scheme appeared in an article in either the *News of the World* or the *Daily Sketch* tabloid (I cannot recall which one), but we did not take it too seriously or pay much attention. Uppermost in my mind at the time was serious revision for my GCE exams at Nonsuch Grammar.

I then went on to take the first year of the A-level course, and never completed further education. It had struck me forcibly that if I had, I would be finishing my schooling aged 19. This was largely due to my earlier chequered education in ten different schools. I had entered in the second year at Nonsuch, and all my friends and peers were a year younger. When I plucked up the courage to seek an interview with our feared headmistress, Miss Dickie (known throughout the school of 800 as The Bird) and informed her that I wanted to leave school in order to take up voluntary missionary work in London, she expressed her disapproval roundly and soundly. She understood my conviction and reluctantly let me go. In retrospect, I wish I had listened to her advice.

This choice meant yet another change for my sisters, but Dad had already set up home again for them, with the help of an older Irish friend, Dorothy. She knew us of old and was a person we had loved and trusted as a family for many years. Valiant Dorothy took up the challenge as his housekeeper, and child-minder for Mary Liz and Penny at New Malden, with much verve and jollity. Mary Liz soon followed Sue to the Anglo-Catholic boarding school of St Stephen's College, at Broadstairs in Kent, while Penny went locally to New Malden Primary.

At that time, my father was Work Study Officer at the nearby Decca Records factory. The pioneer of Work Study, Frank Gilbreth of *Cheaper by the Dozen* fame, had long been one of Dad's role models. Gilbreth had used his experimental methods on his family of twelve children, with mixed success, and had devised a new scheme of saving time and motion by changing the way people think about their work. Dad tried to instil work study thinking into our lives too, which has often served me well since.

When Decca moved their base to High Wycombe, Buckinghamshire, Dad found a pleasant house there, high on a hillside housing estate overlooking Hughenden Valley in which nestles the lovely country mansion once belonging to Benjamin Disraeli.

Mary Liz returned from boarding school, 'very sadly' she recalled, to join Penny in going to a little private school called Piper's Corner, both smartly clad in grey uniforms with red and grey cloaks. The household settled down to a fairly normal lifestyle, and Dorothy made several good friends in the area, as did my father. For a time, all went well. I would visit them from London, where I was then working voluntarily as a telephone operator in Hays Mews, behind Berkeley Square.

Unhappily, after nearly two years, Dad's experiment in re-building home-life was doomed yet again. By this time, I was away in Guildford finishing a three-month bursarship at Miss Temple's Secretarial College. Two days before I was due to leave, I arrived home that evening to be told that my father had just called, and spoken with my friend and landlord Michael. Dad said that he had to move from High Wycombe because he had created an incident which had been reported to the police by a resident on the estate, and a court hearing was pending. He had quit his job and was in the throes of packing up the house so that he, the girls and Dorothy could leave at once. I rang my college principal and explained we had 'financial difficulties' and that I would not be able to finish the last two days because of a sudden change in my family's fortunes.

Quickly, we finished clearing the house at High Wycombe, put the contents in store and left the estate, feeling more than a little ashamed at leaving under a cloud. Our noble friend Dorothy took Mary Liz, Penny and our little cat Benjamin to stay temporarily with a friend of hers in Slough, until my father could arrange for the next step for them all. Benjamin was a half-grown tabby, given to the girls by the Jessop cousins, and he and Dorothy became inseparable friends.

Winter came early that year. I went from London to

Slough to visit Dorothy and my sisters with snow on the ground. We needed to talk over this hiccup in family circumstances with Dorothy, and try to come up with some sort of plan for the future. A similar situation had arisen with Dad in Sutton some years before when he had ended up in court. Once again, his Herculean efforts on behalf of his loved ones were destined to founder on the jagged rocks of problems created by his own doing. His need of counselling to help him learn how to handle his sexual addiction effectively had now become acute, otherwise his younger children would remain victims of constantly fluctuating and disturbing circumstances, however much he loved them.

By the grace and mercy of God, and with the timely intervention and unstinting care of friends and members of our wider Christian family, we were able to find our way through. None of us ever took to drugs, or became alcoholics, or ended up on the streets as was the fate of an increasing number of homeless youngsters, either abandoned by their parents or choosing instead to live among the nation's flotsam and jetsam. There was no time then to think that what was happening in our family was but a microcosm of a far wider field of disasters occurring in society.

In our father's defence, it can be said that he was acutely aware of his failures as a parent, and always quick to admit his faults. He found different ways of saying this to each of his children. While we were packing up the house at High Wycombe, I found a poem that he had written on my fourteenth birthday, which shows how he tried to express this to me:

O Jenny, I think of your birthdays –
Especially two years ago,
When trying to hear what the Lord says,
I suddenly started to know
That something so strange was to happen:
I hadn't the least idea what.

*But God said He'd got a fresh purpose
For you and your life, so fear not.
It started when two days later
You were taken so terribly ill -
Though Mummy and I didn't cater
For something much worse than a chill.
Then God took a hold on your destiny,
Showed through prayer came the power,
And Mummy and I saw His mystery
Working out hour by hour.
Now we are riven and parted:
Self-will and pride have undone
The ties that God lovingly tended -
The two that through Him became one.
I feel that I'm terribly guilty -
Pride, greed and lust still not gone.
I didn't obey what God told me,
And now our old home life is done.
But hope shines anew through this Easter...*

*...There are terrible powers rampaging
That are tearing our world to its core –
Our home is only one sample,
Others are seen by the score...*

We had experienced those 'terrible powers' undermining what was left of our family life, but just now it seemed as though it was my father alone who wielded such powers to wound us. He admitted himself that whenever things were going well, he went off the rails and let himself, and all of us, down badly. The innocent suffer, and, in this case it was the younger members of the family, uprooted yet again and moved on with no just reasons given – their home-life, security and affection seemingly betrayed. I grieved for my younger sisters. My father stood unforgiven by me for the nature over which he had no control, and his contradictory behaviour.

I say contradictory, because to give him his due, Dad

always sought daily, through meditation and Bible reading, the Person he believed and *knew* could lift him above the power of that nature and the difficulties created by it. Yet ... in spite of all his efforts, victory and the remoulding of my father's character was to remain beyond his grasp for some time still. Despite all his mistakes, however, I do believe that had he *not* been bent on this constant search to find God's will for his life, his own fate and that of each of his children might have been very bleak indeed. Without doubt, we were being watched over, and buoyed up by the prayers of many.

A profoundly understanding friend wrote Dad these words during that time of upheaval. I only found them tucked between the pages of his much-scored Bible, after Dad had died:

> *No, Lord, I never will again*
> *Forsake Thy ways,*
> *My oh! so devious heart*
> *Thou know'st*
> *And all my days*
> *Are noted, named and numbered*
> *In Thy book –*
> *Recorded for that hour*
> *When I must look*
> *And recollect with tears*
> *The way I chose to live,*
> *Then helpless pray Thee*
> *If there any hope remains,*
> *Thou may'st forgive.*
> *No, Lord, I never will again...*
> *Yet, frail,*
> *So wilful frail am I,*
> *That even fear to fall,*
> *While yet I cry,*
> *Protesting of an honest new intent.*
> *Lord, could'st Thou permanently shake*
> *And make me see,*

> *When I reject Thy miracle*
> *And refuse Thy grace,*
> *How grievously I harm*
> *Not only me,*
> *But all the human race?*
> *The choice is mine,*
> *Yes, mine.*
> *So shall I choose, this day,*
> *This very point of time,*
> *Irrevocably choose*
> *And take my stand.*
> *Nor wilt Thou scorn*
> *As now I mean and say*
> *'Oh, Lord, I never will again*
> *Betray.'*
>
> G.E.S.

As we grew up, our father's frankness about himself called forth more and more of our understanding, and not a little compassion in my case. I was to learn to love him dearly in the years before he died. But in 1961, just at that moment our small world had fallen apart again, and he was to blame. In hindsight, it is remarkable that none of us was ever out on the street, destitute or without an address. Somehow, somewhere, each of us continued being cared for in the homes of either friends or members of Mum's or Dad's families.

One of my father's better decisions, which must have cost him a small fortune financially, was to send four of his children to boarding schools, at one time or another, in order to provide some security and continuity in their lives. I remained at Nonsuch Grammar, but Richard went to Bembridge School, Isle of Wight, after leaving Sutton Grammar, until he reached sixteen. My three sisters spent several happy years at St Stephen's College, Broadstairs, under the care of a teaching order of Anglo-Catholic nuns. After the High Wycombe debacle, Penny and Mary Liz joined Suzanne at St Stephen's College. Penny was the last to finish her education at SSC, with flying colours in

1969. She went on to do teacher training at Eastbourne. When Mary Liz left SSC, she spent a year in Switzerland at Caux, in the little international school where I had once helped teach. She then returned to London to finish her further education at a crammer in Westminster, and went on to attend the Froebel Institute at Roehampton for the next three years, where she qualified as a teacher.

Whilst I and my youngest sisters were living in Cheam at Wall Cottage, our brother Richard had been going through the Rock 'n Roll (*Blue Suede Shoes*) and fast motor-bike stage of teenage rebellion. Although he had been happy at Bembridge School, he had not shone in his GCEs, and had left school after his exams in favour of earning a living. From the age of three he had wanted to be a farmer, so became an apprentice on the Suffolk farm to which we had been evacuated during the war, where he rapidly became a sensitive and knowledgeable stockman, mainly working with pigs. After seven years training on this farm he was ready to use his skills to further his career, and through a South African veterinary friend emigrated to a Karoo farm in the Cape Province of South Africa. There he set up a piggery on a sheep farm, and within three years was marketing 3,000 bacon pigs annually.

At the same time, our vivacious, blonde and blue-eyed sister Suzanne, who had developed a flair for flower-painting at school, was now pursuing culinary art with notable success in a large London house, and progressed to taking a Cordon Bleu Diploma which stood her in very good stead on her future travels in the States. There she met and married a young Englishman in New Mexico, and when they finally settled in Toronto, Canada, she had a small card printed to the effect that she would 'cook and serve meals in the elegance of your own home.' This statement caught the imagination of the wealthier ladies in the echelons of Upper Canada and she never lacked work from that day onwards.

My path, after leaving school, was to work full-time

with Initiatives of Change. I saw this as a practical way to help other people. But I also hoped that by participating myself in such endeavours, I might learn some way to sort out some of the mental and emotional confusion in my life.

So fractured had our home-life and education become that by this time none of us had attended less than seven schools apiece, and Nonsuch had been my tenth.

Φ

It is worth recording that while we were still living in Iraq, back in 1953, father had the persistent thought that he and my mother would 'find peace in the autumn' of their lives. This phrase had come into his mind in a morning quiet time, months *before* Caddy had borne off his wife. He was to find that peace eventually. But not before he experienced dashed hopes, divorce some three years later, followed by long years of loneliness, much counselling to help him work through suppressed anger and despair – and still that ever-persistent 'trusting in the Lord' to the end.

As a single parent, left to cope with the day-to-day business of bringing up his five children, and despite being at his wits' end much of the time, he did a heroic job in providing for us all, albeit with the help of many friends and relatives. We were his prime motivation. He admitted to me on more than one occasion that, without us to think and care for, he would have committed murder out of hatred for Caddy, and that he reached such depths of despair that he considered suicide.

Truly, we can be proud of all Dad achieved. He proved, more than anyone else I know, the truth that 'change is always possible.' His abiding belief in the love and power of God's forgiveness to bring about those changes in himself and us, to which he clung – even while going through personal hell – sustained him, and his immediate family, to the end.

Although Dad came through many a hardship bringing up his children alone, he was the first to admit that just handling his own caprices of character was a full time job in itself. To cope with ours as well – and that was no easy task – was an incredible feat.

One could not have met a more victorious sinner during the final years of his life, nor a man who understood better the magnitude of moral battles fought against temptation. Before he died, he experienced the reality of a friendship with Jesus Christ which brought balm to his troubled soul. He had been playing an active role in a loving ecumenical religious community situated at Hengrave Hall in Suffolk. This was to become his spiritual home and family.

Dad had suffered from angina for some years, having contracted glandular fever, and then disregarded the need to rest by mowing his cousin's lawn. While at Hengrave, where he was living in a small, unheated cottage, he suffered and survived four heart attacks within several months. I went over from Ascot several times to visit him in hospital in Bury St Edmunds, Suffolk, during the time I was expecting our daughter. While he was still in intensive care from the fourth attack, the Sister Warden at Hengrave (which was run as a conference centre by an order of nuns) asked me to find out from Dad what kind of funeral he would want *should* he die. Practical as ever, he said, 'Oh, cremation, darling. I don't want to take up room in a churchyard. The planet isn't big enough for all of us now.'

He returned to convalesce with his older sister, Janet, at her bungalow in Wiveton, overlooking the rolling fields of his beloved North Norfolk. Mary Liz came over from New Zealand to visit some of her family here, and spent some very happy days there with Dad, despite the cold north winds and snow heralding an early Spring. In the meantime, our mother had gone over to look after Liz's husband and two boys in New Zealand, at Liz's request. The move on Liz's part proved to be timely.

Φ

On a cold March day in 1978, the Oxford and Cambridge Boat Race was well under way. (My father loved the Boat Race and was an enthusiastic Oxford supporter even though his father and brother had both earned oars for rowing at Cambridge.) During this excitement, the telephone rang. It was Dad's sister Janet calling from Norfolk, in tears. Dad had succumbed to a fifth heart seizure. He had been rushed into Cromer hospital where he had died.

I tried to take in... As the shock took hold, I groped for words of comfort for both my aunt and myself. We agreed I must call Mary Liz in New Zealand as soon as possible, since she had been the last to visit him but had returned to New Zealand ten days previously when he had been in good health. As I walked away from the telephone, I heard cheering as the Cambridge boat sank in mid-Thames and Oxford won the race. I thought how Dad would have enjoyed that rare moment, and how strange that he should die today.

To break the news of Dad's passing to Liz on the other side of the globe, unable to give her human comfort except verbally, proved an unenviable task. She was heart-broken. Dad had been the bedrock in hers and Penny's lives, not only materially as best he could, but also emotionally and spiritually. Both sisters were devastated.

A week later, in the quiet grounds at Hengrave Hall, with sheep grazing in nearby fields, we gathered to pay a last resounding tribute to Dad in the lovely chapel of the Hall. The rousing service was led by the Reverend John Tyndale-Biscoe. John, and his wife Margie, had given Dad a home at Gilston Rectory for more than two years, and set his feet on the right road with their loving support and understanding. So on that day of joyous thanksgiving, we could celebrate his unshakable faith in God with the hymns of praise he loved, including his favourite Russian hymn 'How Great Thou Art'.

As we walked to the graveside, carrying Dad's ashes,

our son Andrew, aged four, was deeply puzzled. 'How can Grandpa fit in that little box?' he asked. We laid Dad to rest alongside the graves of several nuns who had passed into glory while living in the Hengrave community.

It is true to say that not one of his children has a scrap of doubt that our Dad finally merited the RAF motto now carved on his gravestone: *Per Ardua ad Astra* (through adversity to the stars). Together with these words we added, 'He loved his Lord.' These summed up perfectly the often tortuous and varied courses of his life, and of his triumphal exit from earthly struggle to reach heaven, pilot that he was.

Hundreds of people gathered in the chapel and then at his graveside – family, old friends and even strangers, reaching way back to his early days in the Air Force. All came out of deepest affection, appreciation for his life and dynamism, and immense gratitude for the sure knowledge that he had come to know, at the last, 'peace in the autumn of his days'. In those final three years of his life, this promise had indeed become a glorious fact.

He attempted to plant his offspring's feet on that same rock of faith. Like the moods of the sea, our often stormy lives have crashed up against it, been broken and re-formed upon it, swirled around it, but more often (in my case anyway) I have drawn comfort and hope from this Rock. We may have found ourselves washed up on different shores, in Canada, New Zealand, South Africa, Portugal, Spain, Scotland and England, but we have known great love from many sources, not least from our parents, and have all found change for the better in our lives.

The balance of Dad's prophecy for peace at the end, however, was yet to be borne out in the life of his ex-wife, Eileen. Would it really be possible for our mother to find that same quality of peace of mind, heart and spirit before she too moved on to another realm?

PART II

Adult years, marriage and forgiveness

13

The London Years

Not 'til the loom is silent, and the shuttles cease to fly,
Shall God unroll the canvas and explain the reason why
The dark threads are as needed in the Weaver's skilful hand,
As the threads of gold and silver in the pattern He has planned.
           Benjamin M. Franklin

I HAVE passed briefly over the strands of the lives interwoven with my own – those of my brother and sisters. As they grew up, they each had their struggles, lessons to learn, destinies to fulfil; each has a unique story to tell. Since this is mine, I must tell it as it happened to me, and include them as our strands interwove.

To rewind the tape to the year before I left school: I had visited — either with my father or independently — several homes in Charles Street and Berkeley Square, Mayfair, which served as the headquarters of Moral Rearmament (MRA) in the United Kingdom. The location was familiar as I remembered being there for a short while after we had arrived home from the States in 1947. At eighteen I was interested in the friendliness of those now working there, and was happy to throw in my lot where there was a need. This often meant serving at tables, or stuffing envelopes for send-outs of letters in the Hays Mews office behind Berkeley Square. Clive of India's magnificent home, 45 Berkeley Square, had been bought as Dr Buchman's London home, and I often helped out there in the Old Kitchen, where Sir Robert Clive had once kept his cow to provide milk for the household. Along the basement corridors were the old air-raid shelters, now store-rooms, where the MRA team had taken shelter from bombing in the war years.

There I met a Scots girl called Alison, whose parents

had been divorced, and with whose story I could immediately identify. She held out a hand of friendship and hope, and we became friends. She was working full-time with Moral Re-Armament, looking after the Scottish family of a shipyard worker from the Clyde. They lived in one of the Charles Street homes, and when Alison invited me to join her in helping to run the large, elegant townhouse, I accepted. I wanted to capture something of what Alison had found which had aided her in handling the hurts she had felt through her own parents' separation.

For the next four years I worked voluntarily for MRA, earning my board-and-lodging by house-keeping in two of these houses, helping with the children when their parents were away, learning how to cook for large numbers, waiting at tables for an amazing variety of people, from diplomats to dustmen. I also operated a switchboard for the telephone system which linked all the houses belonging to the MRA headquarters. I counted it a privilege learning how to serve to the highest standards. Each of the houses was like an embassy of hope in which all nationalities, creeds and colours were graciously received and welcomed as 'royal souls'. Often over a meal with a carefully planned menu, served in a peaceful ambience of confidentiality, key decisions were taken in a person's life, or a new strategy found towards reconciliation between people or even between countries—sometimes the one leading to the other.

While I worked, I watched how people lived out their faith, and how the most unlikely people could work side by side for a big enough aim, through being totally honest with one another. All those I worked alongside lived on the basis of faith and prayer that 'where God guided He provided'. Certainly, with my five-pound dress allowance per month from my father, which he had given me since my sixteenth birthday, I never lacked anything I needed, and was always grateful to step into second-hand clothes.

The latter two years of this voluntary work I spent largely in Switzerland. The beautiful Caux Palace Hotel, now re-named Mountain House, above Montreux and Lausanne, looked out over Lake Geneva to the snow-capped tip of Mont Blanc in France. This inspirational location had been chosen and given in 1947 by Swiss families to Dr Frank Buchman for his work. During the war Switzerland had remained neutral. The round turrets, red-tiled roofs and green lawns of Mountain House were magnificent, and had drawn Disney to use it as the model for the fairy palace in the film Snow White.

This international centre required operators who spoke French, German and Switzerdeutsch as well as English. The main summer conferences there ran into over a thousand people per session. These were accommodated both in Mountain House and the Grand Hotel a 100 metres or so up the mountain behind the main house.

There was much I loved about Switzerland besides the spectacular scenery and its world-famous chocolate (memories of Suzette) and cheeses. Their National day on August 1st was celebrated on the lawns of Mountain House, with the hurling upwards and catching of their national flag. The long alpine horns would echo eerily through the valleys by day, and huge bonfires crackled up into the night sky. Each springtime, the hillsides were carpeted with wild narcissi, and goat- and cow-bells jangled in the pastures; on hot summer days we would carry our lunch out on to the curved stone terrace from the Big Dining room, and always there would be a good Swiss tea served at four o'clock, outside if it was fine. Sometimes on a balmy summer's evening a highlight would be Scottish dancing out on the terrace, led by four Scots sisters from Glasgow. The colourful national costumes of the different Swiss cantons were always in evidence. Every new session of the conferences brought a pageant of people of every race and language seeking answers for themselves and their countries.

In the sub-zero temperatures of winter, the funicular train would chug up from Montreux through Caux, bound for the deep snows on the Rochers de Naye, filled with skis and thick-clad skiers. The children from the Caux School and I spent many happy hours tobogganing down the steep hill tracks, and I watched with mouth agape as two-year olds on skis whistled downhill past the chalet. Next door to the Chalet Patinoire, where I lived for a while, was an ice-rink – skating being another sport we enjoyed. Never to be forgotten were the delicious Gruyère and Emmental cheese fondues, served up at the Col de Jaman restaurant, or often as a birthday celebration in our midst.

I worked hard, and was often up at 4.30 a.m. in order to spend a time of quiet before joining my shift to prepare conference breakfasts. I was also asked to help out with the classes in the little Caux School where children of different nationalities were pupils while their parents travelled abroad with plays or other outreach work. On one occasion, I had the care of a French family of three children, and learned more French in those few weeks than in nine years at school.

I had celebrated my twenty-first birthday in Caux, where my sister Penny had joined me for the happy event. I was still shy and reserved but by then far better at expressing myself and able to relate well to other nationalities. I had made many new friends among whom were some young Japanese who produced strings of tiny paper birds to hang from the ceiling for the occasion. I accumulated some treasures on that birthday, apart from an incredible array of cards and poems. These gifts included *The Joy of Cooking*, a book from a Dutch friend; a beautiful, handmade set of extendable book-ends from India; and a small dark olive-wood cross from a tree in Jerusalem.

Yet despite being so cherished and feted, and the marvellous experience of living in that country, I often felt lonely. I missed my family. It gradually dawned on me that I had not yet stumbled on the secret which I had hoped might be the key to unlock my heart. Still imprisoned by our family's past, I was as far as ever from being able to fulfil what I regarded as an effective role in helping others to find change in their lives (one of the aims of MRA). So where was I heading, and was my life adding up to anything at all? Perhaps the time was coming when I must move on.

I had always sworn I would never become a secretary. Having tried my hand at many other skills, I suddenly had a strong urge to take a secretarial course. Perhaps I could then strike a blow for independence as a wage earner. When I voiced this thought to an English friend in Caux, she suggested I might like to base with her parents in Guildford, Surrey, and explore the secretarial field there. I wrote to my grandmother of my intention. She was so delighted to hear I wanted to take a training course that she promptly offered to fund my studies and maintenance. At last I was going to be 'doing something useful' with my life. She had never approved of my voluntary work.

Φ

That summer at Caux, a group of Chinese students arrived from Taiwan, led by General Ho Ying Chin. Their experiences in Caux inspired them to write a play called The Dragon about their families, many of whom were living behind the Bamboo Curtain. General Ho and Dr Buchman decided this play could speak to the rest of Europe. This would prove to be a major move, which required a team to travel with the Chinese actors, to stage manage the show and support them in this new venture. I travelled with them, selling books, talking to people from the audiences after the performances, and serving meals to the Chinese in the various towns they visited. Their 'baptism of fire' came in Scandinavia. In Denmark they met fierce opposition from young communists who tried several nights to disrupt the show – one night by blowing whistles throughout the performance; another when the backstage crew refused to open the stage curtains, and on a third occasion when they released mice into the laps of the audience. General Ho removed his cast hurriedly across the turbulent waters of the Baltic Sea from Copenhagen to Stockholm, Sweden, where the play had been invited to visit, and was accepted with acclaim.

While we stayed in the beautiful Swedish home of Alnäs, overlooking the wintry grey waters of the sound, I helped serve meals to the Chinese cast. One morning a large meeting was held in the town hall, to which a number of city dignitaries and members of the government were invited. The aim of the meeting, I heard later, was to inspire those present with the vision behind the Chinese drama full of stories giving their hope of change in the Communist world through people becoming different. Hopefully, this would motivate the Swedes to fund its onward programme. Before the meeting ended, baskets were handed round for contributions from the audience. During our travels, each of us had been given a little money for our personal needs in each city, and I had saved up mine so I could buy Christmas presents to send home to my family. As a basket reached me, I felt a strong urge to respond to the need, took a deep breath and emptied my purse for the cause. After all, I was one of those travelling with General Ho's cast. When I realised I had nothing to send my family, I hastened to the ladies' cloakroom and burst into tears. No one knew just what a sacrifice I felt I had made. I kept my misery entirely to myself.

I was to learn a valuable lesson-for-life there in Stockholm. As I passed through the kitchen at Alnäs that same afternoon, one of the Swedish cooks stopped me and said she had had a thought that morning to give me twenty kroner. I was much moved by her generosity. A few minutes later, a message came from a bedridden Swedish friend, asking me to visit her. Inga welcomed me from under her patchwork quilt, sat me down and asked how 'things were going' in my life. We chatted on, and as I left, she handed me an envelope containing fifty kroner. That day I ended up with exactly the amount I had parted with that morning. Only God had known what I had given, and now he was giving it all back. It had happened too fast to think about the principle of 'faith and prayer'. This was more like 'manna from heaven'. Unbelievingly, but joyously, I was able to send home a parcel of little gifts.

From there the play was invited to Norway, and many of us spent Christmas just outside Oslo in the elegant mansion belonging to one of Norway's best-known actresses, who had lent her home for the cast's use. It turned out to be situated close to one of the world's finest ski jumps, and we could watch the experts in breath-taking action.

Finally, the whole operation moved on into Germany, first to Freudenstadt in the Black Forest where in 1938 Dr Buchman had first received the momentous vision, when Europe was talking of re-arming for war, that 'the next great movement in the world would be a movement for moral and spiritual re-armament.' Now, years on, the young Chinese were playing their part in that same vision.

Wherever the play went in Germany, it was well received. We ended up in the industrial heartlands of Dortmund and Dusseldorf. As we journeyed through the country, I marvelled at the industriousness and speed with which that nation had picked itself out of ruins and rebuilt its devastated cities.

It was there that I parted from the Chinese, leaving them to continue their tour, while I took a train, crossed the English Channel, and arrived in Guildford, where I would lodge with the Hallowes family for the next year.

As explained in the previous chapter, at the end of my course the rapid exodus from High Wycombe had left a huge question mark in all our minds about the future. After talking with Dorothy in Slough, she had called up a friend of hers in London to ask whether I might stay with her and her mother while I looked for a job.

The secretarial course had been most timely. I was

now able to take a job as a shorthand typist, and the obvious next step was to find a job and a flat as quickly as possible. Dorothy Stewart had given me the name of her friend in London who had agreed to my spending time there during my search.

In the meantime, my father had taken our youngest sisters back to Reading to be cared for by our Jessop relations, before he eventually decided they should follow Suzanne to the boarding school in Broadstairs, Kent.

Dorothy's friend resided in a prestigious part of London, just off Cadogan Square. This was Leone Exton and her elderly mother, Queen, who was unwell much of the time. When I called them to make arrangements, I could hardly believe the warmth with which Leone welcomed me, also on her mother's behalf. I asked if I might stay a fortnight, while I job-searched and looked for rented accommodation.

At the Brook Street Agency I found a job at once, working in the Copyright department of the music publishers, Boosey & Hawkes in Regent Street. As I turned my mind to flat-hunting, Leone and Queen would not hear of my going off to live in London on my own, and invited me to remain with them. This gesture proved typical of their large-hearted inclusion of all, as I was to discover. How could I refuse such kindness? My thirteen pounds a week and luncheon vouchers (£3.00 per day) was hardly sufficient to pay them rent, but they did not quibble at my contribution. I would walk across Green Park each day to catch the bus from Marble Arch up Oxford Street, and then spend my vouchers across the road from B & H at the Lyons Corner House. I was in clover.

My fortnight's visit to the Extons extended to a ten-year sojourn. During that decade, I was to observe this remarkable family living out their Christian faith as I felt it was meant to be lived. The Extons never spared themselves. Their exuberance for living and their out-- reach to others stretched me and touched my heart. I saw people blossom and their lives change for the better. In my time with them, literally hundreds of visitors climbed the stairs to cross the threshold of their beautiful flat: neighbours, strangers, friends, and—in their extensive family ramifications—cousins, nieces and nephews. Leone often organised parties for buffet dinners, followed by an evening at the Westminster Theatre where Christian plays had been performed since just after the war. The theatre itself had been bought as a living memorial by the families of loved ones killed in the war.

Leone was manageress of the Westminster Theatre restaurant, an integral part of the new Westminster Theatre Arts Centre, built over the consecrated ground of Queen Charlotte's Chapel, just behind the royal mews of Buckingham Palace. She worked long hours, cared for Queen when she came home, and her home was always available to each one of my family as a safe harbour. Mary Liz lived there with us while she finished her A-level education in London. She formed a special bond with Queen, who became an adopted grandmother to us all. My brother and three sisters received from Leone and Queen much-needed stability, loving friendship and wise counsel, as well as generous hospitality whenever needed, throughout the most formative teenage years.

Leone and Queen skilfully fielded many a drama in the Combe family, and remained a living example to us of unconditional love—two words of which my mother was particularly fond. From them we learned about *agape* love, God's own. He expressed love through them in an endless flow of much-needed grace (with our moods and in our doldrums), patience and humour which touched and enriched not only us, but everyone else who knew them. Leone's care for all her restaurant staff demonstrated the same type of love—her involvement in all their lives, divorces, marriages, difficulties—from the kitchen porter to the striking blond waitress who ended up marrying one of the regular restaurant customers.

I had watched her nursing her mother day after day,

and often at night, and asked her once how she managed to do so, always cheerfully, and running a business as well. Her loving philosophy was summed up in her words: 'I want to live so that when Mum goes, I have no regrets.' Queen died peacefully in her own bed in May, 1970.

Those years with the Extons left an indelible imprint on each one of the Combe family, for they were largely responsible for laying the cornerstone for building the strongest family bonds between we five siblings from then on.

During that decade, Richard ventured forth to pig-farm in South Africa, Suzanne to the States and Canada, where she married her Englishman in New Mexico, and went on to live in Toronto and built up her successful catering business; and both Mary Liz and Penny finished their teachers' training at Roehampton and Eastbourne.

While working in London, Mary Liz met a New Zealander, ended up marrying him in Forres, Scotland where she had been staying with our mother, and then moved on to Auckland, New Zealand with her new young family.

A second most important factor in our keeping close strong ties with one another was that, when our father lay in intensive care in Bury St Edmunds following a fourth heart attack, he told Richard: 'You are the man of the family now. Look after your sisters.' Though Rick is eighteen months my junior, he has carried that mantle since Dad's death, and fulfilled that mission to the letter, in his warm-hearted way. Needless to say, he is adored by his four sisters. No matter which continent we land on or how far apart we live, there has remained a fierce love between us. The common difficulties we had weathered together during our upbringing had also served to strengthen those bonds.

After three excellent years working in the music publishing world, I was asked to take up an appointment with a Harley Street dental surgeon as his private secretary. He was writing a book on stress in dentistry, and had some fascinating stories to tell about not only how he learned to deal with stress, but how, as a dentist, he was able to pass on his wisdom and experience to patients. These were drawn from some of England's aristocratic and government circles. In a unique way, some of his convictions quietly influenced many people. After all, in the dentist's chair one is normally rendered silent, so the dentist is free to do the talking.

A year on, Leone needed a secretary in the restaurant, so I worked for her and for her brother-in-law, a Canadian who was the new Arts Centre's director. He also designed all the lighting for the many theatrical productions, and managed the auditions for each one. The variety of my work, both in catering and in the theatre was something I could never have imagined I would end up enjoying so much. During those four years I lived across the road in Buckingham Gate where Leone had taken a flat to be near the restaurant. We worked a thirteen/fourteen hour day, until the current show ended and the restaurant doors closed on the last person leaving the reception after each performance. Our social life was practically nil, since once a month we also did Sunday lunches voluntarily after meetings held in the theatre.

The restaurant served a Businessmen's Special at lunchtime on weekdays which drew in people from several large companies nearby, and we became well acquainted with most of our customers. The days I was working in the restaurant, I talked with many as I showed them to their seats and handed them the menu. Towards the end of four years, I had built up a clientele of favourite customers. Some became friends, and one friendship blossomed into rather more, though as staff we were required to act with discretion. There was little chance to develop such a relationship, and I had to sneak out in the afternoons for a clandestine tea at Fortnum & Mason's or a chat.

Although Leone had remained unmarried, she always knew of my flights of fancy and was on hand to listen to my frustrations and give wise counsel. She saw the wood whenever I got lost in a forest of feelings. She kept my feet on the ground, and prevented me from marrying the man-of-the-moment.

Shortly after this, I received a proposal of marriage from a young man whom I had only known slightly in the past. He told me that while he had been in India doing work for Initiatives of Change, he had become very ill. During his illness, he had thought about me, and immediately began to regain his health. On his return to Britain, he sought me out, and told me he was sure I was the one for him, and that his recovery in India had given him the sound conviction that we should get married.

Though secretly touched by his words and belief in me, I was dumb-struck. He lived out of town, but after six weeks of many letters, we took a wintry walk round St James's Park in London one day, to talk seriously about the future. I had been swept off my feet by Robert's insistence in the rightness of our match, and was confused as to how to proceed, as I had so little time to make up my mind about him. In this instance, Leone was no help, and left me to work things out for myself.

There was a play running at the Westminster Theatre at the time called *Decision at Midnight* by Peter Howard. As I sat through a performance one night, a sentence delivered on-stage leapt out at me: 'When in doubt, don't!' Daylight dawned. I had my answer. My own doubts about the young man were all too evident. I was about to face the hardest thing I had ever done in my life. Over lunch in a nearby Italian restaurant, I had to tell this serious young suitor that I had doubts and could not agree to marry him.

I realised this was not just saying goodbye to a good man, but probably waving farewell to my last chance of ever getting to the altar. I felt by then that my personal position in life was becoming untenable. My brother

Richard had married his lovely English Helen in Johannesburg, and was farming in the Great Karroo; Mary Liz, after a shaky beginning, had wed her Kiwi Eric in Scotland, under Mum's care, and they had made their home in Auckland, with their little son; Sue had settled in Toronto, soon after her lovely winter wedding in New Mexico. Now my youngest sister Penny had just asked me to be chief bridesmaid at her wedding to Pete, a fellow student teacher whose parents were from St Helena.

What was wrong with me, the eldest of the bunch, that I had failed to find a life-partner by then? I had become impatient and disillusioned. I wanted more than anything else to be married, to find someone who would love me and reaffirm me as a person who mattered, provide me with roots, security and continuity in my life. But I had to find out who I was, what my true self was like.

This inner turmoil had come to a head with my refusal to marry Robert. I did not want to stay in England a moment longer. I could not even remain long enough to attend Penny's wedding, and left my darling sister in Dad's hands, and the care of the Tyndale Biscoes. John Tyndale-Biscoe was the rector of Gilston church in Essex, and Penny got married to her Pete from their rectory where Dad was living. I was not proud of abandoning her at such a milestone in her life, and some time later wrote a contrite letter apologising for my selfish and heartless decision. She, in reply, was unreservedly forgiving.

I needed to begin a new chapter in life, so decided to take out all my savings to buy a single ticket to New Zealand to see dear Mary Liz, travelling via South Africa to visit Richard and his new bride. I would work my way as I travelled. I was thirty-one when I left my job at the Arts Centre; my home of ten years with the Extons; the now well-tramped pavements and parks of dear old London, and in time-honoured fashion, set off to seek my fortune.

Quite unbeknown to me, fate was already busy, in the

invisible hand of the Master Weaver. I could see only the rough underside of my life then, and still had so much to learn before I could appreciate the beautiful design being woven in the warp and woof of my destiny....

14

We Meet Again

'Keep your heart open, no matter how painful it is...love will win.' This I did...though there were times when it was so painful I felt my heart was breaking.
Flight into Freedom and Beyond – *Eileen Caddy*

TOWARDS the close of those London years, there had been a breakthrough in the relationship with my mother. By 1969, thirteen years of estrangement had passed between us.

However, at the start of that year in which Nixon was inaugurated as 37th president of the U.S., my brother Richard returned from South Africa en route for our sister Suzanne's wedding to Allan Stormont in New Mexico. While in England he decided to visit our mother in Scotland. Aged twenty-six by then, he had not seen her for almost fourteen years.

On his return, he had reported that Findhorn was 'full of goblins with hob-nailed boots'. Curiosity to see the place for myself, to meet our three half-brothers for the first time, and primarily the longing to renew the long-lost relationship with Mum, had begun to drag at my heartstrings until finally these incentives translated themselves into firm resolve.

Together with a Scottish friend with whom I worked in London, we decided to hire a Mini in her hometown of Aberdeen and tour Scotland. Our route would take us up the east coast to Dornoch, across the Highlands to the west and south to Loch Torridon and the Macgregor stronghold, on southwards to the Kyle of Lochalsh and across to the Isle of Skye to visit the hills of the 'far Cuillins', (about which we had sung in school). Then we would make it back towards our final destinations — Dorien's to end up in Aberdeen to return the Mini and stay with her family there; mine to the Findhorn community, where she would drop me so I could meet up with my mother once more.

Scotland was virgin territory for me, though my five times great grandparents and their nineteen children had lived in Edinburgh, where George Combe owned a brewery below the walls of Edinburgh Castle. I fell in love with the country at once. Even when the rain drove against the windscreen of the little car, or the 'scotch mist' befogged our way on the single roads where we stopped a hundred times at 'passing places only' whenever another car appeared from the opposite direction, we still revelled in the spectacular scenery of towering mountains, often reflected in dark stretches of water below them. When we finally reached the picturesque little bay of Plockton, we turned back northeast to stay a night in Drumnadrochit on Loch Ness (no sign of the monster!) and then drove on towards the Moray Firth. As we drew nearer to Forres, beyond which lay the small fishing village of Findhorn, my stomach began to churn in anticipation of all the hurdles which lay ahead.

We came upon the community, situated between Forres and Findhorn. It nestled within sight of the mouth of the River Findhorn, alongside Findhorn village, sheltered from the North Sea by high sand-dunes rising between habitation and the pebbly coastline. What I found appeared to be an ever-expanding collection of caravans, trailer homes and put-together bungalows which had mushroomed next door to the village.

As my friend drove off back to Aberdeen, my heart beat wildly as I turned to face this new phase in my life. How would my mother and I respond to each other?

Mum had written to me on my twenty-second birthday: 'You (her children) are indeed strangers, and yet I know that when we do eventually meet we shall carry on where we broke off, only older and wiser.' At the time, I had appeared coolly polite in my letter of thanks for hers, and for the first gift I had received from her since our last parting. She had written and published her autobiography in 1968, so the work she had been doing was public knowledge. I read with interest her reactions to myself in her book:

'*The child with the deepest resentment and the one I had most difficulty in reaching when sending out love was the eldest, because she was the one who had taken on the responsibility of replacing me to bring up the family... I had a photograph of all five children which I kept on the mantelpiece.*' She had kept looking at each one in turn, '*radiating love out to them,*' she recalled. But of myself, her conviction was that I was '*the one to pour out love to unstintingly,*' that my heart had been closed because I was afraid of being hurt any more. She had also felt I was '*the key to breaking down all the barriers with the children*'. [1]

Those barriers had been partly built up when Caddy chose to make her his partner; then followed the decision by law, for our protection, at the time of our parents' divorce. But I had formed my own barriers by my inability to handle my feelings, thus taking refuge and miniscule comfort from hiding behind a wall of high moral dudgeon. I had hearkened to the judgements of my father and others during those years, and wrongly adopted them as my own. This had coloured my whole attitude towards my mother, and created distance between us, fuelling a fear of ever facing her again. I had used the excuse that none of my siblings were free to visit her, so I would not upset them by doing so.

Now, in understanding something of the heartbreak she had suffered, I realised how much she had to forgive for my 'cold love of the years.' I wanted desperately to make up for my lack of communication, to tell her I had never stopped loving her in spite of my behaviour, and to prove to her now my change of heart and attitude.

As Mum had predicted, our reunion this time was as though the bleak years of separation simply disappeared like mist evaporating in the early sunshine of morning. The sunshine grew warmer as the days went on and the intervening years slipped away.

Mum was keen to show me some of the visible results of the community's development. As we processed round the premises, she glowed with pride as she pointed out the lay-out of new bungalows with their flourishing and colourful gardens, and the community centre-cum-dining hall and kitchens. (I use the word 'processed' because it appeared to be a royal walk-about during which she introduced me to everyone we met en route as 'my eldest daughter').

The high point of this tour for her was the Sanctuary, a wooden one-storey building, the equivalent of a chapel for the community. However, the interior was devoid of any religious trappings, except for one lovely woven cloth of rainbow colours on one wall. Blue chairs ringed the room in a neat circle. Mum explained that she came here early every morning with others, to meditate. For those present, she would disclose any message or vision she received, and any of her writings were then printed up in news sheets for the rest of the community. (Later, with the development of the Internet, these messages were posted on the Foundation's website.) She told me she conducted workshops during the relentless Experience Weeks which drew hundreds of paying visitors each summer to Findhorn for training.

By then, some television coverage about the comm.-unity's lifestyle, the books she and others had written, and a few newspaper articles by curious journalists, had brought Eileen Caddy and the Findhorn gardens into the public arena. As a consequence, a growing number of young and old had drifted up to Findhorn to discover its spiritual promises, and many then settled down to live there.

Caddy's dynamism was always evident, and he was often to be seen showing round notable visitors. He would not tolerate any 'drones' to remain in the community. Everyone had to be fully employed in one way or another. He was busy fostering an intense interest among horticultural experts who began to flock to the community to see for themselves the community's experiments with soil, seaweed and sun in the first attempts at organic gardening. Many an expert's eyebrow rose as they witnessed the results flourishing in what had been barren, sandy origins. An enormous amount of hard work, leaf mould from the forests and seaweed from the shore, dug deep by sheer physical energy and encouraged (they claimed) by nature spirits, had combined to manifest the wondrously productive gardens.

In one quiet corner was a sizeable Buddha figure and shrine. I mused on how that fat stone-carved figure could possibly influence people who sat on benches to meditate there. The colourful borders throughout were assiduously tended by an army of resident helpers. The extensive vegetable gardens nearby supplied the community, and were Caddy's pride and joy in which he had been known to produce a 40 lb cabbage!

Fortunately, he was in such demand that he kept his distance from me. On one extraordinary occasion though, he strode into their bungalow sitting-room where I was, and asked Mum's whereabouts, which I did not know. He marched over, kissed me hard on the mouth and strode out again, leaving me aghast.

I saw little of my three 'new' teenage brothers, Christopher, Jonathan and David, though what I saw I liked. They each spoke with a Scots accent and were all at Forres Academy during the day, or otherwise highly motivated in their participation in community activities and outdoor pursuits. They all passed on from school to universities. Christopher would develop his skills in medicine and eventually become a highly skilled plastic surgeon. Jonathan 'dropped out' of Uni, but later became a respected teacher in Kinloss School, lived in the community and was intensely interested in its development, particularly environmentally. David took his practical skills across to the States and used them to build beautiful houses for wealthy Californians. He and Jonathan also built a two-storey house for Mum in the centre of the community in later years, which she named Cornerstone.

During those first hours of that first visit, what became clearly evident was my mother's popularity. Each time we met a community resident on our rounds, she was greeted by name with great deference, even reverence, and an affection she obviously had grown to expect as her due. She did not know many of them, but they all knew her, and to each one she seemed to emanate a kind of aura. To her daughter, in the throes of accepting her once more as her mother, this charisma remained invisible.

Mum was eager for news of her first family, and every day we sat out in the sunshine on her patio, filling in the gaps of past years, while we consumed homemade yoghourt, handfuls of peanuts, and lemonade. Our enjoyment of one another's company was like old times. I watched her curiously. She had changed: her merry brown eyes had become 'visionary' eyes, slightly slanted; her voice was pitched higher than I remembered. At times, I found myself sometimes drifting off into a 'dwam' at the hypnotic gentleness of her tone, and she was quick to remark, 'I'm losing you again!' I soon noticed that she would ignore or change a subject which she might have found painful.

On a couple of occasions, I braved the main dining-room to meet members of the community during their 'rabbit-food' meals (as Mum called them) – all vegetarian, largely home-grown, prepared by international teams of 'chefs' — community members who had organised themselves into shifts for lunch or supper.

Mum did not often go to the C.C. (community centre). She cooked for herself, or had a plate carried over for her sometimes from the main kitchen. She loved a good steak or piece of chicken herself, so enjoyed any excuse for an

*The Statue of Liberty
seen when we entered New York harbour in September 1945*

*Our parents with Dr F N D Buchman
when he visited Fort Leavenworth, Kansas*

Our family on Mackinac Island, Lake Michigan

Island House, home of the MRA conference in 1946

*The cabin in which we stayed at
Jim & Ellie Newton's hotel,
Fort Myers Beach, Florida, Christmas 1946*

*Our cook Sarah,
whose home I visited
at Maxwell Fields,
Alabama*

*Return from America
to RAF Hemswell -
Mother, Jenny and
baby Mary Liz
1947/8*

*Our home, Kingstackley, in Cheam, Surrey
after Penny was born, 1951*

*Jenny, Suzanne, Richard and Mary Liz
in the fort that Dad built at Kingstackley*

*Coronation Day of Queen Elizabeth II, June 1953. Iraq RAF School —
five of us with our Coronation trophies*

*Ancient waterwheels by the River Euphrates
helped to irrigate the surrounding agriculture*

How far?

THE BABYLON OF YESTERDAY

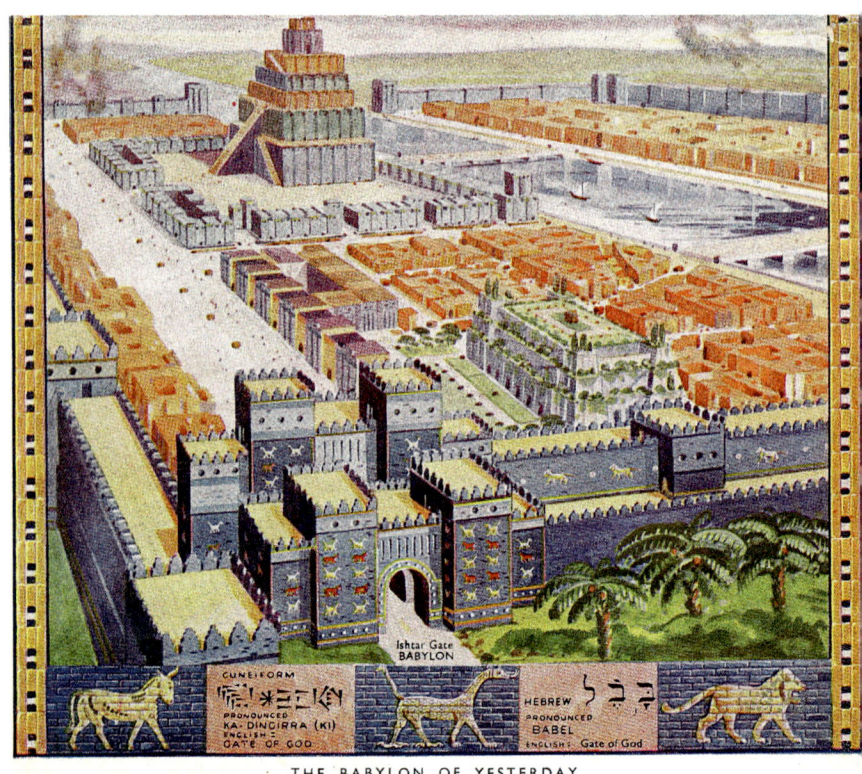

Descending to the excavations

THE BABYLON OF TODAY

What seems to be the remains of the Tower of Babel

A typical Bedouin encampment

After the family dispersed, Dad and Uncle Paddy with Mary Liz, Penny and their Jessop cousins

... and we grew.

occasion to frequent local restaurants in Forres or elsewhere, with her various friends, some of whom were from outside the community.

Workshops took place in the Cluny Hill Hotel in Forres, now community property, or in the C.C. before the Universal Hall was built on community land. These included esoteric subjects (training for eventual initiation, I wondered?), such as Indian dancing, Shamanic, Buddhist and Hindu religious teachings. The practical running of the whole outfit was down to the visitors themselves, organised by the residents into various teams such as home-care, maintenance, gardening, pottery, art and so on.

However, when I looked around at the evidence of the 'alternative' lifestyles of some of the young people: at their scruffiness, hippy clothing and some of the dilapidated caravans they inhabited on the one hand, and at the excellent catering, hard work ethic and high standards talked about by Caddy on the other, the two did not appear to equate. From meeting some of the residents, and the odd remark from my mother, I gathered there was a free-and-easy approach to partner-ships and sexuality in general. 'Tolerance' was a favourite watchword with Mum, though on a personal level, she was to make sure, later on, that two of my sisters, her daughters, got properly wed. All these factors made me more than a little suspicious of what really went on behind the scenes.

I was only dimly aware of the pioneering and inventive spirit behind such developments as the organic gardening. Years ahead, this creative energy would 'manifest' itself (another favourite word of Mum's) in the building of round barrel houses (literally made out of whisky barrel materials), environmentally-friendly homes using hay bales and grassy roofs, and the Living Machine (which recycled all the community's waste water and sewage through growing plants), all of which were not only impressive, but would have far-reaching effects environmentally.

In the meantime, when it came time to leave, the subject of Mum's 'work' had not been broached by either of us. We had simply begun to re-build a long-suspended relationship. My love for my mother had remained intact. However, I was equally clear that in no way would I be drawn into her growing company of adoring disciples. Too many questions remained unanswered.

I did not realise at the time that this first visit would prove a vital step in turning a key for Mary Liz's future, and eventually pave the way for Suzanne and Penny in ending their long separation from Mum.

Meanwhile, I remained in blissful ignorance of the fact that the teachings from the community had begun to fan out globally, and would eventually have an ever-growing subliminal influence on educated thought in society as a whole, in Britain, the U.S., Europe and beyond.

15

A Year of Travel and Revelation

MY adventurous year began in Johannesburg, South Africa, in February 1971. The generous air miles on my one-way ticket to New Zealand allowed me to take in South Africa too. As I landed, I knew already that I had been invited to stay in a home in Westcliffe, one of the many suburbs of Johannesburg, with friends of Leone's, while I worked in Johannesburg.

South Africa was to prove my College of Further Education in Life, Loneliness, and Love. My travels began in the Great Karoo. The endless horizons of that immense country, with its kopjes, sparse vegetation, farming homesteads beside precious, man-made reservoirs were a revelation. The vision for land conservation together with rock-like values and sheer grit and guts of its farming communities, held me in awe.

Richard had built up a new pig-production unit on the farm of a friend, before his marriage. He had designed the sties, shaped and baked the bricks and built them himself, with African help, to house new stock. The success was impressive. My priority was to visit Richard, now married to Helen, an English girl brought up in Aden, Kenya and Zimbabwe.

Richard and Helen had married in Johannesburg the previous year, and were very happy on the farm. Helen proved to be a marvellous seamstress, and I gazed admiringly at her green-and-blue curtains, matching cushions, and the minimal but tasteful furnishings of their new home. Glad as I was to share their happiness and their hospitality, I soon realised that being with them highlighted my own discontent with life. I quickly sensed, also, that my presence set up tension between them. We four sisters all adored our brother, and it appeared that his loyalties between wife and sister were being stretched. Perhaps it was time for me to move on.

The large house in Westcliffe was the home of the Hofmeyr family who welcomed me warmly. I soon learned that these were people who carried the difficulties of that vast and spectacular country close to their hearts. Nelson Mandela was in prison for his radical beliefs in the freedom of his people. Three million white people controlled sixteen million black people in the tight fist of apartheid. Here I learned something of politics, observed the ruthless attitude of the police who often used fear to intimidate their victims, and saw how the lives of indigenous people were counted as cheap.

Change was in the air by then – with television imminent. How would this affect the ordinary people in the townships who lived a simple lifestyle, often in poverty? I learned of tribal warfare; watched the fascinating Mine Dancing displays given by the traditionally dressed miners from their various tribes; I also watched the way the two house servants were treated in my lodgings – with courtesy and respect – and was humbled to learn that one, Joseph, was a prince in his tribe.

I was also learning some salutary facts about myself. For the first time ever I was alone, away from any family responsibilities, and with only a career and uncertain future to consider. I had to get down to work to pay my way as a house guest, and cover daily expenses.

Manpower International sent me first to a small, bleak office above a gold mine, with piles of dun-coloured earth rising behind it, and a layer of dust covering every surface in the offices, piles of papers and typewriters. The only redeeming feature was the cheerful tea-boy, Robert, who plied me with cups of tea every half hour. Robert's rubber plant flourished in the hallway on tea dregs, and threatened to grow through the roof.

Between jobs, I visited Richard and Helen, who planned to take me down to explore the Cape, its wonderful beaches, forests and valleys. We travelled in their van, and I would camp in a lean-to tent on the side. We admired the beautiful Dutch architecture of Stellenbosch with its extensive vineyards. We travelled from Strand in False Bay, along the coast to George where we visited friends we had known in our childhood. Unfortunately, all along the Garden Route, an early rainfall and mists obscured the beauties my family hoped I might enjoy. But the weather conditions resulted in one amazingly spectacular rainbow mirrored five times in a valley. The gloomy weather, combined with the radiance of Richard and Helen's happiness, however, accentuated my sense of solitude, and plunged me into depression. On our return to Zoetvlei, I took the long train journey back to Johannesburg to seek further employment from Manpower.

My second position was with a Greek trading company in down-town Jo'burg, in a large warehouse, where I worked for the managing director next door to his office/board room. This experience was an education in itself, and my introduction to the volatile Greek character. Whenever there was a meeting of the directors, the warehouse would reverberate with furious, raging arguments and send fears of bloody murder through my head while my fingers trembled on the keys. A few minutes later, the apparent opponents would emerge with arms round each other, laughing and joking as though nothing unusual had occurred.

One of the directors took a shine to me, invited me home to meet his wife and have a meal. He took me to my first horseracing event since Iraq days and lost a horrifying amount of money in bets. When he bought me an expensive brooch, I began to feel uncomfortable. Sometime after I left the company to go to Cape Town, he made a point of pursuing me, and I found myself having to shake him off.

When I had first arrived at Westcliffe, a frequent visitor there was a young Dutchman, a friend of the family. He began to think I was a good catch, and sent me a couple of bouquets. I was unprepared for such attention, and it was a challenge to have to tell him that I was not interested.

Meanwhile, among the many Greeks in the trading company, there was a Greek Cypriot who rejoiced in the name of Lucky, and whom I found both good-looking and attractive. He told me he had been living with a woman for ten years while she had been sorting out the legalities of her previous divorce. Recently, they had married at last – and along I came to spoil the party. The feelings between us were mutual. Warning bells rang in my mind, triggered off by his question that I was a Christian, wasn't I?

I knew I was not acting as one. Was this a drawback to our relationship? Or was he of some other religion? I did not stop to ask. I needed to rethink the situation I was in. I knew what I was involved in was wrong, and finally wrote him a letter to tell him that I would not stand between him and his wife, and that the relationship must end. Then I left the company.

Before working in the Cape, I took a break, and returned to the Karoo at the invitation of some good farming friends of my brother, who lived fairly close to them. This family had worked hard to instil the concept of conservation throughout the farming community in that area, where heavy rains and winds did much damage to pasture through erosion for sheep farmers. Their farm nestled among trees by a huge reservoir and was a shining example of the work they had done with both the land and its people over many years. The nearest train station was a long trek from their house, so I was collected in the farm truck by the older of their two sons. During the many miles back to the homestead, our lively conversation ranged over various subjects, and we got along well. He told me his wife was in hospital having just produced their second daughter, prematurely, and mother and child would be away for some time. I was given a warm welcome by the young man's parents, and pitched into farm life.

This began about 5 a.m. with telephone calls between father and his two sons, discussing weather and the plans for the day – just outside my bedroom door. I was taken to the farm school, where the second daughter-in-law was teaching about thirty children of all ages in one classroom. The children looked well and happy. They had just learned a song about a train, which they sang for me. The philosophy on this farm was to care for the family of each farm worker, give them their own homes and plots of land to cultivate, and to educate their children. The work force was consulted each morning about the day's work, and proved both contented and effective. Most had given up drinking alcohol. Drunkenness is one of the most destructive factors, particularly in the Cape among the Cape Coloureds.

One morning early, a note was pushed under my door. It declared the love of the older son and that he was sure it was possible to love both me and his wife. When I had recovered from my surprise, it seemed clear that I must return to Jo'burg – and fast. So I talked with the school teacher, who had been a friend of mine in London, and asked if she or her husband could take me to the station. She drove me there, with all her class in the farm truck, since none of them had set eyes on a train before. As I climbed the steep steps up onto the train (no platform), the children lined themselves alongside the track, and sang their song to the train. The delight and amusement of all the passengers was evident as they dangled out of the windows and waved to them. This was an educational exercise everyone could enjoy.

The new self I was discovering did not impress me. My emotional life was in chaos. I was acting up to this new-found power in myself to attract men, and I liked the effect it had both on them and me. Secretly, I felt ashamed of my feelings, but could not express them to anyone I knew as I felt I would violate their friendship. I could not keep running away from every tricky situation, though. So I resolved, each time I landed myself in one, to return to the only Source I knew, and pray for a way out. After all, I didn't seem able to help myself, so perhaps God could show me what to do. I had neglected my times with Him in the early mornings, and strayed some way from my original faith. At the time, whenever I conversed with my heavenly Father on these sensitive matters, the ground under my knees reverberated with tremors.

The rumblings of explosions in the mines beneath the city of Johannesburg are a feature of life there. The solid veins of gold running deep below the surface seem to solidify in the arteries and hearts beating in the offices of the business world humming above-ground throughout that wealthy land, so rich in both gold and diamonds.

I was often afraid, and felt fragile and powerless. Yet I always arose from my knees with a clear instruction, and had the good sense to obey orders. In two cases, I wrote a letter of apology for standing between husband and wife, and asked for forgiveness. In the third, I was given the words to say on the telephone to the persistent Greek. And the Dutchman stopped visiting Westcliffe.

It began to dawn on me, gradually, that my cries for help were being heard and answered, and that God must love me, or why would He take trouble to give me solutions. Why pick me up by the scruff of the neck whenever I made a wrong choice, and put me back on the right road? For the first time in my life, I truly *felt loved* by Him. I had an actual relationship with Him. I had found my *own* faith. It wasn't a reflection of anyone else's. I began to trust that He must know what was best for my future. This was a revelation! Impatience melted away; I let go of any demand about what *I* felt the future ought to hold; strangely, the major issue of marriage lost its prime importance, and I began to comprehend the meaning of peace.

Another immediate result was a burning compulsion

to write to my father and tell him what I was experiencing. All at once, I was enabled to stand back and look at our relationship and the hellish struggle that had gone on between us. I was free to tell him instead what sort of daughter he really had. I could apologise for my rebellious and divisive ways in the family, and admit that the power-struggle I had set up to win over my siblings' affections was because I had distrusted him and so refused to love him myself. I began to see that I was as much of a miscreant as I had judged him to be, and found I was able to reciprocate, at last, the openness and honesty he had always shown me about himself during those difficult teenage years.

Because of his honesty, I knew he would understand what I was trying to say. Healing and forgiveness crept into our correspondence like a balm. My destructive and judgmental attitudes had been forgiven. I recognised then, from his letters, how truly I was loved by my own father, and how hopeless and despairing of my affection he had often felt. And so, as my time in South Africa drew towards a close, a new love was born in me.

I wanted to say goodbye to Richard, Helen and my God-daughter, baby Patricia, who had moved to Harmony, in the Transvaal, so spent Christmas with them. Harmony was an arid place and a dormitory town for the nearby gold mine and miners. Trees were scarce, so a long tamarisk branch served as our Christmas tree. Richard was friendly with the mine manager, and arranged for me to go on a solo visit down the mine. As we descended by lift, the temperature increased, and I believe (if my memory serves me aright) we went down 7000 feet before we reached the seam of gold being worked by several cheery men, sweating profusely. They seemed glad of a visit, and I watched as they wielded pickaxes at the face and loaded rocks into metal trucks. I would never forget the harsh conditions in which gold is mined in that country. I was given a rock containing gold as a permanent reminder, which I have treasured.

There were still some friends in Cape Town that I wished to visit before departing, so I travelled by train the long journey from Jo'burg down through some spectacular scenery towards the Cape, to that beautiful town below Table Mountain and Devil's Peak. I stayed with the Gladwin family in Claremont, the wife of whom was a sister of the farming friends in the Karoo. They told me that a certain naval officer whom I had known in London, had been to see them recently, and had left ten days before I arrived, on his return from Singapore to England in HMS Forth.

In fact, Peter (Hinton) and I had kept up a friendly, sporadic correspondence since his departure for Singapore. He had learned, early on during his time in Singapore, that my Godfather, with whom I had lost touch, was visiting there, and he had written post-haste to ask for an introduction, so that my Godfather could be invited to a musical play being staged by some young members of Moral Re-Armament. Peter had become involved with arrangements for the cast's accommodation and programme while they were in Singapore.

I had thought his request rather peremptory at the time. My Godfather was a senior officer in the RAF and had been a close friend of my father's during his flying days. (They had broken the Long Distance Flight record together). Begrudgingly, I sent Peter the desired letter anyway, feeling that I was being used as a go-between, especially as I had lost touch with the gentleman in question. Since then, Peter had written several times, and I was somewhat chagrined that we had missed each other in Cape Town by such a short time.

However, the adventures of the Cape were calling: the ascent of Table Mountain (a four-hour climb and an even more challenging two-and-a-half hour descent, with the sea and whole of Cape Town sprawling down below), the elegance of the old Dutch architecture of Stellenbosch, home of South African wineries; the sea trips, and a week with an old South African friend from my days in

Switzerland who was staying in Fish Hoek at the time for a rest. Here I could walk the tranquil beach in the early morning hours, and come back to where Marie had not only provided a good breakfast, but also a patient listening ear as I recounted my spiritual, and not-so-spiritual discoveries and encounters during my months in her country.

While still in the Cape, I began to feel compelled to visit India as my next port of call. My Canadian former boss from London was completing consultancy work there, on the building of a new theatre which had begun while I worked with him in London. The theatre was to be part of an international conference centre called Asia Plateau, in the hills of Maharashtra State, some miles above Poona. The centre had been envisaged and realised by Rajmohan Gandhi, grandson of the Mahatma, who had seen the need to bring Moral Re-Armament to India.

This leg of my journey involved paying only a few extra rand on my air ticket. By the time I returned to Johannesburg, Marie had helped me promise my life to the Almighty, to use as He showed me. I was also clear I should head for Bombay (now Mumbai) and Panchgani. In the process of putting things right with people, I sent an apology to Peter H. for my hoity-toity attitude to his request from Singapore for an introduction to my Godfather, and went on to tell him something of my new decisions and direction.

There was one last commission before I left South Africa. The friend who drove me to Johannesburg airport and saw me off was a young scientist who had been living in Westcliffe, where his mother was based, while I was there. He was also a friend of my brother's and a young man with great potential. I had heard from my brother about drunken orgies with a mutual friend of theirs, and that he seemed to have a problem with drink. We had been out to dinner a couple of times, and had enjoyed a glass of wine or two, or (in his case) three, or four and more... though he had managed to drive me home safely. I was concerned that such a fine brain should be damaged and desecrated by his over-indulgence or even addiction. As I said goodbye to him, I made a verbal promise that I would not touch alcohol again, for his sake. I never heard from him again, but learned later that he had gone to the States, to Harvard University. I was glad for him. It seemed he was still in shape to pursue his high-flying career in science.

I left South Africa with a tight itinerary to accomplish: three weeks to spend in India; just enough time to do a quick hop to look up relations in Perth and Adelaide, Australia, reaching New Zealand the day before my single ticket expired. That is, if all went according to plan.

The flight arrival in Mumbai landed too late to connect with my scheduled flight to Poona. I would be delayed until noon next day, but meanwhile the airline would put me up in a hotel at their expense. As I boarded the shuttle coach, a thin hand reached through the open window. I looked out at a young woman in a sari, baby clutched to her breast, begging. I rummaged in my handbag and passed out my biro and some sweets. I had not had time to acquire any Indian currency by then. This was my first sight of poverty, and introduction to the lively organisation of beggars in that city.

The sounds and smells wafting through the coach window as we drove from airport to hotel were strange, sometimes exotic and sometimes pungent, but all were exciting. The stark contrast between poverty and luxury became evident when we reached the hotel, lavishly furbished and with a large swimming pool overlooking the Indian Ocean.

Fortunately I knew an English couple who were living in Mumbai with their small daughter. With nearly a day to spare, I called them, and they responded at once by turning up complete with swimming gear, to enjoy the pool and keep me company. We went to their apartment for tea, where the small four-year old showed me her

Indian dance routine, solemnly mimicked by her tall father, which had me rolling on the sofa with laughter. That evening, they took me to the Taj Mahal Hotel for dinner. The sultry evening abounded in sumptuous food and surroundings, music and colour such as I had never known existed – a thousand worlds distant from the squalor, the tumbledown beach shanties, and the people lying in the street gutters outside. Out in the streets once more, I was overwhelmed by the seething humanity.

Time came all too quickly to board the flight to Poona. Perhaps this was a military base, for I noticed large boards prohibiting any photographs to be taken. There were two other people at the airport, waiting to go up to Panchgani, so we shared a taxi for the seventy or more miles drive up into the hill country of Maharashtra. This proved a hair-raising roller-coaster as our driver flew up the tortuous roads at breakneck speed, keeping his hand on the horn through every village we passed. Dogs, goats, chickens, children and adults dived out of our way on each side of the unrelenting vehicle. As we wound higher and ever upwards towards the plateau over twisting roads, often without a safety barrier between us and sheer drops over the hillsides, we hardly had time to see the breathtaking vistas at every turn. Our breath was already in short supply, and our toes and hands clutched the floor and seats as we hardly slowed throughout the entire journey.

At last, much shaken and heartily glad to be alive, we cruised through the busy hubbub of Panchgani, home of several schools as well as being a lively market-town. In a great green oasis, amongst palms and bougainvillea just below the plateau, the flat-roofed buildings of Asia Plateau nestled. This was the international centre I had just risked life and limb to visit.

The serenity and graciousness of the spectacular landscape around the centre was mirrored in the grace and warmth with which our Indian hosts greeted us. The calm of the atmosphere and the people living and working there wove a comforting welcome. During the next couple of weeks, I was asked to darn socks for the young men living there, and to serve tables at meal-times, both of which tasks strengthened the homely feeling that I was part of a large family.

Water was precious and scarce, so showers were of the bucket-and-scoop variety, and all the household water recycled outside onto the flourishing gardens. The food consisted mainly of vegetarian curries, simple and delicious. The local mice did not fare so well. I discovered two of them climbing out of a box of Ritz crackers by my bedside one afternoon, and performing a triumphal dance on the sunlit floor in celebration of the banquet they had enjoyed.

The theatre itself was far from finished. Craftsmen from all over the country had assembled there to help. Whole families were at work, carrying loads of bricks on their shoulders to the men up ladders who were building. All were housed in tents and fed with meals cooked at the centre. There were carpenters working on the mud-dust floors of the interior, and wood-carvers chipping out fine traceries of patterns to decorate below the ceilings and the walls.

My former boss was learning to slow down his western idea of normal speed, and drawing on endless reserves of patience he did not know he possessed. Time seemed of no importance in the Indian scheme of things. It was not unusual for an international telephone call to take as long as three days before achieving a connection.

It would be a long time before the building was completed, and I needed to move on to New Delhi where I knew my uncle, with his wife Jill, was serving as the British Naval Attaché.

The trip to Delhi would be by train from Mumbai - a gift of an opportunity to drink in more of this great country. When I reached New Delhi at the end of a long but uneventful journey, I was immediately enchanted by the beautiful white domes and spires architected by Sir

Edwin Lutyens a century earlier.

I stayed within the diplomatic compound with my uncle and aunt, where I could see for myself the remaining influence of the 'British Raj' lifestyle. It was impressive. My uncle had six or more servants, including gardeners, and through them supported about forty or more members of their families.

At dinner, the servants moved noiselessly and served the meal faultlessly, the naval crest on each plate placed carefully at the top of each place-setting. White gloves were worn, and each servant was dressed in a white, starched tunic with a red cummerbund and turban. I recall the grapefruit particularly, as they were crenellated like castle battlements, and the cooking and service were perfection. Next morning, tea was brought to my room by a uniformed Sikh, eyes averted, and laid on a little table at the far end of the bedroom. He reversed out of the door, eyes on the floor.

I particularly remember the conversation at that first dinner, for my uncle suggested that I might go to visit Mother Teresa in Calcutta while I was in India. It had crossed my mind, but my ticket and time were reaching their quota, and I explained the need to continue on to Australia to see my cousins.

Then he surprised me by asking what news I had of Peter Hinton. My uncle had been Captain of HMS Forth in Singapore when Peter was serving there as First Lieutenant. Both my uncle and aunt voiced the hope that Peter and I might 'get to know one another' one day, as we seemed to be 'right' for one another, and had the same 'religious' interests. I explained that the young man in question was back in England by now, and that we had missed in Cape Town, but that I knew no more than that. Their aspirations, voiced as they were in the middle of India, were interesting but pointless since I was destined for the other side of the globe. I gave them no more thought.

I defy any westerner visiting India not to leave it with

a different world-view. For me, life would never be quite the same again. My impressions were of teeming millions, a poverty-lifestyle which needs to be seen to be believed, and an overall placid acceptance of their lot in life; the simplicity and happiness of half-naked children in the street, playing with little pebbles and sticks in the dust; the all-pervading sense of timelessness, where just a stroll through a market-place was enough to realise that trading and lifestyle have remained unchanged by modern civilisation. One small photograph, pinned on the back wall of a stall, boasted the only visible sign of technology anywhere I looked. People dress the same way, carry their water vessels or panniers of vegetables on their heads, spread out a cloth on the ground and squat down to sell their wares or goats, or protesting chickens crammed into tiny crates, exactly as their ancestors have done for thousands of years. Only the dreaming ruins of a temple or a broken bridge over a river might betray the passage of time.

My uncle put his driver, Mohammed, at my disposal. All diplomats were restricted to a twenty-five mile radius of the compound, but he wanted me to see New and Old Delhi, and asked Mohammed to take me in the Bentley to visit the tomb of Mahatma Gandhi, and that of a fellow reformer, the writer and Nobel Prize winning poet, Rabindranath Tagore.

I could not leave Delhi without a visit to Agra to see the Taj Mahal, so Mohammed took me early in the morning to the railway station, helped me buy a ticket and board the crowded train for Agra. Left alone, and the only white face in the carriage, I felt completely at ease with these quiet people. The day-trip included the radiant white marble mausoleum at Agra by the River Yamuna – built in the 17th century by Shah Jahan as a most lavish tribute to his favourite wife - and rightly deemed one of the world's seven wonders; also the Red Fort overlooking the snaking river nearby. After this memorable and enjoyable day out, I found Mohammed at the station to meet me, and he invited me to visit his family in old Delhi on the way back to the compound. I felt greatly honoured, but as dinner was served at eight, I reluctantly declined.

Time came to leave Delhi and fly on to Australia. Before the departure, however, my uncle briefed me that it was customary for a visitor to tip each of the servants. As I descended the wide staircase of the Naval Attaché's rather grand residence, I found the six servants lined up in the hall, and (rather ceremonially, I thought) handed out six envelopes containing my last rupees, one to each, with my thanks for their kindness.

Landing in Perth, Australia, came as a culture shock. My first reaction to Australia was of instant dislike. It was wealthy and brash, and the Australian accent hard and loud by comparison with the gentle Indians. I began to compare the dignity of the Indian ladies in their colourful saris with Australian women. Then I pulled myself together and realised I was making a huge mistake in comparing this country with India.

With this change in attitude, I began to enjoy all that Australia had to offer – the beauty of Perth as a city, and the warmth and friendliness of my new-found cousins there. I visited Rottnest Island to see the wallaby inhabitants; I marvelled at the vastness of the expanses of unpeopled land; was taken to visit a farm where kangaroo and emu ran wild, and saw the tough farming conditions and lifestyle which threw some light on why Women's Lib came to birth in Australia. This was quintessentially a man's world, man-worked, where only the toughest would survive and make a living.

From Perth I flew overland for almost a day to Melbourne, to see friends for twenty-four hours, and then took another plane to fly on to Adelaide to visit more new relations there.

The time in Adelaide was of particular interest. Not only is it a spaciously laid out and well organised city, but the cousins I stayed with there showed me St Peter's

School and the towering Cathedral built of grey stone, both of which had been founded by my great-great-great grandfather, Bishop Augustus Short, Adelaide's first Anglican bishop, in the mid-19th century. The bishop, a dynamo of a man, had worked hard at fund-raising, encouraging bold aims. In fact, a Special Correspondent, who had known Bishop Short in Adelaide and who journeyed to be at his funeral in Warblington, Hampshire, had written of him: '...his works and his fame live, and as long as the Cathedral stands it will stand to the memory of Bishop Short.' Also at the time of my three times great grandfather's death, a former pupil of his in Oxford, one William Ewart Gladstone, paid him this simple tribute: 'There were giants in the earth in those days.' He must have been a very fine person. I felt awed, proud and rather humbled as I gazed at the buildings he had helped to erect.

So ended my brief Australian odyssey, during which I had succeeded in turning all the different addresses, given me when I left England by my father's sister, Janet Gordon, into the relatives I had hoped to meet. It was time to board yet another aircraft, bound for my final destination - Auckland, New Zealand - to land on the opposite side of the globe, the day before my year-long ticket expired.

I longed to see the smiling face of my sister, Mary Liz, again, her enthusiastic Kiwi husband Eric, and my two-year old nephew, Garvin. It seemed an age – two years in fact - since they had moved from Scotland to this end of the world, and I looked forward to staying with their family while I worked in Auckland.

Little did I dream that the next months in the North Island would change the course of my life.

16

Glorious and Incontrovertible Evidence

... I who looked for only God, found thee!
I find thee: I am safe, and strong, and glad.
Sonnets from the Portuguese - *Elizabeth Barrett Browning*

BEACH HAVEN, Auckland, February 1972. I had arrived at last. It was a strange feeling to have reached the other end of the world. People did not pass through New Zealand – they stayed. After all my travels, I found myself not only the furthest I had ever been from home, but feeling isolated. After the novelty of staying with my Kiwi family had worn off, more than once I asked myself what on earth I was doing there!

My younger sister, Mary Liz, and her pharmacist husband Eric had made their home available for the time I was in New Zealand. They were expecting their second child, and finding their two-year old son, Garvin – a sturdy little boy who loved a good western, even then! – lots of fun and hard work. His father, when he was around, and I would take turns in bathing him each evening – a shared duty which involved riotous enjoyment and splashing as part of the operation, not to mention the mopping up afterwards.

On my return from work each day, I would kick my way through the sitting room floor littered with toys. Unimpressed, I would sometimes verbalise my irritation, or criticize my sister's relaxed attitude to house-keeping. I failed miserably to comprehend the output of energy necessary in caring for an active youngster whilst also producing another. I had a lot to learn.

Meanwhile, Eric was working long hours, starting on the bottom rung of the business ladder. Forty years later, it is a delight to see what a great success this has become, with father and son (Garvin now also a pharmacist) working side by side in their extended premises, as well as taking on the running of another business. Eric's vineyard and winery flourish on the hillsides overlooking Ahipara Bay, outside Kaitaia.

Scenically, the North Island is similar to the rolling, sheep-covered hills and long sandy beaches of rural Dorset. Yet the white man's, or Pakeha, history of this fascinating country stretches back only 250 years or so, before which the Maoris had peopled the tough bush country they called the Land of the Long White Cloud. The more I saw of other countries, the more I appreciated the antiquity of the traditions and long history of my home country, her smallness yet wealth and stability, long monarchy, and her remarkable history.

Manpower International had placed me in an employment agency in Queen Street, Auckland, near the waterfront and busy port. I was secretary to the managing director of this small set-up that interviewed and recruited secretaries, among others, to go out to Fiji and the British Solomon Islands to work on a two-year contract. My boss was a kind man, a Unitarian by faith, and a frequent visitor to the jungles and towns of the South Sea Islands. I enjoyed my time in the office, and made new friends among the few female staff. From our floor, we could watch ships come and go, including – on one occasion - the tall Chilean training ship, a replica of a two-hundred year old sailing vessel, which presented a stirring sight as it departed on the early morning tide with all white sails billowing in the morning sunshine.

One day a lucrative post in the British Solomon Islands was advertised, and Mr Cavit (my boss) encouraged me to take it. I was sorely tempted, but something inside me said firmly this was not the time to sign up for a two-year contract abroad, so I declined.

Fortunately, a couple of good friends, whose children I had helped take care of while in one of the Charles Street homes in London, arrived in New Zealand. They were as keen to hear how I was faring as I was to see them again. I was able to talk over my feelings about being in New Zealand, and my renewed frustrations which had arisen because I was living within a family unit where I felt rather like a cuckoo fledgling. 'You are here marking time,' said my friend Stella, from which I understood that there are periods in life when one has to possess one's soul in patience.

And then it happened. On April 23rd, St George's Day, I was sitting up in bed during my morning time of quiet, and a thought dropped into my mind, as clear as if a voice had uttered the words: *If Peter Hinton ever asks you to marry him, say yes.* The thought continued on with clear instructions as to the sort of wife Peter Hinton would need. Fortunately, I noted this all down in my notebook.

Furthest from my thoughts at that time, was any memory of Peter whom I had last seen two years previously, hurriedly departing from the London scene to a posting in Singapore.

The disturbing thought about marriage persisted. I was amazed and excited at such a promise (should it ever work out). I was being offered the best gift imaginable, one for which I had longed. I took it seriously, and allowed this hope to take root in my heart where it became firm conviction. By then, my faith in a loving Father in heaven, which had grown while in South Africa, convinced me that I could pray about this, and God would answer, one way or another. I told no one, in case He didn't.

One morning, not long afterwards, I awoke from a vivid dream. I had been standing in a rose garden near the drive of a large white house. Peter walked out of some French windows round the corner, and came towards me. I smiled in readiness to greet him, delighted to see him again, but he looked straight through me, turned and walked away across the lawn!

No need to be a dream-interpreter to understand this as a clear sign that Peter was not interested in seeing me again. Sadly, I released him from my prayers. Nevertheless, barely two months later, I received a letter from Peter, by now in Belfast, Northern Ireland, asking me to marry him. It began, 'For three years I have been in love with you and have wanted to ask you to marry me...' but he explained that he had to learn 'many lessons' before being 'given the go-ahead to propose to you.'

This letter put me in a panic! I did not know if I loved the man. Nor did I feel I had the necessary make-up of character to hold a marriage together. What if our marriage didn't work as was the case with my parents?

The weekend the fateful letter arrived, my sister and her husband had visitors staying, and were rather busy. Sleep eluded me that particular Saturday night, and finally at 4 a.m., I crept into the sitting room, turned on the standard lamp and leafed back through the pages of my notebook to find the words I had written two months earlier. There they were: *If Peter Hinton ever asks you to marry him, say yes.*

Amazingly, a job description of the kind of wife Peter would need followed: *He needs a loving wife who will stand by him through thick and thin, who will face the Cross (of Christ) beside him and ask nothing for herself, ever - clothes, sex, standing, security, approval. Only on this basis will marriage with Peter work and become one more joyous part of God's plan in whose hand you will be used.*

I reconsidered such a tall order. Should I take a deep breath and make the gigantic leap forward, trusting that those words were a pointer to my destiny? Or not? Somehow, I knew I must jump. I had only my independence to lose. That prophetic forewarning two months before was all I had to go on, but it empowered me to write back to Peter my acceptance, in the exact words received on St George's Day.

I couldn't even remember what he looked like. I had no photograph, no love-letters, nothing except a few letters written from one friend to another since we had first met in 1969. But I trusted the thought must be God-given. I posted that letter with my heart in my mouth.

Glorious & Incontrovertible Evidence

Ten apprehensive days dragged by until I received an excited telephone call with an extremely English voice on the other end shouting, 'Tell the world we are engaged!' Peter was calling from Ireland as though he was using a couple of tins tied together with string, like the telephones we once made as children at Kingstackley, shouting from the top to bottom floors.

It was July 22nd. That same day, my sister was in hospital producing her second son Clive, baby brother to Garvin. I was staying with an old friend nearby as my brother-in-law felt well able to look after himself and Garvin, now two-and-a-half, in Liz's absence.

In Peter's first letter, words tumbled over themselves in his excitement of our proposed union, and the joy at the way our engagement had come about. Apparently, St George's Day was the same date as he had arrived in his new posting in Belfast. '...We will use that story all our lives – it is the most glorious and incontrovertible evidence of God's love and the way He guides. One feels a tremendous sense of awe.'

Our courtship continued over the following two to three months in the form of thirty-five lengthy letters flying back and forth round half the world, giving us ample time to get to know one another better - our likes and dislikes, hobbies (Peter's were fishing, walking and reading), or events in which we were individually involved. I was to discover, for instance, that Peter aspired to poetry when I received the following:

> *How can I tell you all that's in my heart?*
> *I think I must have loved you from the start;*
> *I must have known down all the years*
> *That you would come along to quiet my fears,*
> *And bring me peace and joy and rest*
> *And help me live my very best.*
>
> *I love you so, yet know not how to tell –*

Perhaps it's like a prisoner, from his cell
Released to see the sun and feel the rain,
And know the joy of freedom once again.
Perhaps it's like a ship that's been at sea
And after stormy passage finds a lee;
Or else perhaps a man upon a road
At last discovers how to shed his load.

I know of no trite phrase or honeyed word
That can express my gratitude to God
For all He's given me and you,
To be His chosen instruments we two.
I cannot help but sing and shout His praise
That we His sheep may ever safely graze:
My deepest love I know is safe with you,
And, dearest, you can safely love me too.

During those months, I worked hard to earn enough for the return to Britain. Mary Liz had generously thrown a large engagement shower party of friends, neighbours and the girls from my office. I became the proud owner of many gifts, including a sheepskin rug, some Maori pictures, an electric frying-pan, a hand egg-whisk, a pottery vase given me by Arerina Harowira, a dear Maori friend, and twenty New Zealand tea towels. These were my 'bottom drawer' as a future bride.

Having waited three years already, Peter naturally wanted to get married as soon as possible. I had not earned quite enough, so he sent out some money to make up the difference in my air fare. Three months after his proposal, I was ready to fly back. I had bought a second-hand trunk to send my engagement gifts and most of my clothes back to England by sea as I realised my luggage would be excessively overweight for the return flights. The long journey home, via the States, Canada, Scotland, and finally to Belfast, would complete my first circum-navigation of the globe.

Before leaving Auckland, I had been advised by the

travel agent that a visa to enter America and Canada en route was not necessary. As I reached the head of the queue at the immigration desk at the airport, I was faced with a different story. Panic! The flight was shortly due to take off. To return to the city for a visa would mean missing my flight. My cool-headed brother-in-law, seeing me off and also in the queue, thumbed through my passport while I had palpitations. Lo and behold! Stamped in my passport was a two-year visa, obtained when I had attended my sister Sue's wedding in New Mexico two year's earlier. It still had two days to run – just enough time to get me into the States. A miracle!

So I took off, via Honolulu, duly received a certificate for crossing the International Dateline, and visited friends in Kentucky and Missouri; up to Canada to see my sister Suzanne, now living and working in Toronto; then on to see my mother in Scotland, whom Peter had already visited – 'I *love* your mother. We get on so well,' he had enthused over the phone - and finally across to Belfast to meet my new fiancé.

As the plane circled to land, I saw army Saracens (armoured cars) moving round the airfield and environs, and was reminded that I was entering territory occupied by the British army since the 'troubles' following the uprising of a civil rights movement in 1969.

'How will I greet this virtual stranger?' I asked myself as we landed, my stomach churning. I had not set eyes on him for two years. There he was, tall, lean and handsome, just like the photo he'd sent out to New Zealand (arms crossed and wearing tropical white uniform and cap on board HMS Forth). We kissed and hugged politely. He settled me and my luggage in his car, matter-of-factly, and we drove off. At the top of a hill over-looking smoky Belfast at 8 a.m. on a grey morning, Peter stopped the car. 'I've got something for you', he said, and handed me a little box. It revealed a beautiful engagement ring - four sapphires surrounded by tiny diamonds - which he had kept securely in his safe since visiting Bangkok in HMS

Forth eighteen months earlier. At a reception on board, a jeweller and his wife had been invited, and Peter met them. Next morning, he had gone to their shop to buy a ring, with me in mind. The jeweller asked the size of my finger, and Peter had no idea. 'Well, how tall is the lady?' he asked. Peter measured an approximate height with his hand, and they settled on a size.

As he slipped on the ring that morning, it fitted perfectly. This must be a good omen for the future! I had never possessed such a lovely thing in my life. We drove on to Ardreigh House in Holywood, outside Belfast, where Peter was sharing a bachelor flat with a young businessman. I was to stay in the main house with the owners who were friends of theirs. As we entered the driveway, I recognised immediately the white house, the rose-garden and the lawns exactly as I had pictured them in my dream! Even the French windows were in the same position. I was dumbfounded, and told Peter about my dream. He was surprised, but made no comment.

That night I slept off jet-lag so soundly that I awoke late next morning and rushed up to the flat above, full of shame as I had promised to prepare breakfast for him, his flat-mate and myself. I found Peter calmly setting the table, and offered to finish the job, taking the plates from his hand. He then proceeded to correct the positioning of each plate! 'There's a pattern on the plate. We may as well have the flower facing the right way up!' he pointed out. I realised then that I was marrying into the Navy. 'What a great start to our life together!' I thought, guiltily. Not only had I been late, but I couldn't even set a table properly! What would he think?

A couple of days later, Peter gained permission to cross the Irish border to visit his cousin in Dublin, as well as my beloved great aunt Florence (Auntie in Ireland), to tell them about our engagement. While in Dublin, we went out for a meal on our own, and found ourselves talking about the kind of people we were and the skeletons each of us had in our cupboards. I was thirty-two and Peter thirty-nine, and with seventy-one combined years behind us, we had a lot to talk about and lay out honestly before one another. This lengthy exercise had its painful moments, and neither of us ate much that evening. Both of us believed honesty to be the best policy before we began life together. This process helped us realise that our individual experiences had prepared each of us in a complementary way for full acceptance of the other.

During the evening, Peter offered an explanation for my vivid dream. It transpired that he had met a lovely lady quite recently. She was divorced, with two sons, and he had been so strongly attracted to her that he wanted to marry her. Fortunately, he had the good sense to tell a close friend living in the same house that he wished to propose to this young woman, but his wise friend put him back on the straight and narrow quite firmly, since Peter had told him already that he thought I was the one for him. We worked out together that my strange dream had occurred just at the time he was thinking of taking off with someone else!

Both of us had matured through the lessons learned during those three years of waiting. Honesty proved an ongoing habit after we were married, and one we have adhered to ever since. On several occasions, a particular place or event would often trigger off a memory of an old girl- or boy-friend that had not yet come to light during that first long exchange about our pasts.

We had allowed only five weeks before the wedding ceremony, to fit in with Peter's leave from Northern Ireland. During this time, Peter was to meet some of my siblings and their families, and I his parents, then living in Dorset. At the same time, we needed to sort out all the arrangements for the wedding. He had only one week's leave to get married. Fortunately, he and my father had already done some groundwork together in London for this event, before I arrived back. The Vicar of St Saviour's church in Basil Street, from which I had been confirmed with Leone and her mother, Queen, had written to me in New Zealand when our engagement was announced, and suggested we might have the wedding in his church. This being agreed, Dad and Peter had organised the reception afterwards to be held in the Basil Street Hotel nearby, just behind Harrods, in early December — a rather prestigious place for the wedding, particularly as my father had just been made redundant! The whole thing seemed crazy, but by the time I got home, it was already a fait accompli.

At the first count, Peter had over 400 guests on his wedding list, and mine was about the same, with some duplicated names. We had to be ruthless in deciding who to invite! Only sometime afterwards did I learn that my Aunt Janet, lovingly known as AJ, offered to foot the bill for my father, bless her, and that thanks to her generosity we had been able to proceed as planned. Even so, many valued friends who should have been there remained uninvited because of limited numbers.

This was the only family wedding at which my mother and her husband Peter Caddy, and my three half-brothers were present. The boys and their father wore kilts, and were ushers at the church. It was a great joy to have my mother there, and it was altogether a very happy occasion, in spite of the short time it had taken to arrange. The lovely hand-sewn bridal gown, lent to me by a friend, was a perfect fit, and all the beautiful flowers and bouquets were arranged lovingly by several friends, who could not even be at the reception because of the restriction on numbers.

After our wedding, we were to rent the flat below Peter's bachelor pad, in Holywood, just outside Belfast. This had been the original ballroom of Ardreigh House, now converted into two large bedrooms, a bathroom, small kitchen and spacious living room with a dining room alongside, down several steps. It all seemed very grand, with high ceilings and a view of the lovely garden with its green bank and croquet lawn below the sitting room and kitchen windows. We could just see the waters of Belfast Lough from there.

Amid the confusion and escalating hatred begun by civil rights campaigners and the Irish Republican Army in 1969, we set up home at Christmas-time, 1972. Holywood was a peaceful place to live, but the boom of bombs exploding in Belfast city carried down Belfast Lough as a constant reminder of the growing tensions and killings. Peter had to keep a low profile (he never wore uniform outside the Royal Naval Aircraft Yard, Sydenham, where HMS Maidstone housed the staff of the Royal Navy), and we learned to be extra cautious about where we went and when.

We both made a habit of asking daily for God's wisdom. This taught us to trust and obey hunches. Obedience or disobedience, when living in a war zone, can determine one's life or death. For instance, on one occasion we were expecting a visitor from England to come and stay, and she needed to be collected from the airport. There were two routes to reach it, the most direct and time-saving being through the middle of Belfast. Peter's thought, however, was to go the long way round. At the very time he would have been driving the shorter route, there was a massive explosion in the town centre, and Woolworths disappeared in a pile of rubble. As it was Sunday, no one was killed. Peter arrived home safely with our guest.

This was to be the home in which I was to wrestle with forgiveness for the man I most loathed - my mother's husband. In 1974 our son Andrew was born, in Dundonald, three months before we left for Portsmouth on our way to Peter's next posting in Portugal.

The Portuguese 'Revolution of 25th April' in 1974 had ended many years of dictatorship. Peter was to be appointed from one hot spot to another, at the start of its new government, and Andrew and I were able to accompany him. We were advised to take few belongings as the government was unstable and in case a state of emergency might send us hot-foot back to Britain.

We lived there two-and-a-half years, first in an apartment in Cascais overlooking the Cidadella (originally the monarch's summer palace but now an army barracks), and then in a house out in the country in Murtal where three large white Mountain Pyrenean dogs were kept to guard the house. During that short time, there were no less than six provisional governments and at least one other revolution. We saw the country turn its back on communism; we watched the long, patient queues of people waiting to cast their vote in the first democratic elections; and we made many friends in that amiable country which had been England's faithful ally for over 500 years.

Φ

The following years with the Royal Navy — in Portugal, then back again in Portsmouth where our daughter was born four years later, and finally to the Rock of Gibraltar where Peter qualified as a Spanish interpreter just before the Falklands War began - were as varied, interesting and sometimes hazardous as anyone could have wished. His retirement from the Navy at the end of his Gibraltar posting opened the way for a second career, as bursar at an international school in the south of Spain, where he worked, our two children were educated, and we lived for the next eleven years.

It was there in Spain that the many questions from my past began to clarify. Before our wedding, I had been invited to stay in a gracious home in London by the couple who had visited New Zealand while I was there. One day during that busy time, Stella promised that in our marriage, God was giving us a 'good, good thing.' I was to recall those words often. On our kitchen windowsill stands a Portuguese tile which says: 'Contigo serei feliz' (with you I will be happy). It has accompanied us on our travels, been dropped and broken countless times, and glued together again. It is a daily visual reminder of our partnership which, with all its downs and ups, growing pains and difficulties, has remained glued - not because of our fragile abilities to make it so, I hasten to say, but rather because we have sought wisdom from the Source from whence we believe our union was given.

By laying each of our trials before God, sure in the knowledge that since He brought us together in the first place, He *must* therefore have the solution to each problem arising, we have proved countless times that this formula *works*!

17

The Dynamic of Forgiveness

If one does not forgive, one does not understand; and if one does not understand, one is afraid; and if one is afraid, one hates; and if one hates, one cannot love. And no new beginning on earth is possible without love... The first step then must be forgiveness.
Laurens van der Post in A Far Off Place

OUR two-year service posting in Belfast was to prove a turning point in my life. We were exposed daily to the evidence of hatred and violence between two so-called religious factions. We were living in imminent danger daily, and Peter had to keep a low profile as a naval officer – no uniform until he was aboard his ship, HMS Maidstone. At home, our only protection from any unwelcome intruder was a couple of assegais (spears) in the front hall.

That amazing modern-day saint, Corrie ten Boom, wrote of her fellow victims of Nazi brutality in the last war:

Those who were able to forgive their former enemies were able to return to the outside world and rebuild their lives, no matter what the physical scars. Those who nursed their bitterness remained invalids. It was as simple and as horrible as that. Forgiveness, says Corrie, is the key which unlocks the door of resentment, and the handcuffs of hatred.[1]

In the light of her words, I was one of those 'invalids' – justifiably so, in my opinion. Caddy had taken away from us the person who loved us most, and whom we loved most in the world. I knew I was also 'handcuffed' by my hatred of him for the suffering and damage he had caused each one of us children.

Humanity was once addressed by Jesus, who asked us to weigh all such violent passions in the scales of

Justice, Mercy and Patience. In place of the angry cry 'Revenge!' and fires which can flare into pre-meditated murder, that amazing figure of history some 2,000 years ago bade us plead: 'Our Father in heaven...Forgive us our sins as we forgive those who sin against us.' He asks this of us, knowing what proud people we are. We are convinced we have a perfect human right to harbour a valid grievance, and in our pride, fear or faithlessness shy away from any attempt to understand why we must forgive.

So we forfeit our own spiritual freedom. This can inflict heavy blows on body, mind and tortured spirit because we ignore Conscience (if we still have one). In other words, we consign ourselves to a living death in order to preserve ugliness, bitterness and pride. But is pride really worth it?

Living in Northern Ireland taught me an important lesson on forgiveness. My parents' families had roots in the country, from the time my great great grandfather James Combe and his partner made machinery for the linen industry in Belfast back in the mid-nineteenth century. I had cousins living in the city. Another great great grandfather, Robert George Nicholson, who had built a fine house in Donaghcloney, outside the city, had died in a fire rescuing some of his employees. My mother's family, on the other hand, was from the south, outside Dublin, from Maryborough (now Port Laois). My family bridged the divide between north and south.

At the time we lived there, the killings, tarring and feathering, the tangible fear, the hounding by one so-called religious faction of another, the bombs causing mindless destruction of shops and businesses in the city centres, took place daily all round us. The dominant Protestant marches on July 12th incited hatred from year to year in Catholic hearts. The hatred and fear that had created the Irish Republican Army had poisoned the minds of the next generation, just as hearts and minds had carried similar feelings against Britain down through history. The British army was now in occupation to control the 'troubles', and the Royal Navy patrolled surrounding waters to maintain safe passage for trade to Belfast and Londonderry, and to prevent the landing of IRA arms and explosives.

There grew in me a longing to help others find reconciliation, to bring about peace. I met one woman whose son had been shot in the neck by a sniper climbing over the back wall of his house while he was doing a jigsaw in the kitchen with his son. Incredibly, her tears were of sorrow, not bitterness. I met another feisty lady who had worked in the linen mills set up by my forebear. She described how the linen weavers stood in water all day long to keep the humidity and temperature right for the flax they wove, and how many of them contracted TB and died from their working conditions. She and others with her had initiated a women's Peace Movement. We heard stories of the quiet work being done by the Clonard Monastery in schools to re-educate the historical hatred between Protestant over-lords and Catholic working class. My own aspirations and efforts to help others remained utterly ineffectual in the face of these facts. As one Irishman told a friend of ours, 'In Ireland, feelings are the facts!'

Early on in our two years in Holywood (a small town on the shores of Belfast Lough), my mother was keen to come to visit us. She wanted to bring Caddy, and I did not want him to come. I would not tolerate 'that man' in my house. He remained an utterly reprehensible bounder in my book, who had stolen our mother and robbed my younger sisters of a mother's nurture.

My love for my mother prevailed, however, and I felt obliged, most reluctantly, to accept the package deal so I could be with her again. During their visit, we were to learn a little more about their 'work', though they were reticent in saying anything about it to us. On a trip we made to Lough Erne, we discovered that the island in the middle of the loch had a ruined tower, and while we stood inside it with the guide relating its history, Caddy called it a 'centre of power'. (At the time, we had no idea what he meant.) On several occasions, they went off to visit friends who had been to Findhorn, and we realised that we were a convenient base from which they could further their influence in the Belfast area.

While they were still with us, the full force of the hatred I felt for Peter Caddy hit me, and drove me to my knees one night to wrestle it out with God. I remembered how I longed to help, in a small way, to begin to reconcile the Catholics and Protestants in Northern Ireland. But was I willing to give up the feelings I had harboured for so long towards my mother's husband? If I was going to understand the cost of true reconciliation, and make it real, then surely...?

There and then, I saw the ugly, cancerous growth in my heart for what it was, and decided to surrender it, roots and all, once and for always. I asked God to forgive me for all the years of bitter loathing I had carried for 'that man'. Only at Jesus' crucified feet was I ready to lay down that burden, because He had died to forgive just such hatred.

Next morning, a clear but terrifying thought came into my mind: 'Tell P.C. how much you've hated him for what he did to us, and say sorry.' Unfortunately, I told my husband Peter about this, and once it was out of my mouth, felt compelled to do something about it.

Somewhat to my relief, the chance to talk to Caddy alone never occurred. On the last morning of their visit, however, my Peter suggested tactfully to his mother-in-law, after breakfast, that they might take a last stroll in the beautiful gardens of the house. He knew full well this would be my last chance to carry out my intention.

Left alone facing Caddy, who was relaxing in an armchair opposite, there was now no way of escape. Shaking all over, I managed to stutter out my over-rehearsed words, 'I just want you to know that I have hated you all these years for what you did to my family, and that I am sorry. I was wrong to feel as I did.' At last, I had said it! During the following silence, I felt as though my apology lay in a heap of rushed and jumbled words at his feet. I glanced up to see what impression they had made, and found P.C. staring at me in open-mouthed disbelief. Then he said, 'But I've never done anything wrong in my life. It has all been part of God's plan!'

I was astounded. This lie took me completely unawares and shook me to the core of my being. It was my turn to stare at him in total unbelief. Had he no concept whatsoever of the price we had paid for his actions? Had he no sense of shame, no conscience? What supreme arrogance!

I was remotely aware that he went on to qualify his reasons by some mention of Jesus Christ, and of the 'rightness' of all his own past actions in the light of Jesus' life.

It was a relief when my mother and Peter arrived back from their stroll. Somehow we said 'Goodbye' and waved the Caddys off down the drive. My mother had no inkling of what had just taken place, I am sure. I learned from her recently that Peter never even mentioned our conversation to her. When I told her about it, and what he had said, her comment was: 'Typical Peter!'

Meanwhile, I was left feeling like a piece of seaweed washed up against rocks in a storm — ragged and battered for the rest of that day. I was hurt by Caddy's reaction, deeply hurt, but also puzzled by it. I felt let down and disappointed that no sign of an apology from him had been forthcoming, and wondered why I had bothered to work myself up to such a pitch. My words had made no difference to him anyway.

That night, I discovered that something had begun to happen, deep down in my own heart and spirit — some mysterious release. I found myself praying for the man! I began to see him as a lost soul. (I had never prayed for him before.) A new corridor of understanding and communication had opened up inside me. I heard myself actually asking God to help Peter Caddy — a man who (in my view) had chosen wrong paths throughout his life, who had grasped greedily at every kind of spiritual power, and who I had always believed to be bound for eternal perdition and damnation. These were the first stirrings of compassion for him.

The simple chemistry of obedience to one costly thought had not only dissolved my pride, but had allowed the dynamic of forgiveness to go into operation. Miraculously the shackles had been loosed and the handcuffs of hatred had been unlocked. Hatred no longer had any power to bind me as its prisoner. I was free!

Just as had happened with my father, the opportunity to talk about my feelings to the person who had generated them, tell him why I felt as I did, apologise and admit that my hatred was wrong, no matter what he had done wrong, had brought about a change of heart and attitude in me. Obviously, from his response, what I had said to him had made no difference to him at all. An apology had to be given unconditionally, with no strings attached. I had accepted responsibility for my part in the cycle of hate, and thus the path to restitution had become possible.

Towards the end of our two years in Holywood, our son Andrew was born, complete with the red hair and freckles of an Irishman. I invited Mum to come over to see her grandson, and to help me get adjusted to the unknowns of early motherhood. She had produced eight children by then, and would be a calming and knowledgeable person to have with me at such a time. I was more than happy that she decided to come alone, and we had a busy, practical and reassuring time together.

Interestingly, I discovered that the action of being freed from hatred seemed to hold the key to a far wider understanding of the scenario of history through which we were living in that benighted country.

Almost at once, I was asked by a local church group to talk about my experiences as a service wife in Northern Ireland, so was able to share the hard currency of this experience with them. I had occasion to relate the story of my relationship with Caddy on several occasions afterwards, to illustrate the blue-print God had shown me of what He can and wants to do through obedience and forgiveness. It had relevance to the dynamic of reconciliation.

Perhaps this was just a microcosm of what could happen in a country like Northern Ireland where so many thousands of bitter and hurting souls were hungering in spiritual poverty, waiting to learn the meaning of forgiveness in their land. I longed for the reality of the miracle wrought in me to be multiplied.

Many years before, Dr Frank Buchman had observed that 'When man listens, God speaks; when man obeys, God acts...' The final part of this statement packs the punch: 'When men change, nations change.' Men, trained to kill, need something bigger to live for than war. Since leaving Northern Ireland, we have watched the steady but vigorous attempts by government and people, which in recent years have resulted in bringing about the grounds for peaceful settlement among shattered lives.

The lesson in forgiveness I had learned had been made out of choice, in the context of an occupied, warring country. The need to forgive my parents, however, was puzzling and somewhat bewildering. Both, at one time or another, used the words: 'Am I forgiven?' And: 'Can you forgive me?'

Forgiveness of itself was not a concept I much heeded or felt was necessary for my parents - until after I went to live in Northern Ireland and faced Peter Caddy. If ever forgiveness and I had come face to face it would elude me, much like being shown how to solve a mathematical problem - the concept might make sense for a minute, and then slip away into limbo, leaving me alone with the problem and the panic that I would not have the capacity to solve it.

My father's plea for forgiveness came in the last words he wrote me in a letter ten days before he died in

March, 1978. I found his query perplexing, since we had become close friends while I was in South Africa.

I had begun to write to him about the heartaches and stupidities in which I found myself, while feeling quite lonely in that country. I shared not only my shortcomings with my father by letter, knowing him to be a most understanding fellow-sinner - but also my delight about how God put me right in each instance when I asked for His help. I told him that I had learned from these experiences the simple fact that I had stumbled upon a living God who actually loved me as I was, or why would He have bothered to pick me up by the scruff of the neck and put me back on the right road again? With a new personal faith, I had felt able to open up unreservedly to my father.

Then my engagement in New Zealand and marriage in London in 1972 had given him great happiness. I was the last and the eldest of his five offspring now safely and satisfactorily off his hands!

Towards the end of the 1970s, after we had returned from Peter's second posting, in Portugal, Dad began to suffer a series of heart attacks following years of angina. I was expecting our second child at the time, and Peter had returned to Portugal where he was studying to become a Portuguese interpreter for the Royal Navy. I would drive up to Suffolk from Ascot where we were living temporarily, to visit Dad in Bury Hospital and talk. My father, who adored his grandson Andrew (now aged 4 and named after him), was most excited to hear that a new grandchild was on the way.

Alas, he was not destined to meet his granddaughter, as he died four months before she was born. Some days before his death, we had received a long letter from him telling us about his stay with my aunt and uncle, of their great care for him, his improving health, the present political situation and his delight at seeing golden plovers in the fields outside the window. Then, to my amazement, he ended the letter with, 'Much, much love, you beloved old dear. I do indeed love you! Am I forgiven?'

I pondered and puzzled over this question. It had never occurred to me before that I needed to say words of forgiveness to either of my parents by way of assurance and comfort to them. Both had made clear, over the years, that they felt I stood in judgment of them, but I had taken for granted that the whole change in my attitude towards each was sufficient.

Two factors contributed to their misconception of my judgementalism. I was living and working with people who lived by a high moral code of behaviour, and by whom I was strongly influenced. Nearer the truth was that I used these people as a screen behind which I could hide emotions I was neither willing nor ready to face.

With Dad, we had worked through years of difficulties, and reached a place where I was sure he knew that the past was forgiven because of our close relationship. The growing bond between us was proof enough, to my mind, that forgiveness had been at work between us, surely. It must be quite plain to him that in making him my confidante, I trusted him and that my whole attitude towards him had changed?

Sadly, it took years to understand that behind his last three words to me lay a yearning to hear the actual words of forgiveness spoken. These might have gone some way towards healing his grieving for the missing years of love that had leaked out of our father-daughter relationship. We had never spoken about them, and so he had been unable to slough off the finger-pointing at his guilt. Had I hoisted in this fact, I would have flown to the telephone there and then, when I received his letter, and put the matter right by saying the words he wanted to hear. Long before I was ready to understand his need for that simple 'I forgive you,' he had moved on to his Eternal Home...

In Mum's case, I loved her, had lived very close to her during her struggles with my father, and did not understand what I needed to forgive. At thirteen, one knows little of the ways of the world. I believed I knew at least some of the reasons behind her action, and the rest of the world did not.

The standards I had learned from my mother (honesty, purity, love and unselfishness) were in no way reflected by my mother's behaviour. The one unavoidable fact remained: she had gone out of our lives and would not be returning. That in itself was enough to cope with at the moment. Her loyalty to my father for fifteen years of marriage was another fact. Doubtless, he had driven her into a position where, when Caddy arrived on the scene, she would have been less than human had she been able to withstand his advances. This, I reasoned, was fair enough cause to accept the inevitability of the eventual split in my parents' relationship.

At Mum's departure, all emotions had been quickly drowned out by the sudden thrust of practical demands I saw as my responsibility as the eldest of her five children. It was some years before I trusted myself to the point of deciding to bare my soul to a wise, much respected older friend who had cared for our family through the war and had kept an eye on us all since. In a letter to her, I attempted to lift out of the tangled past some of the confused thoughts and emotions relating to my mother. I admitted that I could not see clearly how to sort out our relationship. My ostrich position was so entrenched by then that I was totally unprepared for the blistering response I received from her:

About your mother, be sure you call a spade a spade and face the truth about her. You will never help her if you feel sorry for her. She is living in adultery, with illegitimate children. It needs Christ's white heat to cut through that much evil. You don't condemn, but you don't condone... She wants to suck you into her orbit and you are never meant to step into it. The only way is for her to step back on to God's ground where you are anchored for life.

I was stunned, like a bird which has thudded against a window pane. No one had dared speak straight from the shoulder like that about my mother before, and such bald facts hurt. Though now in my late teens, emotionally I was still a child facing the objective opinion of an adult who, all too obviously, felt profound anger at the behaviour of a mother who could do such a thing as walk out on her children. She was slating the mother I loved, and I could not handle her anger against her, nor the judgment of her actions. Nor could I understand her expectations of me.

This bombshell exploded from the pen of a woman whom I trusted utterly as someone who sought God's will for her whole life. Surely, then, I needed to accept that this must be the truth? I could not. I adored my mother, and had no equipment with which to counter this fierce attack on her position.

During the ensuing years, I decided to 'let well alone'. Better not to be 'drawn into her orbit' as I had been warned. Only the small demands she made of us down the years were fulfilled: answering letters and birthday cards, and the infrequent telephone call for a birthday. There was little emotional bond between us now. I did not see how the situation could ever be different, though I knew deep down that I still loved her as I had in the past. I just did not know how to show this to the different person she had become in the present.

Mum came to stay with us in Portsmouth after our daughter was born, in 1978. I had again asked for her help, especially as I was suffering from post-natal depression. During this brief visit, my husband and I talked over with her some of the things we, her children, had experienced during those lost years when we had no contact with her. The picture we painted, so hard to express in words, made me tremble as I told her of some of the experiences during our upbringing, and especially with Dad.

But she could not (or would not) take in what I was saying. She remained silent, distant, and seemingly void of imagination. My Peter tried to help her understand better, but found neither comprehension, sympathy, nor even a trace of remorse. She recorded this visit later in her autobiography, by saying that she had been glad I was getting 'all that poison' out of my system. At that time, I could not reconcile my mother with my happy memories of her. She had no feeling. She had changed beyond recognition. Indeed, her conscience now appeared about as dead as Caddy's had been when I talked with him in Northern Ireland.

It was not until we were living and working in Spain, when our mother decided to publish her autobiography entitled *Flight into Freedom* in 1988, that the need to become more involved in her life became necessary. It was only then that I began to understand that there was much from the past for which I would need to forgive her.

Potent words of journalist and author Philip Yancey come to mind when he states: *Forgiveness alone can alter the cycle of blame and pain, breaking the chain of ungrace... Forgiveness offers a way out. It does not settle all the questions of blame and fairness — often it pointedly evades those questions — but it does allow a relationship to start over, to begin anew. Not to forgive imprisons me in the past and locks out all potential for change.*[2]

I was only just launching out on that road of change, but had no notion of the reality of the 'questions of blame and fairness' I had yet to encounter. For my brother and sisters who still saw our mother as they remembered her, and had known her in short snatches of time during the last forty-three years, the path was straightforward. My brother told me he had no difficulty 'forgiving the sinner' without needing to forgive the sin. He was ever a warm-hearted and forgiving person. My sister Suzanne did not feel the need to forgive; sister Mary Liz in New Zealand had recently faced up to the past and found a whole new lifestyle through forgiveness. Penny, who scarcely remembered Mum, had grappled with a mother ideal all her life, and only in her teens was she to meet her. She found the reality fell far short of her ideal. Yet she too had a wonderfully forgiving nature.

My route to understanding our mother was to prove a far stonier and more challenging road to true forgiveness. She and I still had a long way to go as yet, but her published life-story demanded we must walk it together to the end…

PART III

Startling revelations and research

18

All Change!

It is a common weakness that when concrete facts do not match up with our preconceived theories, we prefer to keep our theories and live in an imaginary world, rather than face the facts and alter our theories to suit them. Many lengths are gone to, to preserve our theories, especially in the spiritual realm...

The Challenging Counterfeit *by Raphael Gasson*

BY 1987, I was living in Southern Spain where husband Peter was then working. We had become Iberia-orientated, following his tour of two-and-a-half years with the Royal Navy in Portugal and a similar time spent in his final posting in Gibraltar, where he had learned Spanish. Peter had secured a job as bursar at an international school, twenty minutes from the border with Gibraltar. We rented a groom's cottage on a country estate belonging to one of the school's governors, situated about three miles inland from the Port of Algeciras.

We enjoyed much of the Spanish culture, the language, the warmer climate and a somewhat more relaxed lifestyle than we find in England. But school life was demanding. As bursar, Peter grappled with Spanish accountancy, bureaucracy and education, while I taught religious studies. Our son and daughter were pupils, learning in both Spanish and English.

After three years of commuting back and forth to the school, twenty miles each way daily along the only southern road from Algeciras, the wear-and-tear began to show, particularly in the summer heat. July was the height of the transmigration season, when all the Moroccans employed in Europe return across the Gibraltar Straits to their homeland for a month's vacation.

We were often caught in long traffic queues, called 'caravans'. It could be gruelling. This was one major factor which prompted us to move nearer to the school. Another was a strong hunch that we were meant to get more into the mainstream of the school and community life of Sotogrande where the school was based.

We found a little house within the urbanization of Sotogrande. It took nearly six months and Peter's gratuity on leaving the Navy to purchase it, but just before Christmas in 1986, we left behind the beautiful country estate where we had been poor but happy, and moved into our own first home, ten minutes' walk from the school, and five minutes' bike-ride for the children.

Furthest from my mind, then, was my mother until a note arrived from the Findhorn Press in Scotland, announcing the publication of her autobiography. The note read: '...she (Eileen) would like you to read chapter eight before the book is published,' since that particular chapter 'deals with her relationship with all of you.' Enclosed was the chapter.

I had no idea she had written about her life. This 'blast from the past' began with a 'message' to the effect that Eileen must be very patient and never cease 'to radiate love and more love.' Nor was she to be faint-hearted.... for 'You will be united with your children and glorious will be the uniting. Love will win.'

The chapter covered the period in her life and ours after she went away with Caddy. I was not invited to comment on the facts therein. This was simply an announcement of her intention requiring neither addition nor correction. There were some excusable inaccuracies, as my mother had not always known our movements over the years. In fact, so diverse had been our paths that even we who had walked them found it difficult to remember them all.

The sum of the chapter added up to a pathetic story, mostly related through correspondence with each of us, recounting her sorrowful efforts to reach out for our 'lost' love. She yearned to regain some kind of status in our lives, even if her role as our mother – in the eyes of many – had been forfeited by her behaviour.

At first she had been rebuffed and silenced by the return of all her letters and parcels, unopened. Father had permitted no contact between us and our mother, later backed by the court order after their divorce three years later. Then, I could correspond with her because I was sixteen, but she met with only cool replies from me. I no longer knew how to respond to her. These experiences must have been agonizing for her, yet she clung to her hopeful 'messages', and persevered in keeping sporadic contact with us all. She always remembered our birthdays and wrote, in the hope that some of her love would filter through the censorship and be returned. Unknown to Dad, Richard received most of her letters because he was at boarding school on the Isle of Wight. Otherwise, for the younger family members, those letters were blocked.

One paragraph on page 4 of chapter 8 troubled me. It read: *I was told in guidance: The action you took in leaving Andrew was done under My guidance. Without it you would never have been able to do it...* This statement in particular set warning bells jangling in my head.

In my limited experience, I understood that the essence of God's character was love, and that He was my Heavenly Father. I believed His words to be true, and that He was faithful to His promises. This particular statement put in question those core beliefs. The marriage vows I had taken on my own wedding day were challenged. Belief and trust in those vows would be rendered invalid were I to accept that the God whom I thought I knew and loved, had instructed my mother to leave my father. The Book of Common Prayer states specifically: 'Those whom God has joined together, let no man put asunder.'

My parents' relationship had collapsed in Iraq, and the situation had become too fraught to keep them together for much longer without some Divine intervention, which the advent of Peter Caddy certainly was not. But I could not attribute to God Himself that He had planned the rift and placed Caddy in Mum's path for this purpose. It was unbelievable that the God I knew would have designed the emotional upheaval in the wake of our mother's departure, or actually given His blessing to such a shot-gun union as Mum had made with Caddy. No — the equation she put forward in that statement did not add up in my comprehension. There was an x factor here I did not understand. Was her god the same as mine?

The publication of Mum's autobiography was imminent, and suddenly we were faced with the disclosure of our family's history as seen from her viewpoint. She appeared bent on showing the public what neither she nor the unsuspecting world realised was inaccurate and appeared to me a fabrication. The title of her book was *Flight into Freedom*. But where she used imagination rather than fact about her first five children's lives, I thought it more of a flight into fantasy.

This event sharply focused for me the need to re-think, re-evaluate the past, and try to understand some of the many queries with which we had lived for well over thirty years. It disturbed me that distorted facts were about to be made public. Something had to be done.

While writing a letter to my mother in response, once again I shook all over. The inaccuracies needed correcting, but in doing so, all the old emotions came bubbling to the surface. I found myself seeking to lay before her the facts of how those years had been for us, the truth as I saw it: the sense of loss and lovelessness; how each in his or her own way had struggled to come to terms with life without a mother, knowing that she now belonged elsewhere and could never be ours again.

It had cost emotional pain to write that letter. Yet when her reply came, I remember feeling greatly disappointed. She appeared to glide lightly over all I felt, but in admitting *'though my sins be as scarlet'*, sought my forgiveness. *'I have paid off my karma...When Peter left me I knew the pain and suffering I had caused Dad when I left him... I did deserve it, and...I needed to know what I had put Dad through. I certainly have been through a tremendous amount...and I have learnt so much through it all.'* She made it clear that *'the past is the past and there is nothing I can do to rectify it. It is what is happening NOW that matters.'* She pointed out (gently) that I was *'looking down on her from (my) wisdom and age,'* telling her what she should have done (in other words, judging again). She still believed, however, that all would work out for the best – *'You go your way and I will go mine, and I am sure one day we will all meet in God's love, where there is no separation and all is One.'*

Her autobiography must have gone to print before she received my reply, because none of the corrections I had suggested were implemented. The inaccuracies remained. Interestingly, it was filed under 'occult sciences' in the British Museum Library.

Mum's response to mine produced two results. It had arrived close to Mother's Day, so I sent her a card in which I expressed my forgiveness of her. (What I should have asked was: for what do you wish me to forgive you? I was unclear what she felt her 'scarlet sins' were.) I was soon to discover far more than I could ever have imagined of what her life consisted, but at least the card carried with it a first positive step towards renewing our relationship.

The second result of Mum's letter arose from questioning the statement she made in her chapter eight, which I could not match up with my beliefs – the Christian credo learned originally from her. I needed to understand what had changed her thinking. This exploration was to set up a train of events which opened the window through which I was able to see what lay behind her puzzling statement, and also led to a greater understanding of the exact nature of her work. Out of all this an entirely new picture of the woman I thought I had already 'forgiven,' took shape.

Two months elapsed while I questioned these matters, bewildered emotionally and spiritually. I could not see a way through the differences which had arisen between myself and the parent I truly loved during the first thirteen years of my life, and to whose memory I remained loyal.

Then Mum sent me a book of her messages as a birthday gift, and after the first two pages, I found I was unable to read further. I asked husband Peter why he thought this was, but he admitted, 'I'm out of my depth on this one.'

Finally, when I beseeched the Almighty, there came a prompt reply... I was to talk over my problem with Richard and Connie Smith, an American missionary couple whom we had met recently while living near Algeciras, twenty miles down the road from our new home in Sotogrande. We had all attended the same little church in Algeciras, near their apartment.

After our move to Sotogrande, we had invited the Smiths to join the small Bible discussion group we had formed. We had come across several like-minded people living in the urbanisation, also in pursuit of God's truths for their daily lives.

Richard and Connie were doctors of linguistics employed by Wycliffe Bible Translators. They were attached to two American universities as adjunct professors working with Christian college students from America, Europe and South America whom they were training. Their fascinating work was teaching these students how to go into other cultures and live out their Christian faith instead of preaching it, particularly in Muslim countries where Christian evangelising is prohibited.

Richard had led us in a study on the Book of Acts, about the development of the early Christian church, and he and Connie made the history and picture of that time come alive and relevant to our 20th century living. This fresh way of presenting old truths was wisdom distilled from eleven years living in the jungles of Colombia, four years in Ethiopia and many other far-flung corners where they lived in different cultures while translating the scriptures. Their work was to translate the words of the Bible into the idiom of the culture where they lived, thus bringing God's powerful presence into the midst of tribespeople in ways they could grasp. Living among people whose traditions were dominated by witchcraft and spirits, and who nursed an awesome dread of all kinds of dark influences, had led the Smiths to study widely all forms of the occult, though we were not aware of this at the time.

I had watched this couple as they dealt quietly and matter-of-factly with several human problems shared within our growing discussion group. I was intrigued by their commonsense, questioning approach, their real-life stories, their sagacity, and their sometimes uncomfortably relevant prayers. I felt I could trust them, and believed they might be able to untangle some of the doubts and questions I had about my mother and her work. A ball of wool had rolled at my feet, and I needed to unravel it to get at the truth.

The first step was to request an interview with the Smiths, and how right this proved to be!

One blisteringly hot afternoon, I drove down to Algeciras to the Smiths' rented flat. On the car-seat beside me were the small book my mother had given me, the chapter from her autobiography, and the to-and-fro correspondence we'd had since. When I arrived at their apartment down near the waterfront, the French windows onto the balcony, overlooking the main road running alongside the Port, were tightly closed against the ceaseless sound of traffic, dust and heat waves rising from the street below. The view from the window was magnificent, looking across the roofs of the dockland warehouses and ships in the crescent bay to where the Rock of Gibraltar rose majestically out of the sea on the opposite side. Seagulls swirled and screamed in the deep-blue Mediterranean sky.

It was stiflingly hot inside the little sitting-room, despite the large fan whirring in one corner. Gratefully, I sipped a pint tankard of iced tea I had been given before I could begin to present my case to this dear couple. I hoped the Smiths would gather up the facts and my queries, and knit together the different coloured skeins in some semblance of order, thus skilfully making sense of my story and possibly revealing some fresh insights. They did this far better than I thought possible.

I began with a few broad brush strokes of our family's history so far. Then I introduced them to my mother through a copy of my letter to her, and her reply. When I produced my mother's book of messages, *Opening Doors Within*, Richard opened it, glanced at the first pages and commented: 'This is pure spiritualism.' Surprise No. 1! I had never thought my mother dabbled in spiritualism. I rather suspect neither had she. In the ensuing four hours, I was to undergo many such shock-waves and startling revelations.

At last, with my head reeling and the rest of me feeling emotionally mangled, I climbed into Little Blue (our Renault 4) to drive the twenty-one miles back up the coast. On the way, I tried to assimilate all I had learned. I was in no doubt that the Smiths had hit upon the reality of my mother's position. At the same time, I had been knocked sideways by the truth of it all, and was angered by some of the things said about *my* mother whom they had not even met. I heard myself chuntering, 'But this is my *mother* they're talking about. A spiritualist? Impossible! *And* preposterous! Anyway, they don't know her as I do.' I felt they had presumed upon hallowed ground which had lain untouched for years, and had turned it all over with a rotovator.

When Pandora opened the forbidden box, every type of evil and disease sprang out to 'beset mankind', leaving only Hope at the bottom of the box. Much as Pandora might have felt as she watched all the ugly creatures fly out, I was aghast at what I had just experienced.

My mind was so disorientated after the time with the Smiths that I did not go home at once, but turned the car into the Sotogrande school grounds, knowing I would find quiet there in the school buildings at the end of the day. I sat in an empty classroom and wrote down every point I could remember my friends had just told me.

It took several weeks to evaluate their deductions. They had given me two books, to help me understand the reality of the powerful forces at work in my mother's world. These books opened up for me entirely virgin territory. The truths they described were mind-boggling, but they rang absolutely true. They each raised many different possibilities about the spiritual dimension to our world — all news to me. I was fascinated to read Johanna Michaelsen's account of her brushes with the paranormal, mind control and parapsychology in her book *The Beautiful Side of Evil*. Also, to read former spiritualist priest Raphael Gasson's story of how he came through to an acceptance of Jesus Christ. Both he and Johanna had experienced similar struggles in breaking away from the strangle-hold of spirits, and both had almost died in the attempt. Their stories convinced me of the existence of a spiritual plane, and helped clear up some of my questions. More fortunate than the curious Pandora, I began to see a small glimmer of hope emerging from these startling revelations.

As my understanding grew, so the scattered pieces of the jigsaw puzzle of our lives began to fit into their rightful places, and answers began to match my questions.

Richard had pointed out that my mother's little book was full of spiritualist 'messages' which had come through to her because she was trained as a medium between this and the spirit world. This triggered a memory of her telling me, when I first visited Findhorn in 1969, that she had 'been given' the spiritual name 'Elixir'.

I asked him if he could tell me why I had been unable to read it, just as though I had run into an invisible barrier put there to prevent my seeing the contents. I was to learn two things about this book: a) always to look for the *teaching* in any work I read; and b) that the barrier was a kind of prevention by the Holy Spirit - a form of protection against involvement.

Had I not met such spiritual protection twice before: once when a week's rest from swimming before I contracted polio had prevented a lifetime of physical damage? And again when I had strolled with Sheena Govan-Caddy in Nonsuch Park, forced to listen to all she tried to teach me about twin-souls, free love and planets by way of explanation for my mother and Caddy's love for each other? Perhaps even on a third occasion, when Peter Caddy had set out to woo us children with tales of his exploits, prowess as an athlete, and presents — all of which we had found hard to either believe or accept?

But who was dictating these messages to her, I asked? Where did they come from? The Smiths suggested Eileen was being controlled by a 'spirit of light', and that probably this ruling spirit had gained access to our mother when she had 'lusted after the man'. Her moral and emotional defences had been weakened, and through the chink in her armour pierced by the spirit of lust, a 'spirit of light' had entered to take possession in her spirit. Her function in the spiritual world was to be a channel for this spirit-guide's messages, and through these a power was created which drew people to her as if by magnetism. She literally radiated her spirit's philosophy of 'unconditional love', which would have given her the charisma which was to last till her dying day.

I had always comforted myself with the idea that, even if my mother was surrounded by deluded people, she herself talked of 'Christ-consciousness', Jesus and the 'Mary ray', of God's love and 'unconditional love' in such a way that must prove she had remained partially Christian in word and intent. It came as a mighty shock, therefore, to see that I myself might have been deluded by this belief and by my faith in her words. It was important to understand, stressed my counsellors, that the spirit controlling my mother was not the spirit of God (the Holy

Spirit), but another spirit and one not of His realm.

It was difficult to dislodge from my mind completely the idea that my mother was a follower of Christ. Her lifestyle of self-sacrifice and goodness, of suffering and love, of visions, meditation and guidance, seemed to add up to devoted discipleship. Who was I, then, or indeed they, to judge her? I decided that God alone knew my mother inside out, her intentions, and who she really worshipped. I must therefore trust only Him, and lean on that trust until He revealed His truth to me. After all, I told myself, the Smiths only knew my mother from what I had told them about her, and the little they had read.

Yet, I knew deep in my heart that they were probably right. Perhaps I could accept she had become a spiritualist or a medium. The media saw her as a charismatic leader. I remained puzzled by the fact that she did not seem to fit into any known category I had read or heard about until then, but when all was said and done, she was still my mother.

My stubborn stance began to shift somewhat when I re-considered how the strained and strange mother-daughter relationship had remained in limbo for so many years. Even though she had never tried to influence any of us by her ideas, I had heard she was involved in the New Age movement where she was regarded as a guru, or a high-priestess. Thanks to both press and television, she had by then become something of a celebrity, and had been televised as one of eight Women of Wisdom in a TV series of that name.

In the light of all this, where did this leave our relationship? Always quick to rush in where angels would not, I had asked the Smiths, 'can I not help her see what has happened to her?' Connie made it quite clear, however, that because of my emotional and subjective involvement with Eileen, I could do nothing for her, and then added, 'No one can. She has to be zapped by God!' — her exact descriptive words. I began to see that some kind of spiritual battle was being waged in, as yet, rather misty realms. This proved to be just the beginning of understanding the implications of its significance in our family's circumstances.

The Smiths had lifted one cloud from the scene, however. I had told them how, since the age of thirteen, I had carried a load of guilt and sense of responsibility on my conscience, as I had seen but not tried to prevent the affair going on between Mum and Caddy after we came home from Iraq. (One lady we knew had remarked on the early worry lines on my forehead at that age!) The Smiths explained to me that the guilt I had felt for so long had, in fact, been totally unfounded. They reassured me that no living soul could have done anything to frustrate or prevent my mother's love for Peter Caddy or the combined Caddy-force's diabolical plan. It came as an enormous relief, therefore, to hear them tell me that my behaviour and silence at the time, had not been sinful after all.

So what was I to do next, I asked? They suggested that my part was simply to seek from God what He intended my role to be in this situation, as the child of His I had always been. Perhaps, they suggested, I should write a paper for my siblings, telling them about my findings at Findhorn when I had last visited there?

Also, they helped me understand that our children may have been influenced by their grandmother, since on both occasions at their births, I had asked my mother to help me out for a week or so till I had established a routine. During those periods, they suggested there was a danger they may have received a powerful blessing from her. This was an entirely new concept - that she could possibly have wielded some strange power over them, or 'blessed' them. The Smiths said it would be wise to say a prayer of banishment of any spirit-power over each of them, and replace it with asking God for the Holy Spirit's protection over them instead. I could do this while they were asleep.

The other important point I learned about my

mother's teaching was how to look at it alongside Christ's teaching. I was invited to study the Person of Christ. This would help me sort out the false from the true, the fake from the genuine.

A story is told about a man trained as an expert in detecting forged dollar notes. When he was interviewed on American television, he was introduced to the viewers as an expert in forgery. He quickly countered with, 'No, I am an expert in the genuine article. Only by knowing the real thing can one recognise the phoney.'

By now I felt compelled to explore more about the Real Thing.

Somewhere in his book, Raphael Gasson framed a similar thought, though in a different context, with his words: *Only the real power of God working through His people, through His Spirit, will reveal the second-best efforts of Satan...and will clear the darkened minds of his dupes.*[1]

Some of that 'real power' of discernment was called for right now, as I groped along new, untrammelled pathways towards greater knowledge of the counterfeit world into which my mother had stumbled, utterly innocently and unwittingly, I was sure.

Before I left the Smiths' apartment on that first occasion, they asked me to lay down any right I felt I had to attempt to do anything about my mother's state, and to hand her back to my heavenly Father in trust. For some reason, I found this a nigh impossible exercise to perform. My mind went completely blank. I could not find suitable words for some considerable time. It seemed like an hour, but the Smiths waited. After a long silence, words came out at last, as though dredged up unwillingly from the murky depths of my sub-conscious. I let go of my mother, handing her back to God as His property, not mine—His responsibility, no longer mine.

I accepted fully at the time that I would not be the person to help Mum re-find her Christian faith. I continued to hope, of course, that she would be 'zapped'. The burden of guilt and responsibility had evaporated during counselling, but was replaced by a profound concern as to how this zapping might happen to her before she died.

Meanwhile, the new knowledge I had gleaned had fallen like a landslide across the road between my mother and me. The blockage seemed insurmountable and only increased as I began writing of my discoveries. Old ghosts rose up as long blotted-out memories slowly thawed out, returning to mind. Every book I now read led me further up a mountain in steps towards greater awareness.

I began to discern little by little some of the effects of the Pandora's Box of philosophies Sheena Caddy, her husband, and my mother had opened up onto an unsuspecting world. Then I questioned how the dynamic of forgiveness in all that evil could possibly come about? The loving forgiveness I had offered in words to my mother recently in my Mother's Day card now appeared so much trite nonsense. An entirely new picture had taken shape of the mother I thought I had forgiven.

As I set out on the trail towards the truth, I had little idea how steep and daunting the climb ahead might turn out to be.

19

A Solitary Journey

*And I saw there was an Ocean of Darkness and Death;
but an infinite Ocean of Light and Love flowed over the Ocean of
Darkness; and in that I saw the infinite love of God.*
George Fox (1624–1691)
Vincit omnia veritas – Truth conquers all *(Latin motto)*

I DESPERATELY wanted to discover the 'real thing'. Faced with what seemed a labyrinth of hazy philosophies, where could I find a reliable source? The Smiths had used the Bible as their manual. During two days of counselling, they had intelligently applied chapter and verse relevant to my case. No one had focused a scriptural spotlight on my questions and difficulties before. This approach to the Bible filled me with hope.

They encouraged me to 'look at the teaching' within any work. I had always been a dilettante 'searcher after truth', but now it seemed vital to find out God's viewpoint if I was to understand my mother's work. As I read on, verse after verse in the Bible began speaking almost audibly to my present position. Time and again Jesus said, 'Verily, verily I say unto you...' and 'I am telling you the truth when I tell you...' These were God's words, and they pointed to God's truth. These passages took on new significance as they appeared to relate exactly to my pursuit of it.

I had also been bidden by my mentors to 'study the person of Jesus'. In doing so, I was led to explore the love-theme which was taught by Sheena Caddy, and which featured frequently in my mother's books. Their teaching seemed so plausible. For instance, my mother wrote of Sheena in her autobiography:

Sheena had a mission in life: to transform the world through love. Although I never felt that love, I believe it was there because I saw her help people in their search for spiritual truth...She was firmly convinced that God is within each of us, that we are an expression of God. Her 'training' was to reinforce our faith in this inner God and to encourage us to follow it in our lives.[1] My mother often referred afterwards to 'the God within', a phrase which became her trademark.

A key factor in distinguishing between counterfeit and real love – the forged note or the true currency – seemed to demand a closer study of how Sheena's ideal of 'love' was carried through in the Caddys' lives. Her philosophy about love did not ring true when compared with Jesus' words, 'Love your enemies' Matt.5:4), 'Love your neighbour as yourself' (Matt.19:19), or 'A new command I give you: love one another. As I have loved you, so you must love one another. By this all men will know that you are my disciples, if you love one another,' (John 13:34). In the early church, these commands were obeyed so effectively among Christ's followers that one observer exclaimed, 'See how these Christians love one another!' Christ's love was contagious.

Laying the radiance of Christ's quality of love alongside the difficult and loveless training Sheena had given Eileen, I asked myself what kind of love is it that abducts another woman's child for her own? Had Mum ever questioned, 'What kind of love would remove me from my five children, sometimes cut off my life-line with the man I love, and finally leave me stranded and alone in a tiny, crude cottage on an island (Mull), for months on end with no money and very little to eat?' What kind of love is it that can cause so much misery, and finally make suicide the only alternative to a living hell?

It was understandable, of course, that my mother should feel no love for the former Mrs Caddy, given the extraordinary position she was put in by her. From her autobiography, we learn from Eileen of the shambles Sheena Govan Caddy created out of many people's lives other than Mum's. Reading between the lines, these were workings not of a *loving* heart, but of one full of passion, jealousy, naked hatred, deceit and manipulation. In spite of my mother's words about Sheena's 'vision', it seemed obvious to me that no true love was to be found anywhere in Sheena's all-absorbing and ruthless pursuit of divine leadership. Was this why Sheena felt compelled to make Eileen suffer?

Then I looked into the area of God's laws - natural and supernatural. One evening I was reading a story to our daughter in which the author stated that only in the instance of death would a wild animal ever leave her young. If that was a fact in the natural world, then surely *human* loyalty and a mother's protective instincts should be even more powerful bonds? I deduced from this that a strong *un*-natural element was at work at the time when Eileen walked out of the front door of Kingstackley all those years ago with Caddy. She nearly turned back when her youngest child upstairs had woken and was crying, but a compulsive force was propelling her on, out into the darkness instead – a power beyond sexual attraction and the excitement of touring on holiday with her lover.

Forty or more years ago, society still retained a fairly stable value system: most British people knew right from wrong, good from bad, what was true and what was false. Christian teaching still had its place in education, and the Ten Commandments were regarded with some awe as the basis of law. Nowadays, very few might throw up their hands in horror or even surprise at a mother walking out of her home to go off to live with another man, leaving five children. There might be a shrug of the shoulders maybe, a pang of sorrow expressed on behalf of the 'abandoned', but on the whole we have become desensitized by the media's bombardment in 'East Enders' and other such scripts and tales, often far worse.

I once wrote to the founder of Mission to Marriage, Dave Ames, to ask his views on the present marital status in our country. He replied: '...The minute that people move away from God the least bit, they tend to step right into the most comfortable social trend. Living together has certainly become one of these situations.'

Jesus longed that each one of His followers would show love for Him by obeying His Father's teaching... then 'My Father will love him, and my Father and I will come to him and live with him. Whoever does not love me does not obey my teaching' (John 14:23 NIV). If Jesus' teaching was inspired truth, as I believe it was, then one must question: what was this new kind of love, this new teaching being followed by the Caddys? Assuredly, a very different set of values from those we had learned from our parents.

Returning to the little book *Opening Doors Within* sent me by my mother, the Smiths suggested that it would help clear my mind of unwelcome spiritual influence if I got rid of the book. With it could go any other items which might have occultist connotations. This seemed a bit drastic, but I wanted to do the right thing. I could not read the book anyway, so I burned it on a small bonfire at the foot of the garden. This reminded me of the Middle Ages when converted Christians burned their books on witchcraft in the town square.

Being a slow reader, I found studying hard going. However, trusting implicitly in the Smiths' wisdom and encouragement, I set myself to read the first two books they gave me, about the power of the occult and spiritualism. If these held a key to greater understanding about my mother's work, then persevere I must, and learn I must.

The Challenging Counterfeit by Raphael Gasson was a tough eye-opener on the world of spiritualism. From the age of five, when the author 'saw his first spirit', Gasson had been spiritually sensitive, and eventually had become a medium and then a minister in the spiritualist church. Later, through a series of fascinating experiences, he became a Christian. In order to clear up his past dealings with the 'other world' of spirits and spirit-guides, he knew he must renounce all his dealings with them. In doing so, however, he underwent several gruelling physical life-and-death struggles in which the spirits controlling him very nearly strangled him to death. *These attacks continued for some months,* he recalled... *It was only by my standing upon the promises of God — defying Satan to do his worst — and by pleading the power of the Blood of Christ and by much intercessory prayer being given by the saints, that these evil spirits were eventually overcome.*[2]

Φ

Johanna Michaelsen's *Beautiful Side of Evil* proved even more startling, and rather closer to what I already knew. While living with her family in South America, she too had been 'possessed by spirits' from an early age. In her insatiable search for her 'higher consciousness', Johanna had taken hallucinatory drugs and become involved in mind-control. These drew her on, eventually, towards interest in psychic phenomena and practical participation in parapsychology. She relates how she came through all these experiences, after a similarly horrifying spiritual struggle with forces which also very nearly succeeded in choking her to death.

Both books made clear that a person could be controlled by spirits, but that God's power is stronger and always prevails victoriously over such entities when the victim invokes Jesus' name.

Particularly interesting about Johanna's account, however, was that during her experiments with mind control, she began to have wonderful visions. She would enter her 'psychic laboratory' to talk with her two chosen counsellors, the spirit-guides of Jesus and a Mexican woman who called herself Mamacita (little mother). During a time of prayer one day, after reading 1 John 4 in the Bible, Johanna decided to test these spirits. She recounts what happened next:

I went into my laboratory and summoned my counsellors. 'You are not the Jesus in the Bible, are you,' I challenged the figure of 'Jesus' which stood before me in the shadows (of the laboratory). There was no reply. His eyes were closed. Mamacita stood close by him. 'Then I command you, in the Name of Jesus Christ of Nazareth, tell me: Do you believe that Jesus Christ is God uniquely incarnate in human flesh?' A violent flash - as though from a powerful bomb, brought the walls of my amethyst and gold laboratory down all around me. When I looked up, my counsellors had vanished. Again I looked up the words of Deuteronomy and Leviticus. The question was finally settled. The works of a medium were abominations before God. Neither the psychic perceptions of Mind Control nor Pachita's work (psychic surgery) had its source in God.[3]

What had all this to do with my mother, one might ask? Admittedly she had many visions, which I suspected were the result of Sheena's brain-washing. As far as I knew, though, Mum had not been subjected to any other kind of mind-control or drugs. The path she had travelled was entirely different from Johanna's in her life. Hadn't my mother, much refined by all her suffering, become a force for good? She had told my brother once that she was a white witch - for white magic was 'only used for good purposes.' Goodness was one of her aims, working in perfect harmony with nature and spreading 'love, love, love'. Was it coincidence that at the time, the Beatles were proclaiming a similar message – 'All you need is love — Love is all you need'? Their influence was coming from their guru Maharishi Yogi. The Age of Aquarius was in full swing, and on stage *Hair* was shocking the public.

There was a black thread of self-deception to be seen, weaving its way through the lives of Raphael Gasson and Johanna. This had turned them away from known pathways to explore the esoteric in the forms they had chosen. Other groups appeared to be following suit. Did their experimentations bring them peace of mind, or joy, or certainty, or did they inspire a lust for ever more excitement in their search for spirituality? Both authors had encountered powers which drew them onwards into their tightening grip, until finally each came face to face with Christ as the conqueror of Evil itself.

Was it possible, then, that the hand of deception had been dealt equally successfully to my mother? Had she been led on relentlessly by similar entities from the spirit-world, emanating from Sheena's use of mind-control? Were these the strange powers which had manifested the celebrated Findhorn Garden with its beautiful masque of flowers blossoming among the sand-dunes?

People remarked on the love which seemed to surround my mother like an aura – the love she called 'unconditional.' Her love and lifestyle had drawn people into a community where there was a common longing to do good, to protect our planet, to live in harmony and even hug trees together. They danced, piped, meditated and tranced their way towards a similar goal – 'the dawning of a New Age'. In their avid exploration of every kind of religious, irreligious or pagan ritual, their tolerance *seemed* entirely harmless. Yet, *was* it? Was I discovering here the 'beautiful side of evil'?

I needed to dig deeper and rather more diligently to find satisfactory answers to these questions. I was wading into deeper waters. However, living as we were in Southern Spain, we might as well have been in the middle of the Kalahari as far as resource material, encyclopaedias, and any public library system were concerned. I began to write to publishers and agents in the U.K. and U.S. to order books, and landed myself with several years of extensive reading. As I plodded on, I also learned some uncomfortable facts about myself which came to light. I guess there is bound to be some spin-off from such a challenging learning curve.

I did not enjoy further encounters with the stark facts of how the devil was at work in the world: about what motivated the Bilderbergers, the Illuminati, Freemasons; of how racism and intolerance, hatred and tyranny of oppressed peoples, civil wars and Nazism, with all their subsequent atrocities, were Satan's tools; or of reading up on various occultic practices.

I absorbed as much negativism as I could, but was in danger of getting sucked down myself into the morass of material now available on computer, in books, and by the heightened awareness of the evidence of Satan's wily ways at work in life around me.

I felt as a seagull might have done landing on Smokey Mountain to scratch among the reeking detritus for pickings, and then being driven away by the stench to seek healthier sea breezes and fresh horizons.

Where was I going? A cartoonist's balloon above my head might have read: 'Help! I'm sinking!' I had reached saturation point. Early one morning during a time of quiet thought, I looked down to my left and found myself staring into a black pit. Looking back at me from the darkness was a crowd of chalk-white faces with huge, empty, staring eyes. I knew at once I was peering down at lost souls: ghostly-white faces of thousands upon thousands of souls, lost in a pit of despair into which they had fallen while following shadowy New Age philosophies. It was a vivid and terrible vision – not only for the scared souls thronging in the darkness below, but for me also.

I had first recognised a lost soul during the talk with Peter Caddy in Northern Ireland. But it came as a shock to see he was just one of a multitude of similar souls in pitiable perdition.

The trauma pulled me up sharply. I heeded the warning, and decided I had concentrated over-long on what was wrong, negative and dark. My studies had become too intense. It was time to flip the coin. I needed to counteract the evil by focusing on good. I needed to focus on seeking out veritable, not virtual hope; to find God's solution to despair in order to present a more powerful and attractive way of living. As the Smiths had suggested, I wrote some of my tentative findings about the work of the Findhorn Foundation as a catharsis and to clear my own thinking. I had my brother and sisters mainly in mind. When I presented the paper cheerfully to the first family member, assuming it would be received and read with some interest at least, I met a closed-door reaction with, 'This is my mother, whom I love. I don't want to know anything about her work.' My brother was adamant, but his wife Helen was encouraging. However, his feelings put a brake on sending that particular paper to any of the younger members of my family, in case they resented my investigations as he did. Then my husband confessed he, too, felt at sea, unable to grasp the new facts I sought to discuss with him. So I began to realise that probably others would neither understand nor wish to know about my research either. Subsequent conversations proved this to be so.

It was obvious I needed to go it alone. My favourite proverb came to my aid: *Trust in the Lord with all your heart, and lean not unto thine own understanding.* (Prov.3:3) I could not expect anyone else to be involved.

It was only on our return to live in Britain after fifteen years abroad, that I realised more fully the extent of the 'net-working' of New Age, and the far-reaching effects on people's thinking. Its tentacles reached out through the media, affected changes in companies' policies, and insinuated their way into education; even song lyrics and pop festivals, alternatives in medicine and changing lifestyles reflected this insidious influence.

Of course, having read my mother's autobiography, the next place in which to delve deeper was the past history and characters of her two mentors, Sheena and Peter Caddy. Their beliefs would surely show how the change in thinking, values and character had taken place in Mum's life.

Their individual stories, gleaned from Caddy's autobiography *In Perfect Timing*, and my mother's, from newspaper articles, reports, and the inherited instructive letters from Dom Edmund, all shed light on the core motivation behind the Caddys' convictions, and the growth in the movement of new ageism.

20

Birth of a False Prophet?

Beware of false prophets, which come to you in sheep's clothing, but inwardly they are ravening wolves. Ye shall know them by their fruits...
Jesus Christ - Sermon on the Mount (KJV)

THE person behind the cataclysmic upheaval in my mother's life was not Peter Caddy but his wife, Sheena. When she heard from her husband that he had met Eileen whom he believed to be a spiritual 'sensitive', she encouraged him in his pursuit of this fellow officer's wife. She simply had to wait, like a spider at the centre of its web, for him to lure the unsuspecting victim into it.

What was her motive? Primarily she saw herself as the birthing-mother of a new age, and sensed that Caddy's new girl-friend could have a role in this vision.

New-ageism is a complex of spiritual and consciousness-raising movements which re-surfaced in the 1930s and 40s, covering a range of themes from belief in spiritualism to reincarnation. Sheena studied these themes for some time, and was concocting a strange brew of her own, using her Christian upbringing as a basis.

She had grown up in a Christian missionary home in Edinburgh. She was twelve years younger than the younger of her two brothers. Her busy parents had little time to spend with their daughter – a factor which she related with some feeling years later during a newspaper interview. Despite this, her parents' evangelism and zeal was infectious, and at school she would talk to her friends at break times, passing on Christian convictions and singing hymns with them.

Birth of a False Prophet?

However, by the time she was sixteen – as she told reporter James Allison of the *Sunday Mail*, in 1957 – the tensions of her faith and school work clashed, and resulted in a mental and physical breakdown. Her father, of whom she was particularly fond, took her to Switzerland to recover. After six months, she was well enough to return to school where she excelled in sport and became Sports Captain. She also had a love of music, which she studied up to LRAM standard. This enabled her to start out in life teaching piano.

At the age of 26, she met and fell in love with a young doctor to whom she became engaged. When she discovered she had become pregnant, her fiancé deserted her, and her future seemed to fall apart. She accepted an invitation to go to Canada, where her son was born. Two weeks after the birth, she decided to have the baby adopted – a choice which was to haunt her and have dire consequences later. Understandably, this whole episode appears to have played havoc with her conscience, personality and future direction.

Throughout this time she seems to have confided only in her journal, and probably made any decisions entirely alone. The anguished choice to have her son adopted at birth would overshadow her future. The central fact which became a basic tenet of her teachings was: because *she* had given up all for God, others must make the same sacrifice.

My mother takes up Sheena's story in her autobiography, recounting how, during the war years, Sheena worked in Intelligence in Toronto, and there met a colleague who was to become her greatest friend, Dorothy Maclean. Like must have been attracted to like. By then, Sheena had begun to delve deeply into formerly forbidden highways and byways of arcane heresies, most likely in the search for ways to handle the problems she had come up against in her own life. These led her *away from* the basic Christian truths learned in her younger days.

Dorothy, as a spiritually perceptive person herself and a Sufist, was drawn to this strong personality whose ideas were somewhat similar to hers. During their work together, Sheena often accompanied Dorothy on her missions, as chaperone.

They travelled to London after the war, and Sheena settled into a small flat near Victoria Station, in Lupus Street. Not long afterwards, in 1947, Sheena met Caddy in a restaurant car on a train between Bournemouth and London. She was reading a book he had recently read himself, *The Aquarian Gospel of Jesus the Christ* by Levi H. Dowling, containing strong theosophical and spiritualist teachings. This led to conversation and onwards to the meeting of like-minds and kindred spirits once again. Peter was married, and lived in Bournemouth with his wife Nora and their two children. He had become a Rosicrucian. He began to visit Sheena, magnetized by her spiritual power and knowledge which finally enveloped him—mind, soul, and body. He abandoned his first wife and family in order to be at Sheena's side.

The following six years were to be the fusing together of a one-spirit union between two spiritual power-plants. Caddy had been involved with the occult from childhood and firmly believed man was infallible and could achieve anything if he set his mind to it. This was exactly the kick-start Sheena needed for the development of her dreams.

Sheena had been brought up in a Christian ethos in which she had learned all the right words but they had become hollow, and failed to satisfy her hunger for love from either God or her parents. She craved the love she found in Caddy.

Steeped as she was in scriptural words and phrases learned in her early life, these would provide the *vocabulary* she always used in expressing her ideas. The direction behind her faith had mutated through a distillation process of unhealed wounds and grievances of past experiences, and had become distorted into a kind of martyr-complex. Her primary aim was now to become divine herself, although she said she had 'given up all for God'. When she took the reins of her life into her own hands, the direction of her beliefs changed, and she became obsessed by a thirst for spiritual power.

Caddy was not hood-winked by Sheena's Christian phraseology and the Bible truths she was distorting, even if unconsciously by now, for her arcane purposes. He had been exposed to Methodism from an early age, and had plumped for spiritualism at the age of ten. He knew another pagan when he met one. In Sheena he recognised the mystic and the medium, which evoked his complete worship of her as a high-priestess.

By 1953 it appears that the physical union of their marriage had come to an abrupt end, with a letter she wrote to Caddy explaining that she was becoming a 'divine.'

When James Allison, reporting in an article headlined 'They Call Her the Second Christ' for the *Sunday Mail* on 20th January 1957, asked Sheena why she had married a previously married man, and why her own marriage should also end in divorce, her answer revealed publicly the full import of her aim:

My meeting with Peter was, I know, God-ordained. He was a man who was aware of the coming of the new age which I was struggling to bring to birth. His interests were not limited, as was the average man's, to the material things of life.

God lit a flame of love between us because, I am convinced, he chose Peter to be with me during the following crucial years. I could not have stood the strain of these years without his utter devotion and great protective strength.

But during these six years of marriage I realised that my body was undergoing a re-orientation—a change from the human to the divine. These conditions, caused by tremendous tensions, manifested themselves as nervous illnesses.

I had had many revelations and communications from God, from some of his angels, and from some great souls who had visited this earth in the past. They led me to believe that my other experience as a woman was completed, and that my work for God would be for some time on the invisible or inner plane.

To communicate to Peter that our life as man and wife was over was perhaps the hardest thing I have ever been called upon to do. But during this difficult period there was never a bitter, angry or resentful word or thought between us.

No, indeed! Sheena had asked of Peter what she had been prepared to do herself – 'give up all for God.' Her sway over Peter was total. He responded utterly, first as her lover, then as disciple and slave. He worshipped her as his guru, and eventually, when her nomadic sect, called The Nameless Ones by one newspaper, was formed, he remained her PR man and chief evangelist. In fact, it took a long time for the spiritual power in their union to diminish, even after the many years Peter lived and worked with my mother.

By the time Sheena came into our lives, I believe she was a profoundly complex and damaged person. Her conscience had never come to terms with the effects of her first love affair, rejection and then her lonely pregnancy. Nowhere in her journal did she admit any sense of responsibility for her actions, or repentance of them, and now she was hounded by guilt that she had forfeited motherhood. Her view of God and life had become twisted and unreal, to the point where she convinced herself that God's character and plan for her life were suited to the way her own circumstances and shaping of conscience had developed thus far.

Paul Hawken, an American author who lived in Findhorn for a year and later in the 1970s wrote *The Magic of Findhorn*, described Sheena as ...*a radiantly beautiful woman who had been steeped in religion and Godly pursuits from birth...Born in the 'faith', suckled on service to humanity, and weaned on complete dedication to God's Will, she led a life totally devoted to God.*[1] This description was probably given to him by ex-husband Peter, who always saw her through rose-coloured spectacles.

My mother described Sheena as, 'A good-looking woman, taller than I was, with dark hair and lovely eyes. I remember her as serious and very severe, especially with me.'

However, we children saw a very different side of Sheena, as did our mother later. Admittedly, we were sore at being handed over and looked after by a baby-sitter none of my siblings had met before. At the time, we had no idea we would not see our mother again for some years, or that our instinctive dislike and distrust of Sheena was justified.

My sister Suzanne believed she was a witch. 'She had white skin, black hair and green eyes. She was a witch and I hated her.' On one occasion, Sue made her antipathy to Sheena quite clear. Suzanne had been out in the sun in the garden and come in complaining of a splitting headache. Sheena took her up to the bathroom to look for an aspirin, and asked me to bring up an ice-pack from the fridge to put on Sue's head, at which point Sue shouted at her, 'Go away! I don't want you. I want my Mummy!' and kicked her soundly on the shins.

Sheena may not have been able to handle children, but she had proved capable of wielding strange power over those closest to her: power which could take over their lives and manipulate their destinies. After Mum had gone, two women, ex-disciples of Sheena, appeared unexpectedly to talk with my father. They had some strange tales to tell about the 'goings on' around Sheena. Dad told me about one of these: a gathering of Sheena's minions around her bed when she sat in bed and manifested frogs on her tongue! Dad suspected witchcraft. I believe my father knew a great deal more about Sheena by then than he ever thought fit to pass on to his children.

Strange power indeed, but what generated that power? Why did she use it, and where was this all heading? Many questions would remain unanswered for me and my family until years later.

As I look back, however, I see how exceedingly determined the woman was to execute her plan. It took some courage (or was it madness?), especially since she had no child of her own, to take on five children she did not know. We were told our mother had gone 'on holiday' with Caddy. I was thirteen at the time, and Penny, the youngest, was just two years old.

Around the time my mother left us, Sheena was writing in her journal: *I gave up my baby on 11th February, 1938. Through the nineteen years that have followed I have never forgotten him, nor have I ever given up hope that one day we may meet again. A friend did tell me that she had seen his portrait in a Canadian art gallery. 'It was a beautiful picture,' she said.* [2]

When I talked with 'the friend' Dorothy Maclean recently, she said the portrait was in fact of Sheena's nephew.

Nineteen years on, Sheena found herself unable to identify or sympathise with my mother's anguish when she was forced to undergo a similar process in abandoning *her* five children. Possibly, Mum was a convenient whipping-boy on whom to avenge her guilt? Be that as it may, Mum recalls how Sheena became extremely impatient and intolerant with her when she was unable to come to terms with this maternal wrench, parted from her family by a husband who told her she was 'not fit' to be our mother and must not return.

Given all the known facts of Sheena's history, it is possible to deduce something of how the turmoil of her psychological baggage would cast its shadow over the misshapen footprints of her future. In spite of this, it would appear that, in the 1950s, Sheena's star was definitely in the ascendancy. Her arcane sources had endowed her with an aura of authority in her teaching, and she gained a following.

Undoubtedly she was an intelligent woman whose researches into spiritualism, theosophy, Gnosticism, witchcraft and other power-seeking fields of knowledge, empowered her to harness a mixture of these concepts to suit her ends.

It was a tragedy that, during this process, she had strayed away from the one true God who possessed the power to embrace, forgive and heal the anger, hurt pride and sorrow that had blackened her soul. Although she would have known this well, she was already in the grip of other powers which were bent on dispelling her former beliefs. She refused to give God a free hand in her life or redirect this fresh brand of influential thought.

By deliberately turning her back on what she perceived as sin, a new conviction was spawned — one which sat comfortably with her conscience at last: i.e. if sin does not exist, there is nothing to redeem and nothing from which to be 'saved'. This dealt nicely with any necessity to believe in what Christ had done for her and humanity. Quid pro quo, Raphael Gasson states: ...*the god within becomes one's own judge.*[3]

Sheena had portrayed leadership qualities when at school. It is sad when a born leader becomes flawed, changes direction and takes their followers with them.

As mentioned before, my mother wrote of this period in their lives that Sheena's first mission in life was transforming the world through love. Eileen observed: *As more and more were drawn to her, Sheena's role as spiritual teacher developed. She never gave people advice but encouraged them to discover their own inner direction... She was firmly convinced that God is within each of us, that we are an expression of God. Her 'training' was to reinforce our faith in this inner God and to encourage us to follow it in our lives.*[4]

One by one, Sheena's followers were encouraged to give up wife or husband, children, careers and past lifestyles in order to follow a god-form presented by Sheena. She demanded, of course, that my mother must apply these same exacting principles while she was being trained by Sheena, in order to strengthen and push forward Sheena's work towards the 'dawning of a new age'.

Author Raphael Gasson links this type of teaching to St Paul's first letter written to Timothy, chapter 4, in which Paul warns:

In the latter times some shall depart from the faith, giving heed to seducing spirits and doctrines of demons...having their conscience seared with a hot iron; forbidding to marry and commanding to abstain from meats...

Gasson explains: *Forbidding to marry refers to their (Spiritualists') teaching spiritual affinity, whereby many happy homes have been broken up as a result of the teaching of spirits, that every one has a twin soul. The spirits even go so far as to introduce 'twin-souls' to each other, after which introductions they are encouraged to leave homes, husbands, wives and children, to live together, because it is the will of a spirit guide. The marriage vow is entirely disregarded where necessary, and the result is immorality.* [5]

Our mother's first family had experienced the reality of his words, in action.

I am convinced that wherever Sheena used the word 'god', its hidden meaning had shifted from anything to do with the Holy Trinity, and was as Gasson describes, part of a vision for her new age dream, driven by spirit-forces at work in and around her. In other words, she was being guided by spirits diametrically opposed to the workings of God's Holy Spirit.

In spite of my mother proving to be her most difficult and unwilling follower, Sheena had trained her to be a listener to the so-called voice of God, and therefore as a medium through which the voice's commands could be obeyed. By retaining her power over Peter for some years afterwards, Sheena continued to use Eileen in her plans, though elsewhere she was building up her own sect.

Matters came to a catastrophic head on the Hebridean Isle of Mull in 1956. Sheena and some of her friends took a holiday cottage there and invited Eileen to come and stay, with her two little sons. After the guests had departed they were alone together; but the two women's jealousy and hatred of one another reached such a pitch that Sheena moved to another cottage. Once again, Sheena snatched up the older child. One night, a physical brawl ensued to reclaim him, but the howling storm raging outside forced mother to leave him with Sheena overnight, and return to her own dwelling. Next morning, she went to collect him from Sheena's cottage only to find it deserted. Sheena had left the island, taking the little lad with her.

Seething with fury, anguish, and the feeling that she had been deserted by both God and Peter, Eileen no longer listened to the voice inside her. She found herself marooned on Mull with her second baby. She remained isolated for four or five months with no one to speak to and no money. Fortunately, the village simpleton who had befriended her brought her potatoes and scraps from his own table.

Gradually, valiantly, Mum worked through her bitterness and was able to surrender it to her God. Then she *began to look for the good in everything and it was amazing to see what happened as I went through a complete change of consciousness.*[6] During this time, she realised how Peter had become her raison d'être, and that she had put him 'before God' by making *him* her god.

Finally, on Christmas Day, Caddy arrived on the island to collect her. He was clutching a chicken under his arm for their lunch. They left Mull on New Year's Day 1957, bound for Glasgow.

Dorothy Maclean had been Eileen's only other visitor on the island during those lonely months, and when Peter and Eileen arrived in Glasgow, they shared a tenement house with her and several others. Eileen and Dorothy both felt strongly that the three of them must stay close together *for our spiritual work* and that they would be *led to the land of milk and honey.*[7]

Notably, the spiritual work was to be 'ours' (as my mother wrote in her autobiography). The threesome had now become Peter, Eileen and Dorothy.

While in Glasgow Peter and Eileen decided to get married legally. (Sheena had performed a 'spiritual marriage', as high-priestess, in St Patrick's Chapel in Glastonbury some time before.) At this point, Sheena returned their older son to them and went off to Oban to gather her new disciples around her.

With Caddy's training in the Air Force as a caterer, and my mother's domestic science training, they were able to secure a post at Cluny Hill Hotel, Forres, owned by a large company which had 21 hotels. Peter, as hotel manager, employed Dorothy as his secretary and personal assistant. Tough though their first winter in the hotel proved to be, Cluny Hill did become their 'land of milk and honey', and they raised it from a three- to a four-star rating in five years. It was here that the Caddy's third son was born.

Following their success at Cluny Hill, they were moved on by the same company to manage the rather gloomy Trossachs Hotel in the Highlands. Although they ran the hotel on exactly the same principles, at the end of their first season there, they were sacked, with no reason given. They had asked for a transfer back to Cluny Hill, but now that door had been closed to them.

With only a small caravan for the six of them to live in (Dorothy was still with them), they towed it behind the Lagonda towards Lossiemouth, not knowing what their fate would be. All they had to rely on was a message from the voice to Eileen: *As you take one step at a time, you will find that things work out perfectly.* [8]

They found a caravan park near the fishing village of Findhorn, at the mouth of the River Findhorn, and drew in there to decide what must be done for the future. They decided to settle there and put down roots, and here they sowed the first seeds (both literally and metaphorically) of what was to become the Findhorn Garden. Thus began the first New Age community in Britain, now known as the Findhorn Foundation.

It would be Sheena's rebellious trainee Eileen, the third Mrs Caddy, who eventually stepped into her shoes (albeit reluctantly) to carry Sheena's work and vision forward in this way.

As Sheena had discovered, her thirst for knowledge of the occult could also generate authority and power. It was only when I read the findings of Wanda Marrs in her disturbing book *New Age Lies to Women*, that the significance of Sheena's 'divine triangle' made any sense. The concept appeared to have originated in Babylon several centuries before the Christian era, when the civilization of Babylonia (now central and southern Iraq) was at the height of its power. Wanda Marrs describes its advent in this manner:

Semiramis, Nimrod's queen, was clever and diabolical. She spread far and wide the doctrine that Nimrod had not died. He had merely gone on to a heavenly abode where he sat as God of Gods and Master of All – a man-deity worthy of mankind's devotion and worship. Semiramis' son (Ninus/Tammuz), who later became her incestual husband, was claimed to be the Son of God. This naturally made Semiramis herself the 'Mother of God'. This was the Satanic Trinity: Father, Mother, Son – the prime gods and goddess of a perverse universe. [9]

Here then an unholy trinity had arisen out of the evil character of Queen Semiramis of Babylon. Wanda Marrs places Queen Semiramis fairly and squarely in the Bible's final book, Revelation, where she can be found wearing the harlot's frontlet on her forehead bearing her name as 'Mystery Babylon the Great, Mother of Prostitutes and the Abominations of the Earth'.

Any exiled Jews living in Babylon at the time, would have been affected by her cruelty, and her belief so shockingly different from their own. Their familiarity with the background history of her infamous reign in the wealthiest and most powerful city in the known civilisation would have been borne back to their home country after their release years later. These memories were to remain in the Jewish collective consciousness for centuries.

The Holy Trinity was formed only after the advent and ministry of Jesus Christ, some 500 years later. Jesus talked and taught constantly of His Father in heaven, about Himself as God's Son, and finally, when He left earth, that His spiritual inheritance for all humanity was to be the Comforter, the Holy Spirit. This Holy Trinity was God's solution given to the Jews, to finally supplant the un-holy trinity of the 'mystery religion of Babylon'.

Writing around 90 AD, the prophet John, in chapter 17 of Revelation, describes the similarity of the 'mystery religion of Babylon' with what was taking place in the modern 'Babylon' of that time — Rome. Bible scholar and commentator Dr William Barclay calls this same period *the re-incarnation of evil caused by a series of cruel emperors of the Roman Empire.* [10]

For Sheena a 'divine triangle' became a 'must have'. I can only surmise that this idea had already taken root in her mind. Then, back in 1953, she may have realised its significance while in Glastonbury with Caddy and Eileen in that Upper Room by the Chalice Well. It was certainly one of the foundation stones of her dream.

She was most excited by the affirmation of my mother's 'guidance' from the voice. Certainly she accepted at once that Eileen's voice was paramount, and immediately put her under training as a channel to receive instructions several times daily. This was to become a discipline my mother followed for the rest of her life, and was the basis of her work with Caddy. In 2001 Channel 4's television 'God List' named Eileen as one of the fifty most spiritually influential people in Britain.

What then became of Sheena, the visionary, during the years that Peter, Eileen and Dorothy began to find their feet working together? News of her and her Nameless Ones found its way into the Scottish tabloids.

They had picked up the scandal that one of her devotees had left his wife and daughter in order to join Sheena. Then they became intrigued by her 'way out' teachings and lifestyle which took her from place to place.

She visited Caddy and Eileen only occasionally. Her power over them had waned. Though Peter still loved and worshipped her, he had come to accept – and Eileen had made it patently clear — that there was no room for both Sheena and Eileen, in equal measure, in his life any longer.

Part of the promise Eileen had first received in her message in Glastonbury: 'Trust me. All you do will be very closely linked with Sheena,' had begun to fade, though we know that Eileen's messages were always recorded, typed, and copies known as *The Light* were sent to Sheena's followers. (Scottish press, May 1957).

In one article, written by Liam Regan in the *Sunday Mail* on May 5th 1957, Sheena was reported as calling her disciples 'Children of the New Age.' It was this motley band of people, together with the founding of the Findhorn Community near Forres, that were destined to become forerunners of what became known as New Age. This movement was the full realisation of Sheena's eclectic beliefs, training and mystical vision.

However, she did not live to see her foundational efforts come to fruition. Ironically, she became entangled in her own web of deception and relationships, and was evicted from her little sect — along with the man-of-the-moment who had replaced Caddy in her life — on the grounds that she had broken 'her own rule about human love not interfering with religion.' (So said Mrs Astell, the aggrieved wife of Sheena's lover Fred Astell, to the *Sunday Mail*, 24th August, 1958.)

Her 'divinity' now besmirched, the poor deluded woman who had called herself 'the second Christ', and been hailed as 'Messiah' and 'Redeemer of Mankind' by Caddy and her followers, was hounded until her death by the consequences of her inconsistent lifestyle. The police hunted her for fraud; she was blackmailed by an ex-member of her sect into leaving a good post teaching music at Gordonstoun, one of the country's top public schools, and ended up living alone in a cottage with her white doves. She died of a brain tumour in 1967 at the age of 54. Apparently, there were nineteen mourners at the graveside, three of whom were her two brothers and her sister. It is said that not one of her followers was there to grieve her passing.

Yet Sheena's power did not die with her. Her networking and far-reaching influence lives on. We see evidence of it in every small corner of our society at this present moment. Her syncretic teachings echoed those of theosophist Madame Blavatsky in the nineteenth century, and were fired by the later writings of Alice Bailey (1880-1949). It is worth noting that Bailey claimed that her writings were telepathically dictated to her by her Tibetan spirit-guide Djwal Khul over thirty years.

Sheena's vision and ideas found an easy foothold in the aftermath of WW2, breathing fresh impetus into the pervading mood of despair and disillusion.

By 1980 Sheena's ex-husband Peter Caddy had left my mother and the Findhorn Foundation after 27 years and gone his own way, as we shall see. Of the three founders of the Community only Sheena's oldest friend, Dorothy, now survives — a Canadian in a Californian community, who still holds the baton and runs alongside the many who will run with her.

21

A Wolf in Sheep's Clothing

In the pride of your heart you say, 'I am a god; I sit on the throne of a god...' But you are a man and not a god, though you think you are as wise as a god.
Ezekiel 28:2

AS I write this chapter, I am acutely aware that it concerns the father of my three half brothers. Should they read this, I trust they will remember that my observations were made, and much of my knowledge of him gleaned, before they were born. I hope they will understand my limited perceptions of their father.

I have drawn extensively from his autobiography, as well as my mother's, and am indebted to author Paul Hawken for his more objective insights into Peter's character. This writer spent a year with the community in order to interview the inhabitants and to write his book.[1] Though some of his accounts differ from accounts of similar incidents given elsewhere (in my mother's autobiography, for example), his interviews with Peter provide many broad brush-strokes of the man's upbringing.

It was clear that my mother knew next to nothing about the man with whom she had decided so precipitously to throw in her lot. Following their flight together, her tenuous situation had been rubber-stamped by my father's refusal to allow his wife back into our family circle, thus unwittingly completing Caddy's total conquest.

From the moment he first entered our home in Habbaniya, I had taken an instinctive dislike to Peter Caddy as a person, not only because he later stole away our mother. My later forgiveness of him had been not only for what I regarded as his harmful action towards our family, but also for the man himself. Yet it was only as I dug deeper that I began to understand his background and the choices behind those actions.

I saw Peter as tanned, tall, athletic and good-looking. He could have passed off as a double for Pope John Paul II, though with a character and objectives poles apart from those of His Holiness. The word 'swashbuckler' comes to mind when I think of him. My dictionary defines this as a 'bold, dashing, adventurous, rather unscrupulous fighting man.'

It soon became plain to my mother that Peter was as complex a man as my father had been. Somewhere in her memoirs, she says she found she had jumped out of one frying pan into another. He was jaunty, self-confident and always purposeful. In describing the Valentinian Gnostics centuries earlier, Bishop Irenaeus wrote: 'If anyone yields himself to them like a little sheep, and follows out their practice and their *redemption,* such a person becomes so puffed up that...he walks with a strutting gait and a supercilious countenance, possessing the pompous air of a cock!' [2] Gnosticism was among his many beliefs, especially by the time Sheena had finished his six-year training.

One vivid personal memory of him was of his demonically fast driving, laughing behind the wheel of his Morris Minor Traveller. The Lagonda had long gone. On one occasion when I visited Findhorn, he took two of my half-brothers and me for a ride out into the forest. The car screeched round every corner on two wheels, lustily cheered on by his sons who loved every minute and thought it great sport. I could hardly breathe as I clung, petrified, to the front seat for all my life was worth. Eventually, we stopped at a beautiful spot by some rapids called Randolph's Leap, where we climbed over rocks to the middle of the swirling waters, and sat for a while. When I had regained some composure, I asked Peter whether he ever received his own guidance or did he rely on my mother's messages for his orders? His reply was that he 'always had guidance in action.' I understood this to mean it was *her* guidance he translated into action, not his own.

When Peter was ten, his father Frederick was suffering from suspected rheumatoid arthritis. As his doctor was unable to cure him, he sought help from a healer medium near his home in Ruislip, Middlesex, as a desperate last resort. Frederick Caddy was a staunch Methodist. He took his young son along to a 'spiritual healing' séance. Peter was fascinated when, at the first session, the medium called forth a North American Indian spirit called Silver Deer, from 'the other side'. She asked if anyone had a question to ask the spirit, and Peter piped up, 'How do I win my school boxing match tomorrow?' Silver Deer answered, 'Look him in the eye, and you will know when he is about to hit you!'

Next day, Peter put this instruction to the test, and won the school cup! He was hooked. As Hawken says, 'The ten-year-old boy, accepting the reality of Silver Deer without a doubt, stepped across the 'border' and experienced the birth of a pre-adolescent occultism that was of the most pragmatic and down-to-earth nature.'[3] His father, however, failing to find healing in this direction, returned to his GP who diagnosed kidney stones, the removal of which freed him from pain.

As Peter grew up, strong in physique and will, he remained impervious to his father's fervent Methodism. The harm had already been done. The excitement and magnetism of the occult had taken hold. Caddy frequently spoke of God and of his own life being integral in God's plan for the world, but his steps led him away from the true God into different types of mysticism, as had happened to Sheena. He had been set on course by a dead spirit-guide. How devastated his father must have been to watch the chosen way of his son, knowing he had been responsible for that choice.

At seventeen, Peter took up a five-year catering apprenticeship with J. Lyons & Co. Ltd. He learned most facets of the trade in the kitchens of the Regent Palace Hotel in London, during the course of which he was introduced to the Rosicrucians through his future brother-in-law. He also put himself under the tutelage of Dr Sullivan of the Crotona Fellowship where his interest in all things occultic flourished.

Walter Martin, in his book *The Kingdom of the Cults* says of this secret brotherhood that: 'In fact, there is very little that Rosicrucianism does not seek to enfold within its mythological-magical lore, *yet everything Christian that it touches suffers violence at its hands.* (Italics mine.) 'Most always, the average reader is confused by the fact that Rosicrucian terminology and concepts do have a distinct Christian flavour and sound. But somehow or other, the taste is distinctly different!'[4] So we begin to understand why Christian terminology used by Peter and Sheena, which proved so deceptive to my mother, had no actual Christian truth-base or significance.

Caddy believed in 'divine economy,' a concept whereby there could be no admission of any mistakes in his life, because, as he later explained to me, everything he did was part of 'God's will', and so everything that happened to him, or through him was a part of it. It appeared to me that, in the wake of his actions, others were left to figure out the divine reasoning behind them.

Hawken recounts that Caddy was twenty-two when the Second World War began, and joined the Royal Air Force catering branch as an officer. Dr Sullivan's parting shot to him had been: 'All will be well, but volunteer for nothing,' and he never did. His job and extensive social pursuits throughout the war, which earned him the name of 'playboy of the East' by some, kept him well away from any fighting.

Instead he 'charmed his way right up the pecking order as well as the necking one' with a 'carte blanche ticket...to dances, tennis, swimming, mountaineering, pony trekking, and chances that no boy from Ruislip could turn down', writes Hawken.

He used all the facilities the Air Force could offer him, and enjoyed himself enormously. He took every chance he could to 'delve into places ancient and esoteric in order to further the Training'.[5] He had learned the 'law of cause and effect, where Will merges with Imagination to form the Idea which in the Mind becomes Desire and finally Physical Reality'[6] and he was keen to put this theory to the test.

By this time, Caddy had married Nora. His Rosicrucian brother-in-law, Jim Barnes, had once advised him that 'it took lifetimes of evolution to become a 'realised' man.' When Peter asked whether it could be done in one lifetime his reply was that it was impossibly difficult, to which Peter replied, 'I am *going* to do it in one!' He dedicated himself to this aim: to becoming 'a man totally and completely dedicated to bringing God's Plan into being on Earth. Because he knew he was to be a channel for God's will, he had to perfect himself in body and mind.'[7] He used his ideas to good effect when feeding a million troops, running many miles in hot sun daily, and undertaking arduous climbs in the Himalayas.

'As the ultimate test of both will and body,' writes Hawken, 'Peter organised an expedition to Tibet at the end of the war.' He wished to visit Buddhist Tibet because he thought of it as 'the ancient capital of a world spiritual civilization...the highest reflection of a God-state on earth.'[8] After ten gruelling days of rigorous climatic conditions and feats of physical endurance, Peter and his expedition team had covered the three hundred miles to Gyantse and on to the Rarkor Choide Monastery itself. This monastery was the last one where the Dalai Lama took refuge on his flight from Tibet. Peter claimed that his was the last European expedition, in the late 1940s, permitted before the Chinese began their invasion of Tibet in 1949.

Only a few days after he returned to England, Peter and Sheena met, and his personal search took a new twist. He learned from Sheena to turn inwards to look for the divine, where before his training had been to develop 'through action ... authority and will.'[9] Now, for love of this woman, he went through a 'period of initiation', during which she used mental and spiritual exercises to humble and tame him. Eventually he became a surrendered human being at the feet of his high-priestess. In his own words, he ended up realising: 'One is nothing. The personality is crucified, and the darkness descends. And then comes the fifth initiation, the resurrection and ascension, *when one realises My Father and I are one.*'[10] (Again, following along Christian lines, but resulting in a man who believed he was, like the biblical Lucifer, 'as God Himself'.)

From the original research sent to my father I learned more about Peter's 'master' in occult lore. This was the man calling himself Aureolis, alias Rana, alias Arthur Knight, the actor who was touring with a theatrical company on the South coast. Aureolis claimed necro-mantic succession from the mysterious Comte de Germain whose putative parent had been Prince Roxozci of Transylvania (the latter is probably meant to be Prince Ragoczy of Transylvania). Caddy claimed that through him he 'attained to the 7th Raz', and that while Caddy was still living in Devon, he was chosen as the inheritor of the magic ring of the last high priest of the lost city of Atlantis. This gave him pre-eminence in the occult world, and endowed him with enormous supernatural powers.

In 1957, Caddy told Liam Regan who was reporting for the Scottish *Sunday Mail*, that in marrying Sheena, he: 'gave up all for love of her... You see, nothing is ordinary about Sheena. We were very well suited to one another, but spiritually, I was like a little child to her. It was soon after marrying Sheena that I realised she was the World Teacher.'

He believed his wife Sheena was being prepared for the work of Redeemer of Mankind. Regan recounts Caddy's words, pointing out that Caddy was being spiritually guided by Sheena at the time: 'During our married life Sheena was in the final stages of this preparation, and the strain on her physical and nervous system was very intense. My role was to protect her, to look after her and to give her stability.'

The article, under the heading, A Big Blow, continues: 'Caddy was in the Middle East when a letter came out of the blue. The letter was from Sheena. She wrote saying she realised their relationship could no longer be that of man and wife although there would always be a great bond between them. 'That was a tremendous blow to me,' said Caddy, 'but I knew that whatever she said was the truth. When I received this letter and knew that Sheena was not my soul-mate, I also knew that God would bring me into touch with my future other half.'

Earlier, Caddy had told the reporter, 'Sheena, the woman, longed for a baby but no child was born to them. There were several miscarriages. The forces of good were being attacked by the forces of darkness and evil,' said Caddy. 'They pitted everything against her and prevented her having a baby... Although I was happy with Sheena, it was not easy to be married to perfection, to someone who is always right.'

Some weeks after he first met Eileen, Caddy was stationed in Palestine and walked to the top of a hill overlooking Jerusalem. We will let him tell the story as related to the reporter: 'Some inner voice told me that Eileen was my 'other half' and our future lay together. I thought that this was ridiculous. 'Why', I told myself, 'she is married and has five children, and I don't even love her.'

The article continues: 'Caddy spoke to Eileen and told her of his climb to the mountain top and of the voice. Eileen replied: 'If this is God's will, He will bring it about, and there is nothing you or I can do about it.' (This remark discloses a marked change in my mother's attitude towards Peter by then, as previously she had not encouraged his advances in any way.)

'There was at that moment a 'one-ness' or 'one-ment' between our souls, but it was not on the physical level,' said Caddy.

The next headline in the article reads 'Fate Saw them All on the Same Plane'. Fate? I think not. Anyway, Caddy was there waiting on the airfield in Tripoli, ready to meet our flight home to the United Kingdom in August, 1953. He knew my father had remained in Iraq till the completion of his tour and was due home in October.

For Peter, Eileen's spirituality was magnetic, electrifying, fascinating. Moreover, he found that in winning her he faced a challenge to be wrestled with, and he was by then raring for the match. Every ounce of personal charm and allure was focused on this prize to be won. The 'power' began to work. He gives a full account in his autobiography *In Perfect Timing*... pp. 110 to 111.

At this moment it would be hard to analyse which force was the stronger — the age-old sexual drive, so expertly cloaked by the deeply spiritual charade being played out by Caddy, or the diabolical power being beamed by his actual wife's will and vibrations. Sheena was the puppeteer. Probably both forces formed a pincer movement to produce the final required result. In the same newspaper article, Caddy admits that he 'kept Sheena fully informed of every development of his friendship with Eileen'.

It was careful planning, not fate, that used the occasion of Eileen's 35th birthday celebration, when Sheena's diplomatic migraine prevented her from joining them for dinner and the theatre. And celebrate they did. After the show, Peter drove Eileen back from London to Cheam, and stayed the night — in my parents' bed.

'That was the night they realised they were twin souls,' wrote the same reporter. Peter obligingly explained: 'You see, Eileen knew by this time that we were two halves of a single whole, and that our future must be together.'

Liam Regan zoomed in with one final searching question: 'What made you give up all for love of Sheena and then give up Sheena for another woman?'

Caddy's reply, immediate and extraordinary, shifted the searchlight away from himself and back on to Sheena: 'Either she (Sheena) is the devil and is evil, and moves people about like pawns, or she is not. I say she is NOT. It must be something else. It is simply the power of love. It is simply giving up all for her, so that she and God come first in our lives... We who believe have something which everybody seeks — that is happiness, joy, the teachings of Sheena.'

Although by 1957, when this article appeared, Sheena was away forming her own sect, both Caddy and Eileen declared that they believed Sheena to be divine. She was a 'revelation of divine love', as he put it – 'perfect in the eyes of God... Everything she does is for others without regard to herself.' Sheena had by then adopted the principles of poverty which Jesus had encouraged in his own disciples.

Throughout this interview in 1957, Eileen sat across the table, and endorsed every word Caddy uttered. The same story was told by themselves, rather differently, in *The Magic of Findhorn*, elaborately embroidered by author Paul Hawken. The differing facts throw doubt on the truth of some of those given in the article. It would appear that Eileen did not remember the facts too clearly either. Did it really matter, since the purpose of the article was to take their story into the public domain in order to propagate their work together?

To backtrack four years to the original incident in Glastonbury, part of the message Eileen had received then was: 'You and Peter have a tremendous future together. Trust me. All you do will be very closely linked with Sheena.' When the 'triangle' had become Eileen and Caddy, with Dorothy Maclean, who were attempting to implement in their hotel employment the principles in which they believed, they found these were not always acceptable to the owners of the hotel chain. In his autobiography, Caddy explains that while they were at the Cluny Hill Hotel, he had put his passionate belief in UFOs and aliens into practice by clearing a landing pad for 'flying sauce-boats' (as he called them in his autobiography). This was on a hill behind the hotel. With others, he was trying to make contact with other-planet beings, and preparing for their advent.

Back in 1950, he had submitted a paper to the Air Ministry on this subject, but the article he wrote for the newspapers during their time at the Cluny caused quite a stir, and the subsequent publicity did not go down well with the hotel's proprietors.

After they had been moved to the Trossachs Hotel in the Highlands, Sheena was always hovering in the background, which was unsettling for my mother. Finally, Eileen felt impelled to give Caddy an ultimatum: he must choose between Sheena and herself. Although Caddy's loyalty to Sheena never wavered, and he continued to act on her behalf as her agent, she did not visit them again, as far as I know. He had made his choice.

Apart from this, the hotel seemed to be jinxed, and the staff were unhappy. However hard they tried, an oppressive cloud hung over the place. Then Caddy was asked to leave this position, and rumours of mismanagement were voiced, but never, to my knowledge, substantiated. They were given four hours to pack up and leave.

It was at this low time in their lives that they dragged their little green caravan up from the beach at Findhorn, onto a nearby caravan site between the village of Findhorn and town of Forres on the Moray Firth. With no work, a doubtful reputation, three boys to educate, and living in cramped conditions, life did not look in the least promising. Their Canadian friend Dorothy Maclean was part of the family, and Peter built a small extension on to the caravan as extra accommodation.

The break with Sheena released new energy in Peter and Eileen, and when they settled in the caravan park, they and Dorothy combined all their energies and creative powers to transform a veritable dump around them into a productive area, in order to become self-sufficient. Gradually, people who were attracted by their lifestyle began to move into caravans around them, and an embryo community took shape. My mother was its visionary and spiritual guide, Dorothy the 'spiritual' gardener, and Peter the muscle and brawn behind the creating of what became known as the Findhorn Garden.

Numbers of hippies and drop-outs from society chose to flock to the site in the sixties and seventies, in search of an alternative way to live. Every one of them was put to work, but not all were prepared to put in the hard work necessary to create this new community. Caddy soon sorted out the drones from the workers, and acted as community bouncer.

Meanwhile, the inhabitants of Findhorn village and the country town of Forres watched this strange mushroom growing on their doorstep, and viewed all the proceedings there with increasing suspicion. The sleepy little caravan park fast developed into a hive of building activity. Understandably, the village residents felt threatened and rumours were abounding.

One of the earlier visitors, David Marshall, wrote in his book *New Age versus The Gospel*, 'When I first visited it in 1980 to conduct interviews, the atmosphere of evil had almost been palpable... I had witnessed examples of 'psychic intuition'. The place had seemed to be densely populated with hippy-types of various ages, some of whom I had thought at the time were either under the influence of drugs or actually mind-controlled by the spirits, even as I spoke to them.' [11]

Another frequent visitor to Findhorn, whom David Marshall interviewed later for his book, was Lancashire born Will Baron. As a New Age priest at the time, Baron had advanced from learning 'primal therapy' to 'feeling therapy' in California, and had heard that all kinds of courses from the teachings of the most fashionable (living) guru to channeling dead 'masters' were to be found at Findhorn. On a second visit, Baron had gone to enrol and train in how to infiltrate Christian congregations, because (as he said later): 'Findhorn provides training in all types of psychic healing and occult involvement. It also provides basic training in Christian theology, jargon and methodology...' [12] He lived there for six months.

Will Baron eventually became a Christian through reading Christian literature and the Book of Revelation in the Bible. He had praying parents. He wrote of his experiences in *Deceived by the New Age: the story of a New Age Priest*, described by David Marshall as 'without question, the most successful book against New Age written from a Christian perspective.'

It is little wonder, then, that the local inhabitants in that area of Scotland felt threatened and disturbed by the growth of the Foundation, given the evidence of these and other discerning visitors.

During the years that followed, Caddy came into his own. Much of the growth within the Findhorn Community was due to his incredible energy and force of character on the one hand, always steered by the visions and spiritual power radiating from Eileen on the other. The seeds of thought and vision which Sheena had sown in Caddy, in Dorothy — always her faithful disciple — and then in Eileen during her rebellious training, began to grow, or manifest themselves, under the 'divine guidance' of Eileen, followed up by the human dynamism of Peter, and Dorothy's link with the world of nature spirits, or divas. Around the caravan and those of others who gradually came to join them, sprang up park home

1962 — The green caravan at Findhorn: Dorothy Maclean and Eileen

Peter & Eileen Caddy

Sheena Govan Caddy with baby Christopher

Richard's first visit to Findhorn

Eileen with her three sons Christopher, Jonathan & David

Jenny's first visit to Findhorn and the Caddy family, 1969

Leone Exton Beale whose home in London was for ten years a safe haven for myself and, at times, my siblings.

Mum's 70th Birthday, 1989 with Combes and Jessops

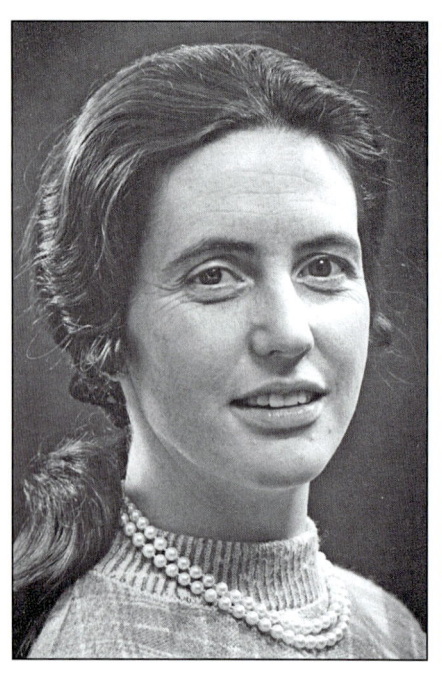

Jenny and Peter at the time of their engagement

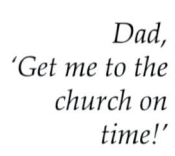

Dad, 'Get me to the church on time!'

Our wedding, 2nd December 1972
Rachel, Jennie, Barry (Best Man), us, Dorien & Jane

Eileen, Jenny, our daughter Georgina (with son Javier), and our son Andrew

*On the eve of Penny's wedding in New Zealand, 2nd April 2010
L to R: Helen & Richard, Penny, Suzanne, Jenny & Peter, Mary Liz & husband Bruce*

A visit to Mum in April 2000 for my birthday

Mum's MBE for 'Services to spiritual inquiry' invested by Air Vice Marshal George Chesworth, Lord Lieutenant of Moray, in 2003

Mum, celebrating her 80th, with all her eight children: David, Jonathan, Christopher, Richard, Penny, Mum, Mary Liz, Jenny, and Suzanne (on the ground)

Eileen's 80th Birthday celebrations at the Old Cowshed in 1997 brought the Caddy and Combe families together

bungalows surrounded by paved paths, lawns, patios, and colourful herbaceous borders.

Incredibly, the Findhorn Garden, created as it was on sandy soil just inland from the sand dunes along the coastline near the river mouth, continued to flourish. Much of Peter's energy was ploughed, literally, into the ground: seaweed collected from the beaches and leaf-mould gathered from the forest floors nearby were dug in to the sand to enrich the poor soil. The aim was to supply produce for a self-supporting community. He worked closely with Dorothy Maclean who had developed a peculiar sensitivity to plant-life and nature, and who received messages about the garden from her 'divas'. Together they began one of the earliest developments in organic gardening. This intrigued and astonished plant and soil experts who began to visit them in order to find out how they achieved such amazing results out of sand, in that exposed, wind-swept part of Scotland.

The success of the carefully tended borders and abundant vegetable plots put the community on the map. It became the subject of several television programmes and radio broadcasts. These, in turn, provided a perfect platform from which to talk about the principles, lifestyle and teachings behind the garden's beauty and productivity. Thus the Findhorn community began its real work — to train each of its growing number of visitors in the eclectic philosophies which come under the title 'New Age'.

Behind the scenes, but more often centre-stage, Caddy tirelessly endeavoured to translate these concepts into mind- and soul-grabbing reality. His persistence in pursuing leads with some of the influential men and women in this country from all walks of life proved him to be a capable roving ambassador for Findhorn. He visited other countries and encouraged the cross-fertilisation of groups and ideas, particularly in the United States, Northern Ireland, New Zealand and Japan.

Thanks to the detailed research of attorney Constance Cumbey, in her book *Hidden Dangers of the Rainbow*, we know that Peter served on the board of the Planetary Citizens organisation, together with leading New Age philosopher David Spangler. He was also on the advisory board of the New Age Unity-in-Diversity Council, of which the Foundation is a member, along with Robert Muller (ex-Deputy Secretary of the UN), Swami Kryananda and others.

Caddy's frequent absences increased, leaving Eileen to bring up their three sons on her own, as well as caring for her community family. The boys were attending Forres Academy, and benefitted from the friendship of the community members for their outdoor pursuits of sailing, hill-walking and mountaineering. One who enjoyed their company was a teacher who filled in for their father as a surrogate parent, and contributed much to developing these skills.

Oddly, as the Findhorn Foundation project began to demand more buildings, more land, and gain greater prestige, Peter's enthusiasm for the Foundation was already on the wane. He gradually drew away from Eileen, and turned his attentions to a young American girl with whom he fell madly in love. But it seems that she was devoted to my mother, and mature enough to realise that a relationship with Peter could not survive in the context of a community. Later, during one of his frequent journeys abroad, he met a 47 year old Californian woman, Shari Secot.

In 1979, just after the community's 17th anniversary of its founding, another newspaper article reported that, in true swashbuckling style, Caddy had called together the community and informed them it was time for him to leave and allow the community to grow up, and that incidentally he was leaving Eileen. He announced he was going on a world tour to visit all the followers of Findhorn, but in fact ended up in Hawaii where he took a long break with Shari Secot to recover his health.

According to an article entitled 'Marriage of Love and Light is Over', written in the Scottish newspaper *Daily Record* in mid-August 1980 nearly a year after this crisis occurred, Caddy is purported to have finally taken off on his 'world-wide lecture career.'

The public announcement of his intentions had sent initial shock-waves throughout the several hundred community residents. After twenty-seven years of partnership, his rather typical approach to cutting ties with the community, and his wife, left my mother in a state of shock and grief amongst the shattered fragments of their once-so-spiritual 'eternal inseparability'. She underwent a long, dark, emotional period during which her sister told me she had taken to the bottle.

Remarkably, Eileen eventually found the inner resources and strength to forgive Peter for his infidelity, and, in time, his future new partners. She summoned up grace enough to visit Shari in Hawaii to try to mend their strained relationship. Despite a broken heart and the humiliation of her position, she and Shari became friends.

Caddy returned to Findhorn again in October 1982 for the 20th anniversary of the founding of the community. The Findhorn Foundation was being run by a council of management which had encountered no difficulties in continuing much as before. Eileen was living at its centre as their guru and inspiration, though now solely as an observer by her own choice. Caddy by then had been 'guided' to leave Shari in Hawaii, and had gone on to marry his fourth wife, Paula McLaughlin, in June 1982. He was in his late sixties when a son was born to them in December 1982.

The next eleven years of Peter's life were spent mainly in Germany. These years have been chronicled in detail by himself, together with his co-author Jeremy Slocombe and, finally, his fifth wife Renata, in his autobiography: *In Perfect Timing. Memoirs of A Man for the Millennium.*

While we were living in Spain, my mother called us in February 1994, to tell us that Peter had just been killed in a car accident. He was 76. He had been to collect his American son from the airport in Germany, when a lorry veered out of a side road and hit the car. His son survived the crash with injuries and concussion; Caddy's biographer, Jeremy Slocombe, also in the car with him, suffered a broken arm and trauma. Peter himself died half an hour later in hospital.

This was shattering news, and Mum's voice broke down as she explained, *'You cannot live twenty seven years with a man like Peter* (whom she had loved so deeply and loyally), *and not feel profoundly shocked by his death.'*

As I replaced the phone, all I could remember of Caddy at that moment were the two terrifying car rides with him. In the light of those memories, the news of his end in a car crash did not come entirely as a surprise. I could not help but imagine that, had he been able to determine his method of dispatch from this life to the next, he might well have chosen that it should be from behind a steering wheel.

22

Against Thy Divine Majesty

Paradigm Shift and Quantum Leap Explained

This is your hour and the power of darkness.
Luke 22:53
*...for we have made lies our refuge, and under falsehood have we hid ourselves...*Isaiah 28:15

RICHARD and Connie Smith had bidden me always 'to look at the teaching behind any idea or belief.' In so doing, I needed to draw on the wisdom of past and present sages in order to be able to discern truth from falsehood or half-truths; genuine faith from the often perilously close resemblance of its counterfeit opponent.

By now, I had studied several authors' writings on the subject of New Age. Particularly enlightening were the carefully investigated and documented findings of attorney Constance E. Cumbey in *Hidden Dangers of the Rainbow*,[1] as well as Randall Baer's *Inside the New Age Nightmare*.[2]

The dangers of my pursuit became evident when I learned that Randall Baer, whose book had just been published, had shortly afterwards killed himself by driving his car over a cliff. This shocking news emphasised the strength of the spiritual grip on a man's soul from those dark 'powers and principalities in the heavenly realms' which will not relinquish their hold without a fight. (In his letter to the Ephesians, Paul warned against such spiritual entities, and the need to seek spiritual protection by putting on 'the full armour of God.' Eph.6:10 *et seq*).

From the experiences of the above two writers, and the third, Johanna Michaelsen in *The Beautiful Side of Evil*,[3] I began to learn something of spiritual dynamics: not only the power of seduction, but the mechanics of mind control techniques with their distortions of the psyche, which must have been at work to capture and enmesh my mother.

Two phrases, or buzz words, kept recurring in these writings: paradigm shift, and quantum leap. Resorting to Chambers dictionary yet again, 'a paradigm is a basic theory, a conceptual framework within which scientific theories are constructed.' Hence, a *paradigm shift* is a sideways movement into a *different conceptual framework.*

The second buzz-phrase, *quantum leap*, was the result of scientist Max Planck's theory on 'the emission and absorption of energy, not continuously but in finite steps' which he called the Quantum Theory. Chambers defined a *quantum jump* or *leap* as 'the sudden transition of an electron, atom, etc. from one energy state to another: a sudden spectacular advance'.

When applied in my mother's case, the evidence of these two concepts was all too apparent. At the beginning of her relationship with the Caddys, she was a ripe plum ready for their picking, as all her traditional ideas of home, marriage and Christian values had been shattered by her adulterous affair with Caddy. Through the state of 'being in love for the first time in my life,' she had been lured away from home and family by her love for Peter Caddy, and then found the front door of her home slammed in her face by her husband, with the words ringing in her ears that she was not fit to be the children's mother. Her *conceptual framework* was upturned, and in chaos. There could be no return. The Caddys had made an all-out attempt to sacrifice her Christian conscience on the altar of their pagan beliefs, and succeeded.

The visit to Glastonbury was a desperate move by them to quieten her mind. As she sat there in the Upper Room at the Chalice Well with Peter and Sheena, the words from Psalm 46 came into her head. She had known the words since childhood: 'Be still and know that I am God.' She had often sought comfort from such words to guide her along the difficult path of family life. Here again was the old familiar inner prompting from memory, to soothe her deep anxieties and fears.

She would have had no inkling, that fateful day, of the counter spiritual energy being generated in that room by the Caddys during her meditation. It was as though, hiding in nearby shadows whispering those words, stood the Arch Deceiver, awaiting the chosen time to turn this moment to his advantage. He now stepped into her psyche, replacing the rest of the verse from Psalm 42 – 'I will be exalted among the heathen, I will be exalted in the earth' — with his own rendering of the age-old promise, of which Peter Caddy wrote later: 'The voice went on:

You have taken a very big step in your life, but if you follow My voice, all will be well. I have brought you and Peter together for a very special purpose, to do specific work for Me. You will work as one, and you will realize this more fully as time goes on. There are few who have been brought together in this way. Don't be afraid, for I am with you.[4]

The familiarity of 'the voice' had not changed, but Eileen was considerably shaken by the import of its message and thought she was going mad. She was in no condition to perceive that her whole known concept of God had *shifted* in that moment, swiftly side-stepping her into a new spiritual field, or *conceptual framework*.

This *sudden spectacular advance* through Eileen's voice-over experience, was exactly what the combined Caddy-force had been looking and waiting for. They interpreted it as complete confirmation of their Plan in choosing Eileen as Peter's 'other half'. They had been spot on target with her spiritual sensitivity.

The *Encyclopaedia of Occultism and Parapsychology* states: 'The essential qualification of a medium is an abnormal sensitiveness, which enables him or her to be readily 'controlled' by disembodied spirits.'[5]

Of course, none of this was apparent to mother as she left the welcome silence of the Upper Room and told what she had heard to the Caddys. They latched on at once, recognizing her 'voice' as a potential power-source of spiritual guidance. Before she had time to evaluate what was afoot, with one on either side, they figuratively, took an arm each and frog-marched my mother into another spiritual realm where she was a total stranger but in which they were perfectly at ease.

'When Eileen shared these words with Sheena and me,' recounts Caddy, in a chapter aptly titled 'Footprints Off the Path'... 'we were both thrilled for her... From then on she began to receive daily messages from this inner voice of the God within; with (sometimes severe) encouragement from Sheena, she gradually came to accept it. This was the clear source that was to guide us step by step along a very difficult and intricate path.'[6]

That seemingly small incident in the upstairs room of a retreat house may not seem significant in itself. In the spiritual world, however, it must have been like a Rift Valley shift in the earth's crust, altering its contours. During Mum's upbringing there had been No-Go areas in her beliefs, into which the scriptures clearly warned not to wander — necromancy, divination, interpreting omens, engaging in witchcraft and casting of spells, consulting mediums or spiritists. But she had come under new management from a 'god within', or her 'higher consciousness' as Sheena would have recognised immediately. In this spirit world, other spirits were free to guide her now, sometimes gently, sometimes more forcibly, but always *away from* any influence central to her Christian belief.

Back then in 1953/4, given Eileen's state of mental and emotional upheaval, I would imagine she never knew she had stepped into another domain, under a different ruler already well known by the Caddys. Here that fallen angel of light, Lucifer — best recognised in the Bible as Prince of this World — reigned supreme. (Lucifer's name was to recur many times in later years when one of his prime advocates and promoters, David Spangler, visited Findhorn in the early 70s.)

For Eileen there were few, if any, recognisable landmarks in this new spirit-led world. It did not belong to the God she had known though she recognised some of the language, for much of the phraseology used by Sheena sounded familiar. Otherwise, where sure paths and moral fences had stretched securely before her, there were now gaping holes. Only gradually did she grasp the changes in her thinking and also in her circumstances. With the Caddys as guardians, teachers and interpreters of this strange limbo-land into which she had been catapulted, she had unwittingly performed an almighty *quantum leap* into the unknown.

While Caddy resumed his Air Force career, and became more elusive, he appointed Sheena, his own teacher, to train up the new recruit. As Sheena's stranglehold tightened, she used emotional blackmail to discipline my mother, who wrote of this time:

Finally the sickening reality would hit me again: If I left here, Sheena would make absolutely certain that I never saw Peter again. I couldn't stand that, not after all I'd been through to be with him. I daren't do anything that would cause me to lose him... So I gave Sheena complete power over me... [7]

She was expected to be on duty twenty-four hours a day, acting as Sheena's carer through her sporadic illnesses, to be perfect in all she did for her, always punctual for her 'listening' sessions three times a day, and punctilious in writing out every message or vision and relaying them to Sheena.

I'm certain now that it was my resistance to everything that made it so painful. One time I was so overwrought that my right arm became paralysed for over a week... Another time I had a vivid dream from which I awoke crying. I dreamt that pus was flowing out of my mouth and I was in great pain...three days later a boil swelled up in my mouth and after about a week it burst and the pus flowed out, just as it did in my dream. [8]

In 1954, when she was neither married to Caddy nor divorced from my father, she found she was pregnant. Her child would be illegitimate. This fact further compounded her agony of mind. She was at her wit's end to know how to cope. She wrote: *At that time, in the mid-1950s having a baby out of wedlock was the ultimate crime against decent society. And a divorce from Andrew was still a long way off... My thoughts kept turning to the Ten Commandments. The word 'adultery' plagued me. The voice said I was doing the right thing, but how* could *all be well?'* [9]

The publication of Caddy's memoirs in 1996 helped put in place a number of missing pieces in the jig-saw of Eileen's life. One piece was that resourceful Sheena saw Eileen's pregnancy as a chance to claim a 'spiritual child' of her own, and arranged a second visit to Glastonbury in October 1954, in order to get Peter and Eileen 'wed'. This would also help progress her own agenda.

The threesome visited St Patrick's Chapel, standing among towering ruins in the hallowed and ancient grounds of Glastonbury Abbey. In Caddy's words: 'Sheena performed a spiritual marriage for us; in the same chapel, Eileen received in meditation *'His name shall be Christopher Michael,'* so we knew that the baby would be a boy!' [10]

So it was here in this small chapel that self-appointed priestess Sheena exchanged the small gold band from my parents' marriage, for a strange band worked in silver with a black serpent etched on it.

Only a year later, when we joined our mother at my uncle's cottage in Reading for the summer holidays, under the happy misapprehension that she had returned to us once more, I noticed this ring on her finger.[11] We were not to know that even then the Caddy-force were plotting other plans for her, which did *not* include her first family.

What we also did not know at the time of Mum's return to us in 1955 was that Sheena had abducted Caddy and Mum's first son, born in her flat in 1954, under the pretext that Eileen 'was not fit to be his mother,' echoing the exact words thrown at her by my father after she had left us. Sheena's insatiable desire for ever more knowledge of the 'divine' combined with jealousy of Eileen's love for Peter, drove her on ruthlessly. I believe these were the prime factors which had spurred her in her rigorous training and indoctrination of her protégée.

What my mother would not have known either, was that she was being used by Sheena who had been unable to produce a child of her own due to a miscarriage. Sheena stole the baby as part of the Plan to advance her spiritual power, towards fulfilling her vision for the new age. She had earlier become involved in a brief but bizarre affair with a friend of Peter's and herself, one Walter Bullock, who had become the Supreme Magus of the Rosicrucian Order Crotona Fellowship. Bullock was convinced he should be the father of the next Messiah, and that Sheena was to be the mother – an unhappy trial for all three parties, which ended in an ectopic pregnancy and thus no birth of the next 'messiah'.

Sheena's extraordinary measures came sickeningly close to destroying Eileen altogether. Driven to total distraction by Sheena's handling of both Peter and their child, she chose suicide as the only avenue of escape from Sheena's clutches. Thanks only to my uncle's timely visit, she had been saved.

Following the Caddys' retrieval of our unhappy mother from her brother's farm, she was given back her baby for a short while, but for the first two years of his life, the little boy was shuttled back and forth between Sheena, regarding herself as his 'spiritual' and therefore rightful mother, and his biological parents.

In all the turmoil of these events, I would claim it was largely due to my mother's innate stubbornness and Irish rebelliousness that Sheena failed to mould her grudging trainee into the type of ascetic, divine oracle the Caddys hoped Eileen would become. It is also something of a wonder how she had the strength of mind and character to survive at all in the pit they had dug for her existence.

Some years later, after reading the words by exspiritualist author Raphael Gasson, I recalled some of Sheena's efforts at indoctrinating me in Nonsuch Park with ideas about Caddy and my mother being twin souls, about free love and that theirs was the uniting of two beings from different planets. As a family, we had seen the stark truth of Gasson's words.

It seems as though a calculated stratagem to make Eileen 'give up everything for God' had been set in motion by the combined Caddy-force, which demanded that any parental ties with her first family *must* be eradicated totally from her conscience and memory for her to operate effectively in her new role as a medium – a scheme which, happily for us, proved unsuccessful in the long term. Therefore, we too had been caught up as victims in the *paradigm shift* engineered by Sheena who was co-operating (as I now realised) with the 'divine guidance' of 'other' spirits. Thus mother was forced into making the *quantum leap* which divided us from her, once and for all... or so Sheena hoped. The fact remained that Mum disappeared out of our lives for many years to come.

In the long run, such a callously diabolical notion was bound to fail. Surely the victorious power of the Holy Spirit through Christ's death and resurrection must always prevail over such schemes. Eventually, Sheena's philosophy within the cult of her later disciples, The Nameless Ones which she led as their 'female messiah' (Caddy's words), also took a nose-dive into oblivion. Her self-sought (or perhaps 'spirit-appointed'?) divinity foundered on human fallibility when she failed to apply her spirit-guided teachings to her own behaviour.

Sheena may have died a lonely and broken woman in 1967, but long before then she had secured the eventual outcome of her dream by handing on the baton of responsibility for a new age to her ex-husband and my mother.

23

A Bucketful of Frogs

It is the contention of this writer that for the first time in history there is a viable movement... that truly meets all the scriptural requirements for the antichrist and the political movement that will bring him on the world scene.
Hidden Dangers of the Rainbow — Constance E. Cumbey

Truth is incontrovertible. Panic may resent it; ignorance may deride it; malice may distort it. But there it is.
Winston S. Churchill

IN the forty-eight years following Mum's 'conversion', the out-rippling of those seemingly insignificant events in Glastonbury, followed by the Caddys' obedience to their fresh power-source in Eileen's 'messages', had a subliminal effect on educated thinking globally.

Although as time went on Eileen reverted to some of her earlier Christian beliefs, her principle of tolerance meant attempting to weave them in amongst the ideas of Hinduism, Buddhism and Theosophy she had learned about from Sheena and through travelling. Presumably, everyone had to feel comfortable, so though those Christian tenets became blurred and diluted, they still popped up in her teachings, along with phrases such as Christ-consciousness, the Mary Ray (the vibrations emanating from the figure of Mary, mother of Jesus), and the ever-present 'unconditional love'. My three brothers, who grew up in the community, have admitted in my hearing, 'Mum is confused'.

A very few noticed the gradual changes being wrought by Findhorn teachings. When we were in Northern Ireland in 1973/4, a visiting author, journalist and broadcaster gave a talk in Belfast Cathedral about the start of his own change after meeting Mother Teresa in Calcutta. As we walked out of the building later, his author wife and I met. During our conversation she described society as being like a bucketful of frogs. The water in the bucket was being slowly heated and the frogs did not realise it. But if one frog was dropped into that same temperature, it would hit the surface and leap out.

At the time, I did not fully grasp her meaning. However, thanks to the timely enlightenment from the Smiths, while studying the subject of my mother's work, I realised how those insights related to modernism in every-day life.

Working in the international school in Spain, I had seen for myself how children's minds were being put under assault through their reading matter, and through the countless animated films then rife on Spanish children's television — films mainly produced in Japan for the European market. Innocent young minds were being initiated subconsciously into an ever-heightened tolerance of evil. The name of just one of the creatures who featured often in the Spanish films was a skeletal figure called Primaeval, who ruled over several demonic entities with various powers. Demons appeared to be the 'in' thing.

If the media were to be believed, established religion was fast on the wane; a heresy was circulating that creatures and the created were to be worshipped in place of exalting God Himself as our Creator; the ideas of theosophist Alice Bailey, by now adopted liberally into the New Age agenda, taught that any adherents of the three Abrahamic religions — Jewish, Muslim or Christian, called by her 'the hierarchy' — were not only to be marginalised, but were destined to 'be externalised' eventually to some higher spiritual plane where they could not interfere with the formation of a One World Religion.

Did this indicate the basis for the governmental decision, in English-speaking schools, to ease out

Christian education in favour of teaching *all* religions? This would then permit children freedom to choose for themselves what to believe, or – in their confusion – nothing.

A comment by Billy Graham's daughter, Anne Graham, reinforces the unholy pickle we find ourselves in, particularly with the younger generation. When asked on an American TV show how God could let such major disasters as those wrought by Hurricane Katrina happen, she replied: *I believe God is deeply saddened by this, just as we are, but for years we've been telling God to get out of our schools, to get out of our government and to get out of our lives. And being the gentleman He is, I believe He has calmly backed out. How can we expect God to give us His blessing and His protection if we demand He leave us alone?*

Even the commendable move towards the Abrahamic faiths working together for a better society could be misused as a blind step towards a 'one world religion' by unwary inter-faith worshippers. Constance Cumbey, in her informative book *Hidden Dangers of the Rainbow*[1] writes that the principal aims of the New Age Movement include: A New World Order, a New World Religion, and a New Age Christ (who is neither Jesus nor 'Christ'). Interestingly, Russian president Mikhail Gorbachev mentioned *his* belief in 'a new world order' some time before the Berlin Wall was reduced to rubble.

Even the hallowed halls of Anglican and Methodist training colleges for future priesthood seemed vulnerable to New Age thinking. One young Methodist minister in Gibraltar told us how he had been confronted during his theological training by confused teaching. His lecturers had given him a hard time because he had stood up in defence of what he considered to be Biblical truth. As a result, he felt compelled to study the New Age movement for his thesis, so as to expose the fact that even theology was being undermined by its insidious influence.

I believe it is accepted that some aspiring priests have lost their faith while in theological college. Certainly, another friend of ours studying at a bible college to become a preacher was just such a casualty, no thanks to an anti-God book by A. N. Wilson he was given to read as part of his course. Only after years of faithful prayer by his wife and friends was his belief in Christ restored.

Gradually, oriental influences and practices have become acceptable throughout society in England. Alternative lifestyles are increasingly sought by young and old alike who cannot, or will not, conform to tried and tested ways because of the excitement of exploration into all subjects taboo. The discovery of unlimited resources of 'spirituality' is now acceptable. What the unwitting seeker does *not* see is that he or she may be being introduced into a spirit-controlled world.

When ex-new age priest Will Baron was asked by David Marshall what, in a few words, he thought was the danger posed by the New Age Movement, he replied: 'The principal danger? Demonic control through Eastern meditation techniques of men, and through men, demonic control of the world.'[2]

St Paul understood better than today's church what goes on in the spiritual world when he commanded the church in decadent Ephesus to: 'be strong in the Lord, and in the power of his might. Put on the full armour of God so that you can take your stand against the wiles of the devil. For our struggle is not against flesh and blood, but against the spiritual forces of evil in the heavenly realms...' (Ephesians 6:11-12). I pick up on this warning in the next chapter.

As Malcolm Muggeridge once remarked, England can no longer rejoice in the name Christendom. Like the bucketful of frogs, society was largely unaware of what was actually happening within its framework.

I question the wisdom of Will Baron's irreverent description of the Findhorn Foundation as being 'the Vatican City of the New Age Movement.' However, the Findhorn community had opened flood-gates when it undoubtedly became a training base. It had already spawned other such communities elsewhere in Scotland and in California. The visitors who came there searching, left with new ideas and fresh possibilities of advancement along a spiritual path. They could set about worshipping mother earth and *her* creations and energies (the Gaia theory), or seeking new powers through wizardry and witchcraft. Others reverted to pagan rites of over 2000 years ago and became Druids, and still others explored eastern religions and arts, medicinal and martial. Cut free from their original moorings, they launched out on a swelling tide of different philosophies and beliefs, in search of a non-challenging form of spirituality which presented no moral cost to themselves.

While living and working in London in the early '60s, I walked round the flat humming, 'This is the Age of Aquarius', and 'Krishna, hari krishna', two songs which topped the pop charts. Publicity given to the Beatles' infatuation with Eastern religion and their guru was hugely influential on the young at that time. Across the stage footlights of *Oh, Calcutta* and *Hair*, audiences were being ushered out of the astrological age of the Fish (Pisces, symbol of Christianity), into an age of relativism symbolised by the Water-Bearer, Aquarius. Astrologers informed us we were being subjected to the stern auspices of the planet Saturn, and to the planet of change and disturbance, Uranus. Everything was changing fast, and numbers of young people took their lead from their heroes, the Beatles, and dropped out of society to go in search of their own gurus.

When I visited India in the early seventies, I saw many such Europeans sitting along the walls of Bombay (Mumbai) airport – shamelessly dirty, unshaven and unkempt in a Hindu country where few would dare to look likewise, for the Hindu puts 'cleanliness next to godliness', and the women walk with the pride of a goddess, in beautiful saris.

At the time, I for one was content to 'go with the flow', not even vaguely aware of being led by the nose into a new age.

Not until I met the Smiths did I begin to see the process my mother had experienced, way back in 1953, on her first visit to Glastonbury — and what has subsequently happened to thousands of other pilgrim souls exploring the labyrinthine paths of New Age spirituality.

An early researcher into New Age had pointed out to my father an interesting theory which could have been partially true in Eileen's particular case, but fitted the Caddys. It is voiced by John Michell in his book *The View Over Atlantis* where he claims: 'People whose occult adventures subsequently turn out to be purely subjective or illusory have usually started out in the first instance as liars and later *fallen victim to those fantasies to which they have become psychologically adjusted.*' [3]

Mum had been accused of unreality by one influential friend during the war years. Denial of reality is, perhaps, the first step towards living the lie of self-delusion. But remember, too, that Eileen was seduced into a deluded state by the wiles of Eros, quickly followed by the imposition of Peter and Sheena's fantastic beliefs, and therefore became the 'victim' of *their* beliefs to which she *must* 'psychologically adjust' in order to survive.

I have attempted to explain the phrases 'paradigm shift' and 'quantum leap' - terms often used nowadays, and not only in New Age circles. In understanding my mother's case as being among the earlier of such experiences, I believe that our present times have accelerated in reflecting her experience. Men, women and children are shifted sideways from the plumb-line of their Christian faith and values, onto the road of self-deception, swayed by the powerful influences of the media in all its forms, falsified information for the sake of a good story, by the flood of new games on the market, as fast and furiously as rumours and gossip spread. The more comfortable or stimulating form of spirituality they happen upon grabs their imaginations. They go on to forget God, His wisdom and words echoing down the centuries, and consign them to the four walls of churches. After all, who needs God when there is an attractive array of comfortable spiritual alternatives from which to choose?

Many such seekers in the 1960's came to believe that Dr Timothy Leary's psychedelic experiments with LSD would put the halcyon state of 'higher consciousness' within their grasp. Laid firmly at his door are the countless tragically misguided attempts to follow the seductively beckoning finger towards those ever-ascending states of mind. Once hooked, they were addicted to escaping from the real world, but then became ruthless in their efforts to fund their expensive habit, with fearful consequences throughout society. Many deceived and wasted young lives have been lost in the quicksands of ever-shifting lifestyles and beliefs.

Twins we once knew tried to kick their drug habit, but found themselves trapped in the powerful and threatening grip of their 'pusher'. Overcome by confusion and despair, they gassed themselves, leaving behind bewildered parents and sibling – loved ones questioning deep in their beings: Why?

Before that, Aleister Crowley (1875–1947) had proved himself to be just as dangerous as Leary, through his total commitment to the occult and black magic. Wikipedia says he was, *'perhaps the most controversial and misunderstood personality to figure in the new era of modern day witchcraft'*. The carnage caused by such men, in the vanguard of the fast-accelerating, relentless and merciless march towards the 'dawn of a new age', amounts to what is perhaps the greatest tragedy of our times.

More than 200 years ago, Quaker William Penn was claiming: 'Right is right even if everyone is against it; and wrong is wrong even if everyone is for it.' The once lively conscience of our nation, boasting its present broadmindedness, can no longer discern right from wrong. Yet we tolerate evil at our peril.

In Alexander Solzhenitsyn's *The First Circle,* Volodin, talking of communist methods of brain-washing warned:

'We have only one conscience – and a crippled conscience is as irretrievable as a lost life'.

Let us hold on to the hope our nation's conscience *can* be restored, and that his observation proves wrong in the light of what that towering warrior St Paul said — that 'all things are possible' with God.

The truth is that the forces of evil have never relented since the human race began. Again I say it: Never underestimate the manipulative strategies of the devil and his seductive wiles at work in today's world. They are targeted at the younger generation in particular because youth represents our global future. Most of those he uses have no idea what runs them, and often 'do what they do not want to do,' because the moral guide-lines of what was once believed to be Right or Wrong have been almost eradicated.

Are there those remaining who will have the courage to stand up to the heat of battle for what is right? The poet Susan Lenzkes describes her hopeful vision that this could still be so in the following words: '...the flashing of warriors' swords would be seen everywhere as the powerful Sword of the Spirit slashes at evil to make way for truth and light.' She continues: 'While we can't yet see what happens in the heavens, we can begin to see what *prayer* accomplishes on earth.'

Towards the finale of the epic *The Lion, the Witch and the Wardrobe* by C.S.Lewis, the author depicts a similar and memorable battle of Armageddon over the dead body of the heroic Lion, Aslan. History will show us how close this picture represents the Truth in our times.

Meanwhile, the baton races onwards, and our story must continue…

24

Fresh Insights

For we wrestle not against flesh & blood, but against principalities, against powers, against the rulers of the darkness of this world, against spiritual wickedness in high places.
Paul's Letter to the Ephesians 6:12 (KJV)

THE concept of spiritual warfare between heavenly realms and humanity dawned as something of a revelation. In two of Frank Peretti's novels – *Piercing the Darkness* and *This Present Darkness* – the author reveals a disturbing picture of forces of evil at work in the lives of his characters; of angelic warriors sent from heaven to sort them out; and of the essential role of prayer to achieve defeat and final victory. As I delved deeper into New Age practices, I gradually became more alert to powers released and spiritual tensions in 'high places'. Strange happenings, which once I might have shrugged off as merely a little out of the ordinary, or coincidence, now took on particular significance.

Several such incidents occurred to people either known to us, or reported from reliable sources.

Before I first went alone to Findhorn to visit my mother, I wrote to my American friends, Richard and Connie Smith. Winging back from them came the response that they would pray for my protection during that time, and they suggested it would be as well to ask others to do the same.

At Findhorn you will be in the evil one's territory. Keep in mind that your time there will be a spiritual battle – even if it doesn't seem so...Once there, that you ask God to surround you, and your whole family, with his hedge of protection so that evil forces cannot attack or interfere with you or your mother... Innocent appearing interruptions can really be spiritual forces working – phones ringing just at the wrong time, one of the children getting hurt, etc...Keep aware of God's timing. Also watch for thoughts in your head that confuse or tell you (that) you are wasting your time, etc. Such thoughts at that time will be from the evil one. Silently reject those messages and command that spirit to leave, in Jesus' name.

Not long before our return from Spain, Gibraltar TV presented a BBC TV children's series. Though we lived in Spain by then, we could receive programmes transmitted from Gibraltar. This particular series demonstrated how power through a form of witchcraft could be used. By the time we realised what was being put across, it was too late to censor the programme for our own children.

Another brush with the occult came to our notice while still in Spain, when one of my sisters — then living in Scotland near our mother — rang us to say she was concerned that her bright younger son had become obsessed with the game Dungeons and Dragons, and was unable to concentrate on his schoolwork. His teachers had complained how badly he was doing. Unbeknown to my sister, the content of this game was occult-based giving false choices which a player must make (including murder) in order to win. The result was bound to introduce some kind of spiritual confusion in an imaginative child's mind. When my sister realised the nature of the game as well as the powerful hold this had over her son, she was able to ban it altogether, and our gifted nephew began to improve at school once more.

Soon after this, in a telephone conversation with my mother in Findhorn, I attempted to explain about the harmful influence of the occult at work in her grandson's life. Her immediate response was: 'Oh, I don't know anything about that.' 'But Mum,' I protested, 'you are surrounded by the occult at Findhorn. It's all round you.' 'No. I wouldn't know anything about that,' she insisted. 'That belongs to the darkness. I only live in the light!' I wondered then if she understood how many people she had introduced into the world of 'darkness', while she continued to 'live in the light'.

A young class-mate of our son in Spain got drawn into a spiritualist church by two of her friends. The next news we heard she was under heavy sedation in a psychiatric hospital. It took her months to recover. It is so easy to dabble in the spirit world, but it can result in much psychological damage and it can become almost impossible to withdraw, as Raphael Gasson and Johanna Michaelsen had found. Demons never let go of a captive without a fight.

Soon after I began my research, I wandered into a classroom in the international school where I was helping to teach. The children were out at break-time, but lying on their desks were their current reading books. Every book, except two, was written about witches, wizards, monsters, or crystal balls, and this was long before J.K. Rowling began her writing.

The children had ordered their books through the school from the Puffin Book Club. Puffin's colourful pamphlet advertised twenty-two new books, eighteen of which were on these particular subjects. When I wrote to Puffin's director querying their agenda, I received a peeved reply about such literature being commercially fashionable at the time. Notably, however, such concentrated coverage of this type did not reappear in their leaflets.

Then Harry Potter swept onto the market. Through her lively imagination, J.K. Rowling has introduced the present generation to an attractive world of wizardry and witchcraft. An enormous section of both young and older readers have been carried away by her fascinating teachings through books and films. Only when I picked up a book by Richard Abanes in which he reveals something of her childhood leanings, and gives a comprehensive analysis of the use of the occult in her books,[1] was my suspicion as to the agenda behind her imaginings confirmed.

Other authors have blazed a similar literary trail, of course. She does not stand alone, except in that she has made literary history by her popularity and widely acclaimed contribution to the film industry in recent years.

After our return to Dorset, friends of ours were staying with us while they house-hunted in the area. They had been over many properties. One day they returned with a tale of a house they had visited in the village of Burley, Hampshire. As they walked through it, the evil vibrations which hit them were so strong that the husband began to feel physically sick. Hanging from the beams of the old cottage were many pagan artefacts. They realised they were visiting the house of a witch. Later they discovered that Burley, situated on the edge of the New Forest, had become a magnetic centre for witchcraft.

Driving through Burley village, near Hallowe'en time, I had noticed that every other shop dripped with strings of weird beads, strange figurines, masks, pointed black hats and ghostly outfits. The 'vibrations' in the high street shops were powerful, and I shuddered as we passed quickly through.

Even before this, I had learned that England's leading witch, Doreen Valiente (1922-1999), an early initiate of Gerald Gardner in the 1950s, had lived in the New Forest, and was deemed the 'mother of modern witchcraft and wicca'.

It is not surprising, therefore, that psychic fairs are advertised throughout the surrounding towns and villages quite frequently, though few may have realised that they are living in an area with strong pagan cults. It struck me that it was no coincidence that we were then living on the Dorset/Hampshire border, not far from that particular village.

One day, when searching the internet for the Rosicrucian Order Crotona Fellowship which had such a hold on the Caddys, we discovered that the Order had moved from Liverpool to Dorset in 1935, under the direction of Gerald Sullivan (1890-1942). They had built the Ashrama Hall and the Christchurch Garden Theatre at Somerford in Christchurch, and members studied occult sciences and esoteric subjects there under the leadership of Sullivan. He also wrote mystical plays under the name of Alex Mathews, staged at the Garden Theatre. One member there during the late 1930s was Gerald Gardner (1884-1964) who 'claimed to have been initiated into a New Forest coven by another member of the Crotona Fellowship.'

As I read this, my memory harked back to that first meeting between Sheena Govan and Peter Caddy on a train from Bournemouth to London. Peter lived in Bournemouth with first wife Nora at the time. Sheena lived in London. Had she visited this area in connection with Rosicrucian business at the time, or as a student of witchcraft, I wondered? Back in 1953, I recalled my father mentioning the incident, related to him by two of Sheena's ex-disciples, which had prompted him to 'suspect witchcraft'. Then I remembered that Peter Caddy had told in his book about his first wife's brother-in-law, with whom he found an instant rapport on spiritual matters, and of how he had 'offered the hand of friendship in my early spiritual training. He ensured I read all the right material... and I read... everything available at that time, including Madam Blavatsky's *Secret Doctrine*, the arcane books by Alice Bailey, and Max Heindel's *Rosicrucian Cosmo-Conception*.' [2]

Self-deception can all too easily draw others down the same path. Hence the formation of some tragic cults in recent years, in which more than one self-deluded leader has led his following to commit mass suicide.[3]

Near to home, a new friend, grieving for an adult daughter 'lost' to a cult, introduced us to the work of the Cult Information Centre and to the book written by Ian Haworth (himself an ex-cult member), *Cults: A Practical Guide*. I learned there are more than 500 cults operating in Britain alone, so that on a per capita basis the problem with cults in the UK is on a par with that of the United States, where there are believed to be five times as many cults and five times as many people. When I queried whether the Cult Information Centre had heard of the Findhorn Foundation, it became apparent that they had, having been contacted by people expressing concern about Findhorn's activities.

Something similar appears to be happening in the Islamic community where self-delusion appears to have opened the way to a devilish lust for power by some, distorting truth and converting it to terrorism. We see fanatical Imams firing up the revolutionary energies of the unwary; suicidal bombings by their poor dupes who have been indoctrinated into believing that their violent form of martyrdom leads them directly to Paradise – usually along with a multitude of innocent bystanders who believe only in the peace proclaimed by their faith. The Koran does *not* teach violence. In a Yemeni court, a Muslim judge challenged imprisoned terrorist offenders to find, in five days, where their so-called teachings appeared in the Koran. After much study they failed the test, but it had re-directed their thinking.

The psychiatric therapist, Dr M. Scott Peck in his book *People of the Lie – The Hope for Healing Human Evil*, describes his encounters with patients during his work 'who are not merely ill but manifestly evil.'[4]

We are told how Jesus healed people 'possessed' by spirits — blind and dumb spirits, demonic spirits, spirits which, when they encountered him, knew him at once as the Son of God, even though Jesus was not even accepted as a prophet in his own hometown. The healing power Christ offered was, and still is, a very real hope for people who realise, or whose family suspects, they may have some form of possession. I was shortly to discover something of the ministry of exorcism in the church by those who have a vocation in this dangerous but rewarding work.

Finally, exploring further afield, I needed to look no further than the pages of a daily newspaper to see the same kind of inexplicable 'happenings' as I have mentioned. I found myself scanning shelves of videos and DVDs in a supermarket or household, noting their electrifying titles. A review of children's computer games, films and television programmes they watch showed what ideas are being fed into impressionable minds; the content of many new films threw light on desensitisation, so heightening the potential for violent or murderous behaviour in our streets. While browsing through the large selection of books in the Mind, Body and Spirit section in one of the bigger bookshops, it was obvious how many authors were passing on New Age philosophies through a variety of attractive activities. I found my raised level of awareness in these areas was proving most uncomfortable.

When studying the person of Christ, however, (as bidden by the Smiths), the two disciplines Jesus taught became a mainstay: to 'Love the Lord your God with all your heart and with all your soul and with all your mind and with all your strength,' and to 'Love your neighbour as yourself'. They struck me as the ultimate blue-print for how to live. I have found none better or more challenging as yet. Like Christian in John Bunyan's *Pilgrim's Progress*, the hazards we may meet on life's journey seem unending. But, as Christian found, a fresh way forward was about to open up. I came across a sign-post pointing a pathway onwards and upwards, and so am able to echo Bunyan's Apology for his book in his words:

And now, before I do put up my pen,
I'll shew the profit of my book, and then
Commit both thee and it unto that hand
That pulls the strong down, and makes weak ones stand.

PART IV

*God's leading towards healing;
new relationships, a demise, and destinies*

25

A Pathway towards Healing

To forgive is like cleansing a wound - all the infection goes and the wound is then able to heal over the weeks and months, instead of remaining open and festering. The healed failure, the forgiven sin become the place where Christ's power rests upon us like a tent pitched over our weakness (2 Cor:12,19). The thickened scar tissue is stronger than the original undamaged flesh.
From the *Emmaus Course*, Part 14, Learning to Love

WITH my immediate family I had been abroad for most of fifteen years, eleven of which were living in Spain. In 1994, following her last visit to us there, my husband Peter's mother, Kitty, had begun to fail in health. As she took her leave at Malaga airport, she was adamant that we did not need to see her to her flight gate. However, both the time of departure and the gate were changed. In finding her way to the new departure lounge, she had toppled down the only escalator in the airport and subsequently ended up in a nearby nursing home. She had been badly shaken, and had a lacerated leg and cuts to her hand. Five days later, I flew home with her as her 'nurse'. During the next ten days, it became clear that she would need major support from then on.

At the same time our daughter had just finished her GCSEs in Spain at the International School where Peter was the bursar, and the school itself was changing hands. The time seemed right for us to return to England to be near Kitty, and for Georgina to finish her further education.

The next three years saw major changes in the Hinton family's lives. Kitty bought a small flat within walking distance of her house in Ferndown, Dorset. She moved at the age of eighty-five, leaving her house available for us.

Georgina went off happily as a boarder at the Royal Hospital School at Holbrook, Suffolk, to study for her 'A' Levels. Due to our residence in Spain, our son Andrew was an EU student and had chosen to change universities after a year, from Manchester to Kent. He gave up his dream of becoming a millionaire by the age of twenty-one reading Financial Services, in favour of a degree in International Relations and Politics in Canterbury, an altogether preferable location for him.

Husband Peter had taken a sabbatical year out, but towards the year's end was offered a job as a senior editor of *Burke's Peerage & Baronetage*. This delighted him as he had always been interested in heraldry and genealogy and so was able to enjoy this, his third career, for the next nine years.

Adjustment to English life was a brief culture shock after a more relaxed lifestyle in Spain. Although houses there had been protected by elaborate wrought-iron grills on all ground-floor windows, and the urbanization we lived in was patrolled by security guards, the weather, space, and emphasis on enjoying life made a huge difference to one's attitude to living. Our daughter found the grey skies in England dreary and cold. Everyone around us seemed more wary and insecure than we remembered from our time in Southsea in 1982. Our kind Ferndown neighbours warned us to keep the front door locked at all times, and never to leave the garage door open.

Compensations, however, included deliveries of a daily newspaper, and milk to the doorstep. Kitty's membership of the prestigious Ferndown golf club nearby where she played bridge, ensured Andrew could become a member. He had become a proficient golfer during our years in Spain. His name is on the Ferndown Club's honours board as Junior Champion in one of their competitions.

Our home was next to Parley Common, an environmental site where sand lizards and butterflies are protected. Kitty's love of gardening had left us with a mature garden which sported a painter's paletteful of colour in spring and summer months. Yet in our children's estimation we were now living in the 'geriatric centre of the universe', surrounded by many retirement homes.

In December 1995, sixteen months after our return, our darling Kitty died, aged eighty-six. Her fall at Malaga airport, her brave move to release her house for us, and the onset of dementia had finally taken their toll. Since she had moved to her flat, she had walked up the small hill between her flat and house almost daily. She would stay for a meal and see her little stray cat which she had left with us. The numbers of friends and family gathered at her memorial service proved how much she had been loved.

Georgina finished her exams and took a gap year before going on to study languages at Southampton University. Being fluent in Spanish, she chose to work in a home for abandoned children in Paraguay.

Andrew finished his degree and then decided to take a year before settling down to a serious career. He lived at home and learned the rudiments of landscape gardening hands-on with a nearby company.

The Ferndown house was only our second home since we were married. We put our own stamp on it by modernising it. Within a year of finishing the refurbishment, however, an unexpected change in our circumstances proved that this had been a timely and fortunate foresight. After three years there, we were house-hunting for a larger place to accommodate our extending family, and would be shortly on the move again.

While we were still in Spain, and now that we were back in England, my mother and I corresponded and telephoned infrequently. In 1987, there had been a family gathering of her siblings and mine at my farming brother's home, Porthouse Farm in Herefordshire. We were in the throes of school holidays in Spain at that time, and were unable to get over for the occasion. We had suggested, instead, that our gift to her could be to visit us, and we would pay her air fare. Her upbringing in Egypt had accustomed her to sun and heat. She revelled in it.

After all the discussions about my mother I'd had with Richard and Connie Smith, I mentioned our invitation to them, hoping they would wish to meet her. I was brought up with a jolt when Connie asked, 'Do you really want that spirit in your home?'

I asked myself what effect might their grandmother have on our children whom they did not yet know? Would our home become a launching pad for her ideas in Spain among our friends, as Caddy and Mum had used our home in Northern Ireland years before? How would I handle our daughter-mother relationship after my enlightenment about her involvement in new age activities?

Undoubtedly, I had not taken into account that my fresh knowledge of the nature of her work had created a barrier in our understanding. Of course we would need to thrash it out at some point, but perhaps a holiday abroad for her was not the time. After some heart-searching, and the disappointment of not seeing her, I called her to say we had had a set-back in our plans which made the timing unfeasible. Fortunately she agreed that if it was meant to work out, it would happen at the right time. We continued to keep lines of communications open.

On one occasion, I had been back in UK for a visit, and able to attend Uncle Paddy's funeral in Reading. As Mum was unable to be there, we could not meet, but she rang later. I could describe to her in detail his family's send-off: the mango under one arm in the coffin (he loved mangoes); the crematorium ceremony in which his favourite song, 'Paddy McGinty's Goat' featured; and the co-incidental Red Arrows' fly-past as the coffin disappeared, reminding us of Paddy's wartime military service.

Towards the end of 1996, Richard in Bromyard and Suzanne in Toronto, hatched a plan for a big Combe/

Jessop (Mum's maiden name) family gathering at Richard's lovely home, The Old Cowshed, to celebrate our mother's eightieth birthday due in August 1997. As this event loomed up in conversation among us, I began to panic. After too many years I did not know how to respond to meeting Mum again, or to the proposed plans for the party. Should I boycott the do as I had done for her seventieth, or should I attend? What would the effect be on Mum and the rest of the wider family if I did? Could I prevent my own family from being there? Despite the past, she was their grandmother, and my mother. I could no longer remain emotionally objective.

The records of Mum's first family's lives were not without blemish. They stood at three broken marriages, two instances of single parenthood (one saved by a last-ditch marriage), depression and mental confusion, and more. Negative forces had been at work creating havoc in all our lives, and would continue to do so unless a powerful panacea could be found. Sceptical as ever, I did not see how a party celebration, 80 or not, could possibly make any difference.

In consternation, I wrote to my erstwhile mentors, Richard and Connie, for advice. Back from the States came their calming words:

When mother is around, be kind and considerate as you would with any lady her age and who happens to be your mother, but don't comment on the past or let it stand in the way of the present moment – you are only responsible for the <u>present moment</u>; act as Christ would...

I was grateful for their wisdom. It pointed a way forward. But could I implement their words? I still remained adrift and feeling far distant from any certainty of how to face their challenge.

Even before Christmas 1996, the forthcoming party was in its early planning stage. Then, unexpectedly, a further door swung open. As I pondered the way forward to my next meeting with Mum, a strong feeling impressed itself upon me that I should talk to psychiatrist Dr

Kenneth McAll, two of whose books I had read some years before. His wife Frances (a medical doctor) had been a friend of mine for some years and had treated me professionally on several return visits from Gibraltar and Spain. I remembered her husband's work in the spiritual field of psychiatry, and felt he might hold some key to unlocking the darker side of our past.

I had met Dr McAll once at a wedding, when his silence and penetrating stare had seemed intimidating. So it was with some trepidation that we invited him and his wife over from their home in the New Forest to lunch with us in Ferndown. It was just before Christmas, and our son Andrew was with us. During luncheon, Ken McAll related several stories, two of which struck me particularly. He spoke of his latest ventures into Native American territories, scene of past terrible battles, where he had been invited to bring peace by holding a Eucharist service for the unhappy, tortured souls still roaming those sites. He had turned his strong belief in God's power being released through the Communion Service, towards healing the violently executed, unshriven dead. This ministry would reach their souls and lay them finally to rest. He had applied this restorative power in case after case with the living also.

He told us how he had once been becalmed in a ship in the area of the infamous Bermuda Triangle in the Atlantic, where ships and aeroplanes had disappeared mysteriously over the years. He and the crew had been mystified by the sound of mournful singing rising from the sea. Later research showed that during slave-trading days, slaves had been thrown overboard there to drown. After a talk at a monastery in Yorkshire, at which he mentioned this fact, a Mass was said next morning, 'when we could apologise to God for what our ancestors had done in the past.'[1] Three bishops then suggested that other churches pray also in this way. The Bishop of Bermuda arranged a similar service in his cathedral and another was held at sea for the souls of the murdered slaves. They too were committed to God and released into eternity by the healing power of prayer and celebration of Christ's life, death and resurrection. In the subsequent 10 years no more unexplained disasters were reported in the Bermuda Triangle.[2]

Ken had been a medical missionary in China and an internee under the Japanese with his family in the war. During these experiences he had seen the ever-present availability of God's power in any situation: to reconcile, to heal troubled minds and spirits, as well as bodies. His later study of psychiatry only deepened his conviction of how the amazing power of the Holy Spirit, the Comforter, could be harnessed to bring spiritual release from curses or any ancestral horrors.

The McAlls' visit triggered questions in my mind which required yet further discussion. We arranged another meeting for after Christmas. Meanwhile, I re-read Ken's *Healing the Family Tree* in which he gave case-histories of 'incurable' patients who had been victims of ancestral control. I passed the book on to my brother Richard to read, hoping he would reach the same conclusion as I had – that when we five siblings gathered in August for Mum's birthday, we might arrange a special healing Eucharist. The purpose would be to break the cycle of negative power and influence in each of our lives.

In January 1997 my husband Peter and I visited the McAlls' at their interesting home deep in the forest. The house had once belonged to Sir Arthur Conan Doyle, and early on in the McAlls' time there, a family member had encountered Conan Doyle's restless spirit, looking for his 'red book'. Her reassurance that she would let him know if they found it put an end to any further visitations.

During a riveting session over tea, Ken McAll asked many questions and mapped out my family tree. Had there been abortions or miscarriages in the family? Had there been any occult influence in our history? How did my mother and the Caddys feature in our lives? Out came the family's story.

We talked about Peter Caddy, and I told how his Christian father Frederick had once deviated from his faith by seeking healing for chronic arthritis from their neighbour, a spiritualist medium. And how his ten year old son, Peter, had gone along to the séance and had become hooked by the excitement of witnessing the workings of occultic power. Dr McAll suggested that we should intercede for both Frederick and Peter Caddy, then and there, by praying for their souls. Ken prayed.

We talked on and on, covering a pageant of people in our family, and my Peter threw in queries about some of his own family too. Five-and-a-half hours later, we stepped back into the darkening New Forest, our minds reeling from the intensity of the session.

Next day, the following comment by Dr William Barclay struck a chord: *What happens to a man in the afterlife is inextricably bound up with what he has done in this life...* The chilling words lodged in my mind. I wondered whether there might be yet another practical step I was meant to take on my own, on behalf of Frederick Caddy and his son, Peter.

Next Sunday, I approached the Communion rail in church with the idea of taking both father and son there in my mind. As I received the bread and wine, I promised Jesus I would 'stand in the gap' for them. (Ezekiel 22: v 30 recounts how God 'sought for a man among them, that should make up the hedge and stand in the gap before Him for the land, that He should not destroy it...') Could this spiritual act, this experiment, perhaps start some kind of healing process in the spiritual realms for the Caddys, I wondered hopefully?

Three days earlier I had been in touch by phone with Mum asking her forgiveness for my 'cold love of the years'. Her response had been lovingly forgiving. I had also just written her a letter about a book I had recently read on managing back pain, because Mum had become prone to terrible back spasms. I had sent her the book, and rashly suggested she might ask for Christ's healing from this condition. She rang back immediately with a severe verbal rap on the knuckles: 'Whoa – I want your love, but not your probing.' One step forward had fallen back six.

A month later, I found Peter Caddy's autobiography in the local library and began reading about his life and my mother's. When I reached the part where Sheena Caddy had performed a marriage in 1954 between Mum and Caddy in St Patrick's Chapel at Glastonbury, I felt compelled to visit the place — simply to walk and pray in my mother's footsteps of all those years before.

My patient husband was willing to make the visit, so armed with Caddy's book and a suitcase, we set off to spend a weekend at Abbey House, an Anglican Retreat centre at Glastonbury. We found we had landed in a silent retreat by members of a Catholic church from Ferndown. This proved somewhat of a blessing in that our only chance to talk was either in our bedroom or outside the building, exploring the old town of Glastonbury.

As we wandered down the streets, we noticed that many curtained windows or front doors were adorned with pagan symbols. We lunched in a hotel and were assailed by its creepy ambience. Afterwards we climbed Burr Tor to breathe more freely and take in a wider view of the surrounding countryside – green, tranquil and peaceful, with sheep grazing in the sunshine. It was hard to imagine that the timeless plain of Avalon below had been where the mythical and spiritual had clashed from the dawn of time.

The Saxons, who had been converted to Christianity, conquered Somerset under the reign of King Ina in the 7th century. The King is reputed to have built a small church at Glastonbury, later enlarged to an abbey. After a rather chequered career in and out of the royal courts, a locally born monk called Dunstan became Abbot of Glastonbury. During his administration, he reformed not only his abbey but monastic life throughout England, and went on to become the Archbishop of Canterbury. He later became one of the greatest Saints of the Anglo-Saxon Church. As Abbot, he set the abbey on the road to becoming the richest medieval monastery in England before it was dissolved by King Henry VIII in the 16th century.

As we know it in its present day, the environs of this ancient site have become a magnetic, and sometimes muddy, venue for the world of popular music festivals.

There was plenty of time for quiet reading during the silent retreat. As I continued browsing Caddy's book, fresh knowledge of his character and exploits, together with the hi-jacking of my mother, forced me to realise I needed to forgive him anew. Was I ready to do so? I needed more time to think.

As we wandered round the towering abbey ruins, we discovered the small Chapel of St Patrick remained intact. We entered and sat a while within its profound silence. I could picture my mother, heavily pregnant and confused, being brought there by the Caddys in 1954. She was loaded with guilt that she was about to produce a child out of wedlock (my parents only divorced in 1956). Both Mum and Caddy recalled in their books the wedding ceremony performed by Sheena as the high priestess and divinity she believed herself to be, in a desperate effort to salve Mum's conscience. I saw the deed as part of Sheena's brain-washing process.

When leaving the little chapel, a box marked Prayer Requests caught my eye. A note beside it stated that requests would be read out for prayer the following Tuesday by the chaplain. Knowing more of Caddy's track record by now, the circumstances of the so-called marriage, and feeling both scepticism and sadness at my mother's state of mind at the time, to drop a prayer in the box would be another form of intercession for the past, so I wrote: 'Dearest Lord, for Eileen – let the scales fall from her eyes so that she may know Jesus Christ as her Saviour and Friend. In His name I ask. Amen.'

The following morning, we were in the beautiful cathedral of Wells for a sung Eucharist. This was an inspirational setting, with full choir, thundering and uplifting music from the organist, and a memorable sermon preached by the Precentor, Canon Lucas, on the energy of the Holy Spirit. He likened His energy to a magnet placed beneath iron filings, leaping between poles and bringing the filings into a pattern, just as God's power could also work in our lives if we ask Him.

Once again, I felt compelled to place all my turmoil over my mother and Caddy at the Communion rail. This was becoming a habit.

There was time before a silent lunch to continue reading Caddy's memoirs. The very existence of the book itself bothered me. I crept away through the silent retreat house, and took it down to the basement chapel – a hideaway arched room resembling my memory of an air-raid shelter, with a tiny grille at the window. An icon of Christ was propped up by the altar on the floor. I laid the book before it and asked Jesus to intercede for me, to forgive this man for all his words. This would be the last time.

When I arose from kneeling, all the adverse feelings which had hit me like an avalanche when reading Caddy's rendering of events concerning my family had vanished. I had done all I could for him, and my own spirit. Any other result was now out of my hands.

Mission accomplished, I was at peace. I was free to join in wholeheartedly with the planning and preparations for the clan-gathering due to take place in honour of our mother in August, six months hence.

Meanwhile, 'back at the ranch', certain dramas were taking place within my close family.

We had booked to visit Vancouver Island, in Canada, but first needed to sell the Ferndown house and find somewhere bigger. Amazingly, the house sold quickly and satisfactorily to the first couple who saw it. Fortunately, they were in no hurry to move in, as we were due to leave for Canada the following day with no time to house-hunt. As we flew out, taking our daughter with us, we knew we would have some weeks' grace to find our next abode when we returned – which we did.

August 1997 was approaching fast, so before we left for Canada, Georgina and I designed and drew up the invitations for Mum's birthday so they could be duly circulated. The theme was to be a hot-air balloon with our mother in the basket, taking off into the future! We planned as a family to contribute to such a venture for her, but then read of another grandmother who had similarly celebrated her birthday a few weeks before. The balloon had hit a pylon and she had died. So we canned that idea, but as our part in the preparations was the décor, we made a little helium balloon with a basket to hover above each table instead. This done, we took ourselves off to Victoria, B.C.

Five weeks after our return, we had bought and moved into *Treetops*, a large bungalow with all the space we needed. We hastily threw ourselves into the new house with only a week to get settled in. Then we drove off to Herefordshire to help my brother and his wife prepare their home in Bromyard for the forthcoming birthday celebration for Mum.

26

Celebration!

Together with these things, the most important part of your new life is to love each other. Love is what holds everything together in perfect unity... And always be thankful.
Colossians 3:14-15c

IT is a saga of its own how Richard and Helen, with little money, had bought a grade II listed cowshed on more than three acres of land in July, 1994. It was a cattle byre, with dung on the floor and concrete feeding troughs. Architected by Helen, they both worked hard to transform it into a magnificent home. It was in a prime location, sitting on a ridge, with windows looking over rolling fields and the Bromyard Downs on one side, and on the other, the Malvern Hills rose in the misty distance. Rick told me that theirs is a story of faith where God provided all they needed for the venture.

Soon after the purchase of what they called The Old Cowshed, Porthouse Farm, the huge pig and chicken unit in Bromyard which Richard managed, was closed. This freed him to continue work on the house, where he did some of the building work himself and most of the finishing off as the work progressed.

Meanwhile, his ever-resourceful wife Helen had taken a degree in Social Sciences, while also supervising the reconstruction of their new home. The lower end of the building was a barn where the calves were born. In 1999 this was made into a two-storey semi-detached house which they duly named The Calfcote.

By 1997 Richard had established a flourishing Bed-and-Breakfast business, after doing a six-week course with the Tourist Board. As a perfect Mine Host, he enjoyed a steady flow of people from as far afield as

Japan, Holland, Poland and Hungary, as well as Britain. They never lacked bookings, and business was flourishing.

This was the perfect venue for a large family gathering for our mother's eightieth birthday celebration. Undoubtedly, it would be a memorable occasion, with family coming from Scotland, Spain, Canada and New Zealand. It would require a lot of preparation. Richard had reconstructed the tin-roofed barn next to the house into a building with metal walls, as a store and workshop. This was the largest space available for the party and needed to be cleared.

As numbers grew, the five bedrooms, three bathrooms, and a gallery over the spacious dining-cum-kitchen area were too small, despite the ever-expandable walls. Many of us were to be accommodated either in tents or as guests nearby with friendly neighbours.

Helen was working all hours for a big fruit-producing farm elsewhere, so was not there to help direct the willing hands which arrived from all corners to put the occasion together. Richard became foreman, being the only person who knew how the whole operation would work.

He had managed to find flags of all the countries represented, and had erected six white flag poles on the back lawn within sight of the entrance. The flags greeted all-comers, and fluttered continually throughout the whole week of festivities: Irish (for Mum), Scottish, Canadian, New Zealand, the U.S. and the Union Flag.

By the middle of August, the Old Cowshed was a whirl of activity. The enormous barn was decorated, and the kitchen hummed with creative culinary ideas. Mum was due to drive from Scotland with her sister Torrie for the celebration, and about 80 of us would gather for dinner in the barn, followed by Scottish dancing.

In the midst of the bustle, our eldest half-brother Christopher, now a highly successful plastic surgeon, had caught wind of the gathering and called Richard to ask if he and his family could be invited; whereupon his two younger brothers decided to come with their families, one from the U.S. and the other from Scotland. This would be the first, and only, occasion when our mother and her eight offspring and their families would be together.

This idea did not meet with mother's approval. She had wanted a small celebration with her sons in Scotland, with the Findhorn community, and an entirely separate event down south with her first family. Mum's efforts to keep her first and second families apart were quickly overridden, however, by Richard and his three brothers' enthusiasm.

Tent City grew up overnight in the field next door to the Old Cowshed. The New Zealand contingent set off on an expedition to the nearest river in nearby Wales to find big river-stones as the base for 'putting down the hangi'[1] which would continue the celebrations the day after the birthday. Spotlights and coloured lighting were arranged around the barn walls to light the dinner and Scottish dancing in the evening. Each round table was decorated with the six flags, and a hot-air balloon floated above each, trailing streamers from a basket filled with sweets. The table seating was planned and each place named. The barn stood transformed into a banqueting hall.

Out in the yard there was a hog roast on a spit, and a couple of Kiwi nephews gathered wood for a bonfire to heat the river-stones for next day's traditional Maori feast. All was set for an exciting and colourful party that evening, and celebrations for the days ahead.

As the Scottish academic year is divided into four, and the Michaelmas term starts in August, our half-brother Jonathan, a teacher, needed to be back in Scotland early for the beginning of term. It was therefore decided to have the main dinner party on Saturday, August 23rd instead of Mum's birthday three days later.

A tea on the Cowshed lawn in warm sunshine was followed by a photo-call for the entire clan. While gathering for this, Mum's sister-in-law, Joan Jessop —

who had played such an integral role in holding our family together over the early years after Mum's departure — arrived from Reading. She was recovering from a hip operation, and had been unsure she would be able to come, so her advent represented an enormous effort on her part, and joy on ours. None of us realised at the time what a sacrifice she made to be there. Three weeks later, we were shocked to hear she had died peacefully of an aneurism.

The dinner was a salmon-and-salad buffet followed by a unique dessert: a huge boot-shaped cake for 'the old woman who lived in a shoe and had so many children she didn't know what to do'! In the icing, Suzanne had placed photos of Mum's eight children as infants, and Mum had to guess which was who.

During the dinner, at five-minute intervals, one of Mum's eight children would pop up and verbalise his or her appreciative memories of our mother, and express our wishes for her future with a toast. Memorable among these were Christopher's words about 'our global family' and the 'web' which had brought us all together! Richard remembers that Mary Liz found this a particularly difficult and emotional moment, and the youngest, David, broke down in tears as he talked about the stability our mother had given him, and ended by saying he hoped 'she would stay with us forever.'

Then back went the tables and chairs, and our kilted brothers, with Jonathan as the caller, led the merry company in Scottish dancing until well past midnight. The birthday queen sat through some of the Scottish dancing, but retired early with her sister Torrie. For many, the night was still young and the festivities would continue until early next day.

For Mum, though, the whole exciting event had proved too much. When I crept in to see her early next morning, she was writhing in agony with one of her back spasms. The osteoporosis – which she refused to admit she had – had been triggered by her emotions as much as by the length of time sitting the previous evening. 'It feels like things clawing up and down my back!' she gasped. 'Morphine. I must have morphine.'

A local doctor was called in, but he would not prescribe it. The recent Dr Shipman affair had caused the medical profession to use the drug with added caution. The GP tried administering Pethadine at first, but when the pain persisted, her son Dr Christopher was called up to talk with him, and he was persuaded to capitulate.

Eileen was prone to such attacks for which morphine had proved the only solution. She would curl up and sleep for two days, without food or liquid, until the pain abated. These were becoming more frequent of late. She had read the book on healing back pain, in which the doctor-author claimed much of the pain could be connected with emotions and attitudes – in other words, were psychosomatic. Mum recognised now that they occurred particularly when she was faced with a situation she could not handle, and had thereafter identified the spasms as psychosomatic. Whenever I went to Scotland to see her in the ensuing years, she would have one of her turns either before or after the visit. I realised that there was a far deeper underlying cause than simply osteoporotic collapse.

When the hangi took place the following lunchtime, Mum was not there to enjoy this Maori tradition laid on for her. It was such a novelty and success, however, that the forty or so guests hardly noticed her absence.

Since the early hours, meat and vegetables had been buried on a metal tray, placed on top of red-hot stones, and strewn with willow branches to give them a smoky flavour. Wet sacks and earth were then piled on top. The heat from the stones tenderised the chicken, pork chops and vegetables, all wrapped in muslin bags, which were perfectly cooked six hours later. With the sun beating down on the gathering, the hangi was uncovered and we sat round in the August warmth, enjoying both food and good company.

As it transpired, there had been neither time nor opportunity during our time together for Richard and me to prime our siblings about the reasons for arranging a special Eucharist to absolve family problems from the past. This did not prevent Richard, Helen, Peter and I from attending Bromyard church, for an eight o'clock communion service on Sunday, Mum's actual birthday. There we could give thanks for the way her celebrations had come together, asking for absolution of past family problems, and praying for Mum. Her recent 'turn' after the event had cast a shadowy reminder over us all of her increasing frailty.

As the time came for each family to leave The Old Cowshed, the front courtyard echoed with fond farewells and last-minute snapshots. Jonathan, with Alison and baby Caitlin, was the first to leave, with a long drive ahead up to Findhorn. Then Christopher and Judith with their merry crew of four 'tea caddies' (Timothy, Thalia, Tegan and Travis), drove back to Sheffield; David, Kacie and their son Aaron flew back to California where David was building expensive houses for the rich and famous; Torrie's son Michael, with wife Daphne and their golden retriever Bonny, drove back to Yapton near the South Coast, while Mike's sister Jane and her family headed back to Flin Flon in Canada.

The remainder of us helped put the Old Cowshed back to rights again. Mum came out of her cocoon, and announced that now she was 'ready to die' having had the joyous experience of seeing her first and second families united under the same roof! She told us then that she had been praying for this for years, in spite of her previously stated wish for the two families to celebrate separately. She grew stronger each day of her week's recuperation. Her sister Torrie remained with her until Mum had recovered strength enough to drive back to Nottingham. She stayed only briefly with Torrie, insistent that she must get back to Findhorn for an important meeting.

We Hintons had already made tracks for home to prepare hastily so that some of our New Zealand and Canadian family members could visit our new home while they were still on this side of the globe. We scurried round, sorting out furniture and belongings, pots and pans, to get ourselves operational after the upheaval of our recent move. The drive to Heathrow airport from our village was, conveniently, less than two hours from Alderholt.

During a happy visit from our New Zealand branch of the family we set to and turned a games room into a nursery, using heavy green velvet curtains from the Ferndown house to create a bed-sitting room for our daughter, and nursery on the other side of the curtain for our forthcoming grandson. The baby was due in October, and the new arrangement provided their own quarters out of earshot of the 'oldies'.

Our grandson's arrival was cause for great rejoicing. Javier was much beloved by us all from the beginning. He and his mother lived with us for the next eighteen months. He had thick black hair and sparkling dark eyes, and was fast-growing, jolly and noisy, always on the move. He seemed busily intent on bringing up his mother and grandparents, always making the most of the joyful business of living. He laughed at a good joke, and enjoyed music – from a lively Latin American tempo to gentler nursery songs and rhymes.

When he and his mother departed to a home of their own, he had gained a new 'Daddy' and a family home-life. We watched him go with sadness, for he left a huge gap in our lives.

But I digress. My personal family is but a small sketch in the corner of a far wider canvas – a minor detail in a painting in which other colourful and influential figures take precedence in our family history. At this time, we are following along a path towards the healing of our past: in relationships, attitudes, and the ditching of old baggage, in order to find (in the words of the old spiritual) the

Balm in Gilead which could turn wounds into 'honourable scars'.

This pilgrimage takes us onwards, opening not only 'doors within' but many other doors along the way.

27

Further Steps along the Path

Though healed, the soul's wounds are still seen by God, not as wounds but as honourable scars...
From *Revelations of Divine Love*, Ch. 39, by Mother Julian of Norwich

IN the coming years, mother's eightieth anniversary proved to have been an important milestone along the road to reconciliation between the Combe and Caddy families. Not only had it given us the chance to get to know one another, but undoubtedly beneath the surface of this memorable family event, certain dynamics had been operating. The eight of us had been brought together by the united love the eight of us had for our mother, but also by her faithful love for each of us down the years. Direct contact with each other had caused a 'paradigm shift' in our relationships. We became acquainted with the lives, work and families of our half-brothers, and they with ours, which were forged between us during those few precious days, amidst the fun, creativity and ease of social exchange.

There was a tacit agreement between us to leave behind any estrangement and baggage created by our parents' past. The whole occasion had acted like an invisible spiritual compass. It changed our direction and pointed us to a new road, along which we could decide how each could make the best out of the final years of our mother's life.

It would not all happen at once, of course. There needed to be a 'settling process' during which the new seeds could grow. For me, it was in the millennium year 2000, when a dormant seed of confidence and love sprouted into life. I was extremely glad that Mum's death-wish, made two years earlier about 'being ready to die now', had not been granted, for she was still very much with us!

The exuberant millennium festivities had begun to wane, and spring-time – my favourite season of the year — was in the air, when that seed began to unfurl and identify itself as a yearning to be with my mother for my sixtieth birthday. She was only twenty-two years older than me, and I felt that as her first-born, being with her for that anniversary could bring us closer. We needed time together to just 'be', and to talk; to ask each other questions, and rebuild our still all-too-distant ties, not just of blood, but of affinity. She was genuinely thrilled when I telephoned to ask her if Peter and I could visit.

From Dorset, it is a 584 mile hike up through England to Morayshire. We stayed a night either way to rest the driver. This way we could appreciate fully the beauty of the Lake District, its hills and dales, and the blossoming of new life on both sides of the border. As we neared the colder north, the early lambs were dressed in little orange raincoats. There was snow on the heights along the deep blue of the Moray Firth, but lower down the sun-warmed land was visibly waking, ready to don its colourful clothes of yellow daffodils, purple crocuses, and white and pink blossom, almost three weeks later than the more southerly spring blooms and warmer climate we had left behind us in Dorset.

During this varied and happy visit with Mum, we toured the Moray Firth with her, through Lossiemouth and Nairn, past the gates of Gordonstoun School where Prince Charles had been educated, familiarising ourselves with the towns and pine forests, and enjoying a noticeable lack of traffic. We explored Elgin, and lunched one day at Johnsons of Elgin, Mum's favourite and, of course, most expensive store. Mum was ever generous, and wished to buy me a birthday gift. Knowing how I feel the cold, most of her presents were warm clothing! We were not permitted to leave without a Viyella shirt for Peter, and a red cashmere cardigan for me, thanks to the continuous flow of royalties on her several books, no doubt, and her small pension.

For my birthday, we dined out at one of her favourite restaurants near Nairn, and included some of her community friends. One guest was a young man who had been with the Moonies. She had a way of gathering unusual people around her.

Two of her closest friends were Helmut and Karin, a South African couple and she wanted us to meet them. They no longer lived in the community but had remained frequent visitors to Mum, to whom they were devoted. Big Helmut was a long-distance coach driver, and kept us amused with his stories of his passengers, one of whom was called Mr Mukerjee, whose accent Helmut would often mimic on or off the telephone. Helmut was also a fisherman, and whisked Peter out on a nearby loch one day, while his wife Karin, Mum and I lunched at a popular garden centre in Forres. This couple became firm friends, and stood by me and my mother countless times in the next nine years – whether during discussions over cups of coffee, or taxi-ings, jokes and meals. Helmut was a great handyman, and never tired of doing jobs in Mum's house, while Karin took on her laundry and ironing, and eventually became her house-keeper and cook when Mum's health began to fail. Through their many acts of kindness, they were bent on showing her their gratitude, and seemed quite at ease including us under the same umbrella.

One afternoon, Peter and I drove over to the Benedictine Abbey at Pluscarden, some five miles away. This was a shot in the dark because I had been corresponding with one of the monks there for some years. It had been Dom Edmund's valuable research into the history of the Findhorn Foundation, its growth and occultist influence which had started me on the same path.

He had been delighted when one day he heard from a bishop friend of his about Eileen's ex-husband, Andrew and had written immediately to my father about his concerns. Since inheriting these letters from Dad, I had kept in touch with Pluscarden long after Dom Edmund had passed into glory at the ripe old age of 86. From what I had learned from his honest appraisal of the Foundation, I was certain that if I asked for their prayers specifically, the brothers would carry their concerns for Findhorn in this way.

That day Peter and I met the Abbot, an historian. He offered to give us a conducted tour of the abbey, and told us they often had visitors from the Findhorn community because it was considered by them to be a favourite place of 'spiritual power'. The church, with its central square tower climbing high above the vaulted ceiling, had been restored in recent years — as had the entire abbey — by the monks themselves, and was very beautiful. At one point while in the church, twenty or so white-robed monks descended the stone steps down into the nave chanting, and Father Abbot excused himself to join their worship, while we listened.

Later, he invited us to his office, where we discussed the community over a cup of tea. He was interested to meet Eileen Caddy's daughter, and we were able to give him a picture of the little we knew about life in the community. By the time we left him, we felt we had made another friend.

My next visit to see Mum was in November 2002, for the 40th anniversary of the beginnings of the community, begun in 1962 with the arrival of the Caddys' green caravan. This time I went alone, but not unarmed! I had sought advice from Richard and Connie Smith on how to 'be' with my mother. As was their wont, back came their e-mail. They suggested I ask praying friends to keep me in their thoughts, which I did. They continued: *When we were in Colombia in a tribe that paid allegiance to a female spirit, we were not bothered – but our very presence (as Christians) made a difference in their lives. The Indians noticed it even when we didn't. So as a child of light, you will make a difference – but only take on the issues that God gives you at that time, meaning be very sensitive to the Holy Spirit's guidance.* I was warned by them to be aware of uncalled for interruptions and distractions if we were discussing anything of depth or meaning from the past.

I was glad of this briefing, especially when, on the night I arrived, Mum took me straight into the huge, packed Universal Hall, built like a giant tepee in the middle of the community. My mother was so thrilled to have her eldest daughter with her, that as we sat down on the front row of benches, she introduced me to everyone in the audience around us. She grasped my hand and hung on tightly throughout the proceedings, much to my discomfiture. I soon became accustomed to this love-sign, as she often held the hand of any person she loved.

The entertainment itself was fun in parts: a skit on the days of my mother's early morning sorties to the public lavatory as a place for peaceful meditation; a clever and amusing song entitled 'We have Philosophies', and a rather strange presentation of weird art by two female artists. The best impromptu act, to my mind, was Mum's pure white cat, Crystal, walking across the stage in search of her owner. She was retrieved by the M.C., Mike Scott, one of the pop group The Water Boys, who lived next door to Mum and adored Crystal.

On that visit there was much talk of imminent war with Iraq. From nearby Kinloss Airbase, the constant roar of aircraft taking-off from 5 a.m. every morning, and the drumming of engines overhead were an ever-present reminder of pilots preparing for, or returning from, reconnaissance. Within the community, everyone talked about 'peace'! I found myself walking an emotional tightrope, unsure of every word I spoke with Mum or step I took with members of the community.

At my first lunch in the community centre, I met Dorothy Maclean again. This was the occasion when I asked her about the portrait of Douglas Govan, hanging in a gallery in Toronto, and Dorothy assured me that this was Sheena's nephew, not her son.

The following day, I visited Mum early, before her carer had helped her dress. She was rested and at her most receptive, so my early morning visits were to become a normal pattern. That day, we touched on the time she had returned after an absence of two years, when we all thought she had come back to us forever. She admitted then, 'I was pregnant with Jonathan.' I had suspected this at the time but was glad to have the matter confirmed. Another time, she admitted to me at least twice, maybe three times: 'I was terrified of Sheena.'

On another visit, I landed in a hornet's nest! Mum's middle son, Jonathan, who lived on the community site, had become her financial adviser, and had Power of Attorney to help her make decisions. Soon after I arrived, I learned from Mum that on the day before, Jonathan had discovered from the bank stubs of her cheque book that she was spending incredible amounts of money on scams, the lottery, and *Reader's Digest* offers of prizes of £20,000. When questioned about this by Jonathan, she said she was trying to win money because 'the Foundation was in debt', at which her son grew angry and walked out, slamming the front door. Although he had every right to challenge her, she was furious.

I asked Jonathan to come round while Mum was sleeping, and he explained the circumstances. He followed this up by procuring a recent bank statement of her outgoing payments from the Royal Bank of Scotland in Forres. The record made sad reading. She, like so many older people, was being gradually fleeced by unscrupulous companies offering promises of cheap goods for her money.

Her bedside chest-of-drawers was crammed full of boxes of the cheap, sparkling jewellery she had purchased – earrings, bracelets, necklaces, brooches, gold chains – all sent in answer to a request for £10 here and £10 there. As our church's annual Christmas bazaar was due in December, I asked her whether she would like to donate some of this squirrel's hoard for a charitable purpose. She agreed readily, and we went through them all. I returned home with a suitcase full of the pieces, which made a lovely display on what became the winning stall at the bazaar that year.

However, this was not the end of the problem. Mum had been bitten hard by the gambling bug and already her upstairs bedroom cupboards were full of household goods still in their boxes unused, clothes she did not need, and dozens of *Reader's Digest* compendiums. Jonathan was at his wits' end, and we decided that all Mum's mail needed to be censored by those who were with her at the time of its delivery. One of her postal fans was a persistent astrologer touting for financial support. The 'search' policy was instigated, with the help of her secretary, Rosie. For the rest of her life only the letters and cards from her hundreds of international fans filtered into her hands.

This debacle engendered an interesting conversation about her trusting to luck and the lottery rather than to God as her Provider. Puzzled by this unspiritual approach to finance, I told Mum the story, recounted in Chapter 13, of what had happened when I gave away the 70 kroner in Sweden which I had carefully saved for my siblings' Christmas presents. I said that I had never doubted God's provision after that.

Mum's ideas changed gradually, and she decided that what she really wanted to do was leave a large inheritance to her eight children, and that this had been her prime motivation. She was always generous, to a fault, bless her.

On another occasion, we talked about her favourite theme of unconditional love. She said how she must become a 'clean, pure channel for God to send out love to Bush, Blair and Saddam Hussein,' and that she was the intercessor. She told me that 'The Father is love, God is love, and love changes everything and everybody'. At which I suggested that God can also deliver 'tough love'.

'Oh yes, often. I know. I am the pure, clean channel through which He can work,' was the reply.

I explained that interceding was different for me. I would ask God to do the work, through Jesus, using His Holy Spirit. Then I asked her, 'What are these 'Christ energies' you talk about, Mum?' Her answer, again, was about being 'the channel for the energy to work from the divine centre.'

This all seemed too vague to me. I remained unconvinced by her words and countered, 'To me, Jesus/God is a Person, not a 'centre'...God Himself is on the throne of His Kingdom, and Jesus is at His right hand, and the earth is the footstool at His feet.'

Then I painted a picture for her of the time my husband Peter and I had been in the Holy Land, mounting the rough-hewn steps from the Kidron Valley in Jerusalem to the Chief Priest, Caiaphas's house. These were actual steps trodden by Jesus when he was taken for trial before his crucifixion. I said that walking where he had walked had affected me profoundly. Jesus had stepped out of the pages of the Bible as a real Person, and there was I, on the very same steps where He had been. They would have been the steps up to the city, or down to the Mount of Olives, or the short cut to see his friends in Bethany.

Just at this moment (as Richard and Connie Smith had predicted could happen) a couple of visitors walked in unannounced. My mother greeted them with: 'Jenny has just been trying to tell me about Jesus!' I can hear the mockery in her voice even now.

It was then that the full realisation hit me that she and I each believed in a different Jesus: that one was real to me but unreal to her, and vice versa. She had told me that she felt more comfortable in the spiritual world than the real world. I had wondered then whether this was where she could escape successfully from some of the harsher realities of her everyday life. Had she been trained to create in her imagination an entirely different belief system of virtual reality where she felt at ease and in control? Perhaps this was why her teachings were founded on half truths; the other half came from an endless medley of those philosophies I had heard being sung about. In one of his poems Tennyson, echoes these wonderings with a similar conclusion:

...*a lie which is half a truth is ever the blackest of lies,*
That a lie which is all a lie may be met and fought with outright,
But a lie which is part a truth is a harder matter to fight.[1]

In most matters, however, I found Mum was extremely matter-of-fact and practical — about her forthcoming demise, for instance. Years in advance of any illness, she asked her friend Craig to measure up a coffin for her. On one of my visits, she walked me round to his house to see it. On another visit, we discussed who she wanted to take her funeral, and decided that Ken Hills, a Northern Irish ex-vicar friend, should conduct the service, at Inverness Crematorium. I suggested the local Church of Scotland minister, whom Peter and I had met, as a possible candidate, but this notion did not sit well with Jonathan. He conceded, however, that Ken Hills might be asked to be the celebrant, if he could get away from his home duties in time.

Mum had written out a Living Will as early as 1992, in which she asked that she should not be kept alive if she fell ill and was dying, and that her death should be a time of celebration for all who knew her and her work.

She did not wish any of her family to feel obliged to celebrate with the community at that time. We belonged to a different 'lifetime' (she often referred to things happening to her 'in another lifetime'). Instead, we should hold some kind of memorial to her wherever we should be when she died. Once again, she did not wish the two families or lifetimes to mix.

In 2004, two important events happened. The most exciting for Mum and the community, was the evaluation of how the world appeared to see her. In Her Majesty's New Year's honours list Mum was awarded the M.B.E. 'for her service to spiritual inquiry'. She was 86 by then. When she heard the news, she chose not to travel to London to receive this honour from the Queen as she preferred to receive it in the place that 'had been her home and labour of love for more than forty years,' wrote the *Findhorn Community News*. So in March, seated on a golden chair, she received her M.B.E.

The investiture was conducted by the Queen's representative, the Lord Lieutenant of Moray, Air Vice Marshal George Chesworth. Mum had known the Chesworths for some years, since their children had been at school together in Forres. The Community News continues: '...Surrounded by wider family and representatives of the media, the award crowns her life work of encouraging all to find God within themselves.... Frail, though elegant as ever in a lilac suit, Eileen said she was surprised by news of the award and dedicated it to God.'

In October of that year, Peter and I drove north again to see Mum with our daughter and grandson who were very keen to get to know her better. Neither Georgina nor Javier had seen her since Georgina's wedding in 2000, and Javi had been just under three years old at the time. We used the half-term break as a birthday treat for Javi, just seven years old, to visit his great grandmother. For the journey, Javi's two-and-a-half month old Border Collie, Misty, came too, lying across the car's back window ledge. Every lay-by marked 'P' for parking meant a stop for Misty to pay a visit, so it was a slow, two-day journey with a night-stop en route. On arrival at the Foundation, we had to obtain special permission to keep the dog in the bungalow allotted to us, called 'Genesis'. It was thus named because it had been the first actual building on the foundation's site. It was where Mum, Peter Caddy and their boys had first moved in and put down roots after the cramped years in the caravan.

Two years previously, I had left Mum in a very poor state of health, suffering from one of her back attacks and bed-ridden for some days after my departure. This was to be a much happier visit, with Mum up and active, more able to cope with her ailments. She had told Helmut and Karin of our coming. True to form, keen fisherman Helmut took Peter and Javi for an enjoyable day's fishing; we also visited Loch Ness in the hopes of a sighting of the legendary monster, but had to content ourselves at the lochside with an inflated look-alike in a small pond, and others' photographs of the real thing! These were displayed in the magnificent millennium exhibition hall dedicated to the elusive creature.

We also visited a big farm near Aviemore which trained Border Collies for work, first teaching them to herd ducks before they were permitted to round up the ever-decreasing flocks of sheep on the fells. Misty sat with her back to the demonstration, intent only on the motley selection of collies patiently awaiting their turn to perform.

Our daughter, interested at the time in Buddhism, found much to draw her to the Foundation, as did the many Japanese visitors who came each year. Shambala, the Buddhist centre across the road from the Foundation, was grooming the seven-year old daughter of the owners to become the next Dalai Lama. I gathered recently that Shambala had closed due to lack of funds. On each of my visits, I noticed gradual changes in Mum's health and physique. An early riser, she would dress and sit in her room meditating beside a candle. Then at 6 a.m. walk to the Sanctuary nearby, where she was joined by a handful of community members for meditation, and to learn about any message or vision she might receive. After a fall in the snow, she employed an elegant umbrella to steady her dawn walks, whatever the weather. Later on, when she had lost the sight of an eye through diabetes, her neighbour, Mike Scott, would call for her at six and accompany her to the Sanctuary. Then, more frequently now, a back spasm would prevent even meditating in her room, and the whole exercise gradually came to a halt.

During the same year she became more immobilised, Channel 4 TV, in pursuit of way-out and freakish programmes, sent a film crew to the Foundation. They spent five weeks living with the community, studying its inner workings and activities and filming hundreds of hours of footage. By November 2004 their findings had been pared down to just three hours of the more sensational aspects of the community's lifestyle. *The Haven* was screened in three episodes, covering all the Foundation's alternatives on offer.

Towards the end of the final episode, they had filmed a Council meeting of the responsible members discussing how the community would function if and when their mother-figure died. At the point of filming, Eileen had been very ill with one of her worst spasms and the community was worried about her future health, and where future leadership would come from. By the time *The Haven* series came on television, Mum had recovered enough to watch all three episodes. After the final episode, she was on her way to bed, so amused by the Council's dilemma that she literally 'fell about laughing.' Her carer was in another room when Mum keeled over and broke her hip.

After an operation to pin the fragile bones of her hip, the fall proved to be the beginning of a more rapid decline in her health. She was bedridden for many weeks. Fortunately, the health services in Morayshire are generous in their provision for older people to remain in their own homes for as long as possible, and they certainly came up trumps for our mother. She now needed twenty-four hour caring, and had up to ten devoted carers from the community and Forres in her retinue. Doctors and physiotherapists from the Forres Medical Centre were always on hand and attentive. Alison from Cumberland, who lived in Forres with her family, took up the medical reins as her stalwart nurse for the next two years.

During each subsequent visit, Mum and I grew a little closer. On two of these, her sister Torrie, my godmother, and I went together and shared a bungalow in the community. These were times often of simply sitting and listening to the two sisters reminiscing about their halcyon childhood days in Alexandria, Egypt. One memory I recall was of the thrilling times they had being rowed out to The Ark, an old hospital ship abandoned by either Nelson or Bonaparte (they couldn't remember which) after one of their battles at Aboukir Bay around 1798. Their Uncle Alec had bought and renovated The Ark. The children would be rowed there by an Arab, who kept an eye on them for a couple of nights and cooked them atrocious meals, while they had a whale of a time. They loved swimming at night in the phosphorescent waters.

Unfortunately, serious schooling put an end to such enjoyable capers, when Mum was ten and Paddy was twelve. She, Paddy and Rex were sent on the long trip back to Ireland alone, clutching passports and very little luggage, to stay with Aunt Florence to be 'properly educated'.

These two occasions were also a bonding time with my aunt with whom I got on remarkably well - a practical, down-to-earth person who spoke her mind, had the same sense of humour and with whom I shared ideas about how we could set the world to rights. Unimpeded by any efforts to rebuild a relationship, I found her a far easier person to relate to than my own mother.

With decreased mobility, Mum had to resort to a wheelchair, and finally a hoist was used to move her from room to room. As she remarked, she had to learn to 'be' rather than 'do', and often found this hard to accept and frustrating. However, this 'be-ing' presented the golden opportunity I needed – the time when I was able to become more fully involved in her life; to take up the role of a true daughter; the precious time to know my mother in greater depth as the person she had by then become – no longer the mother of forty years ago, idealised in my memory.

The next months were destined to show how she, and we, were able to translate her decline into a time of acceptance and contentment.

For Eileen

Eileen there in Scotland braw,
Holding court at Cornerstone,
Your family spread beyond this shore:
But you are not alone.

The Caddy clan and many a Combe,
Fraser, Bell and George,
And Hinton, whose wedding you'll recall —
A new era helped to forge.

We've all a long way come since then,
Old hurts have been forgotten;
United are the girls and men,
The eight that you've begotten.

You're loved by all both near and far —
Your many-featured kin;
To them you are a brightling star
Who's loved through sick and sin!

Just rest assured your failing health
Is not the final story:
Your Saviour who is Christ the Lord
Will welcome you to Glory.

P.J.H.
3.7.06

28

A Long Summer of Bitter-sweet Content

The bud may have a bitter taste,
but sweet will be the flow'r.
Olney Hymns – William Cowper

DURING many walks throughout the summer of 2006 I was to become more familiar with the fishing village of Findhorn, at the mouth of the wide estuary of the River Findhorn. During the eighteenth century it was a major port, but became less navigable for large vessels as the movement of sand reduced the depth of the estuary's mouth. Nowadays, instead of herring fishing, leisure craft are moored along its banks, sheltered by the pine forest of Culbin Sands situated on the far side of the estuary. It is a tranquil, gnat-free corner of Scotland in the summer. The winter months can be wild, so the fishermen's houses are built to withstand the strong winds.

Earlier that year, Jonathan had asked whether I would stand in for him as family representative at Findhorn. He and his family wished to celebrate his 50th birthday travelling for two months in Australia and Bali. He was well aware that Mum would probably not be alive when he returned.

Until then my visits had been brief, interspersed by letters and frequent phone calls over the years, so the quality time spent together as mother and daughter had been fragmented, and later visits often clouded by a back spasm. I looked forward to what promised to be an opportunity when I could have her more to myself and spend precious leisure time with her as one of her carers; it would also be a chance to meet and work with some of the residents, and learn more of how the community operated on a daily basis.

The realization that Mum's time in this world was getting short focused her family's thoughts on how best to spend that time. I suggested to my brother Richard that he and I might visit her together. I also hoped that Mum's sister Torrie would come with us, as she had done before on a couple of occasions. By now, however, Mum's health had deteriorated, and Torrie preferred to remember her as she had been the last time she had seen her, so declined.

Richard and I set off in May. He flew from Birmingham and I from Luton, to meet in Inverness. We were collected by our sterling friend Helmut. When we reached Findhorn and Mum's bedside, she was at a very low ebb and heavily drugged by morphine following another dreaded attack. This was particularly disappoint-ing for Richard, who felt quite strongly that he would probably not see her again.

Once more it appeared that our imminent arrival had triggered a back spasm, although Mum had looked forward to our coming with delight. Such an osteoporotic collapse had occurred several times before one or other of her first family turned up to see her. If they were, in fact, psychosomatic as she now claimed, they were surely a sign that there were unhealed and painful incidents from her past, triggered by our presence and still surfacing in her psyche. Excruciating and debilitating as these spasms were, she remained adamant that she did not have osteoporosis of the spine!

Undaunted by the set-back, Richard and I joined the community for a meal. We had to hold hands in a huge circle before the meal to 'give thanks', and then line up to help ourselves to salads, lentils, chickpeas and pasta. Most of the produce we ate was home-grown. Being a gregarious person, Richard chatted with everybody including founder-member Dorothy Maclean who had come over from her community in California for a visit.

We stayed in one of the guest bungalows, and used the time of Mum's recovery to walk the sand dunes and pebbly beaches, sometimes joined by friend Veronica's boisterous golden retriever, Candy. Veronica, who lived in Findhorn village, was indisposed with an acute back problem and always grateful for a dog-walker. Whenever able, she took care of Mum's garden around her house, often lying horizontally on a rug to ease her own back pain! Veronica's love for Mum and gardening was stronger than her own suffering, and if she couldn't get across to tend Mum's garden, she brimmed over with ideas which her friend Kristy, Mum's Australian carer, would implement for her.

In other ways, the visit had its compensations. We both enjoyed getting to know Jonathan and his family better. When they had visited Rick's Old Cowshed for Mum's 80th, Richard had discovered Jonathan's love of sailing, and had lent him the boat he had inherited from Aunt Janet, Dad's sister. Now Jonathan had his own dinghy, moored in the Findhorn estuary, and he took Richard out sailing for a day while I stayed with Mum.

I was sad for Rick that his precious moments with Mum were few on that occasion. It was as though we were both witnessing her life-blood draining away. My brief times with her were spent mainly at her bedside holding her hand, praying silently for her strength to return, and assuring her, in her wakeful intervals, of my love for her.

During our visit, Helmut and his wife Karin, and Mum's secretary Rosie, all busy people, gave us great and gracious support, generous in both time and understanding. But I was glad Torrie was not with us on that occasion, as it would have been distressing for her to see her sister as she was then.

I believed God had never fully let go of Mum and that her faith in Him (as she saw Him to be) had never wavered. Her mind was often confused, brought on by antibiotics given for urinary infections. It was not surprising, considering all the brain-washing she had been subjected to by Sheena in the past, let alone wading through mine-fields of emotions and philosophies. All we could do now was to pray that He would be merciful with her when she passed over into eternity, which looked all too imminent.

As Richard and I took our departure, Barbara, one of her carers, told us we needed to give our mother 'permission to go': a comforting way of telling us *we* needed to let her go rather than try to hold on to her. I was getting used to the sadness I had felt on previous occasions at the prospect of this being our last 'goodbye'. This proved to be so for my brother, but turned out not to be so for myself.

Jonathan was due to leave Scotland late in June, and I had booked to be there for a week of briefing on June 7th. He wanted to pass on his mantle of responsibility in his absence, and perhaps it was fitting that it should fall on the shoulders of the eldest of her family.

When I arrived at Mum's house, *Cornerstone*, our youngest brother David and his wife Kacie, a chiropractor, with their son Aaron, were just leaving Mum's bedroom, knowing they would not be able to visit her again from the States. This was an emotional moment for David. I had met Kacie once before. At that moment, she seemed oblivious to David's feelings. She grabbed me round the waist, pressed me against her side and commanded: 'This is how you must lift her!' and swept out. Next morning, I went to their caravan to see them off to Aberdeen, but their departure was earlier than they had told me, and I missed the chance to say goodbye to David. It left me wondering whether they had resented my presence.

Mum's health was very poor by now, but she welcomed me smilingly. She was hardly eating, very thin, almost skeletal and deathly white. But the fact she was there at all was a joy.

There was much to discuss with Jonathan before he went on his travels – the organisation for all Mum's carers who were in her employ but paid by the Moray Health Services; and the funeral arrangements he had put in place. I needed to know what both Mum and the community expected to happen if her death occurred during his absence, and what legal formalities would be entailed. We decided that Mike Scott would write an obituary for the press as he was in charge of the community archives. We needed to locate a spot where she wanted her ashes buried in St Barbe's Wood nearby. In her Living Will she had also asked that an oak sapling be planted in her memory, with a simple plaque with her name and the dates she was born and died.

After a week at Findhorn, I flew home, confident that all would run smoothly in my absence. I was due to arrive back a week later for a longer spell, to take over from Jonathan. The night before I returned there, Mum's carer Barbara rang to say that mother was 'ready to go, and very depressed.' As I took off from Luton next day, my thoughts turned to the funeral service and what might be its content. I was not sure what I would find when I arrived there once more. But all was well, and my presence seemed to give my Mum fresh impetus to rally yet again, and get on with the business of living!
Jonathan and his family took off on their globe-trot. At the time, Mum's health and spirits went up and down like a yo-yo, and I could only act as an encourager, while trying to grasp the contingency plans he had put in place for her and her caring team.

During the following summer months, I commuted between home in Dorset and Inverness, all flights paid for by Mum. This involved a coach from Ringwood to Heathrow in the early hours, changing coach at Heathrow for Luton, and then taking a mid-day flight to Scotland.
I quickly discovered what being a true daughter to my mother meant. I was plunged into involvement in her domestic needs, health-care, tactfully stemming a constant stream of would-be visitors and hanging a No Visitors notice on the front-door during her worst

afternoons. On better days, I would ask Mum whether she wanted a particular guest, and only then allow them to see her.

I met and talked with each of her eight or so devoted carers – two from Germany, including the community doctor, an American, an Austrian, one from Australia and another from Switzerland. All were searchers for deeper meaning in life, and had gravitated to Findhorn and become residents there. Through conversations with them all and Mum's many visitors, I made several good friends. Most people were both kind and eager to help whenever necessary – which turned out to be quite often.

Although I found myself fully accepted by everyone, I realized that I was coasting on the love and respect all had for Eileen. My role evolved as a useful liaison for Mum on any domestic decisions that needed to be made, and a buffer for any questions with which she need not be bothered. Her nurse Alison and her carers had their daily rota and medication routine well under way, and they kept a careful diary of her progress. Their detailed care was impressive. Her meals were covered either by the carers, or by housekeeper Karin, who knew all Mum's favourite meals and kept the little deep-freeze well stocked. Karin also looked after the washing and ironing, and keeping the house clean. Mum's long-standing friend John Willoner, was responsible for collecting her many prescriptions, and was a frequent warm-hearted comforter to us both.

Each person around her made a marked effort to maintain the peace and dignity of their patient in this final phase of her long life, however tetchy she became, which fortunately was not too often. I learned to withdraw from the room whenever one of them brought news or problems to her bedside. She was interested in their lives, and treated each one as a son or daughter. They were, after all, her alternative family.

Any shopping, banking, a fresh contract for one of the carers, collecting any necessary items from the on-site

Phoenix Shop with the community's eco-money, fell to my lot. The organization of the garden and its fencing, sorting out someone to cut down some pines outside her bedroom window, any general maintenance, the purchase of a new microwave and toaster, and the much appreciated gift from her family and members of the community of a recliner chair for Mum, were all part of my duties. I also covered the night shifts, since I slept in the upstairs bedroom, but had time off in the afternoons to either sleep or walk.

At night there was an alarm near my pillow, connected to her room so I could hear her breathing and the tinkle of her bell whenever she needed help. Most nights were broken, and she was always awake early. When she stirred, I got her breakfast, and we spent time together. She enjoyed porridge, toast and a cup of tea.

Those early morning times became precious. We discussed things from the past. We talked about Dad and the difficult life they had together which she had felt she never handled adequately; of my own fraught relationship with him which lay behind his final question in a letter to me 'Am I forgiven?' Of course he had been forgiven, but I had never actually *told* him so. I admitted it was I who needed to be forgiven in that case. I asked Mum whether she had ever forgiven herself for leaving us. This proved too painful a probe, and she quickly changed the subject.

Another time, something I read to her from one of St Paul's letters, sparked a reaction: 'I don't like Paul,' she exclaimed. This led to a discussion about his conversion, his blindness, and how Ananias lovingly sought him out and how the 'scales fell from Paul's eyes'. (Inwardly, I longed for the 'scales' to fall from hers.) I reminded her it was she who had once given me my first Bible. It had pictures, and I used it to study in Religious Instruction, with our teacher Mr Clark, at Northlace School when I was eight and nine. These lessons began my own spiritual pilgrimage.

Her life in Alexandria featured several times. I learned about her uncle and aunt, Alec and Lelly, Christian Scientists who had exercised a strong influence on her mother; of how bossy her mother used to be, and of her mother's death after their arrival back in England; of the tragedy of Uncle Rex's epilepsy which Christian Science methods had been unable to cure. Rex's illness worsened until he used to bite his tongue and shake all over. Then followed the tragedy of the asylum he went into after their mother died because Mum and Paddy could not cope with his fits, though Paddy remained a regular visitor to the home. Rex died, aged 22, 'of a broken heart,' Mum recalled, unemotionally.

Her cool response was an echo of a similar lack of sympathy when Mum had visited us in Portsmouth after our daughter was born. I had attempted then to explain what our lives had been like growing up without a mother. In her memoirs later, she regarded this as 'poison' I had needed to get out of my system.

We talked over our relationship. I learned that I had told my aunt that Mum was 'a wicked woman!' This must have been deeply wounding for her. I had also told Torrie that I thought Mum's work was 'run by the devil,' and that I had been very anti-Mum in the very earliest days after her departure, which was probably true.

'Do you think so now?' she queried. I countered with how I thought she had been hi-jacked by the Caddys for their own ends, to which her reply was simply, 'Oh dear!' She found any reference to this terrible episode in her life too harrowing to dredge up, and had long since blotted it out. So we left it at that — I with the realisation of how shattered she must have been by the way I seemed to have turned against her after she left us the second time.

One morning she told me she had heard: 'Wonderful music, and they were all happy.' This sounded like soul-talk, and I wondered whether she was on the verge of dying. Then it dawned on me she was hallucinating. A recent urinary infection had necessitated a strong antibiotic. Although her mind was normally clear, at times it wandered. For instance, she often mistook her bedroom for the one upstairs where I was sleeping, and on another occasion saw an imaginary figure at the foot of her bed.

Gradually, though, she became stronger and better. It was a pleasure to see her get about in a wheelchair and watch television. We watched various DVDs and live programmes, including the Wimbledon tennis final between Federer and Nadal in which Federer became fourth-time champion. We enjoyed the film *My Big Fat Greek Wedding*. Her TV favourites were *Bargain Hunt*, *Flog It!* and any of the nature series. On one occasion early in 2005, with snow falling outside, we watched the Papal Inaugural Mass of Pope Benedict XVI. This kept her riveted with fascination for a couple of hours.

Veronica had a carpenter friend who built a ramp for Mum's wheelchair so we could roll her down through the patio doors into her garden. At 9.30 a.m. he was measuring up, and by 3.30 p.m. he had it built, varnished and in place. So Mum was able to spend hours outside in the sun-trap of her patio. There she could soak up the sunshine, enjoy her climbing roses and the riot of coloured plants in the herbaceous borders. Veronica and Kristy had been busy planting up her spring and summer garden, and we had added some sunflowers. Watering the garden on a summer evening became another of my tasks.

A favourite pastime was feeding and watching birds, and Mum was delighted when they visited the bird-bath for a drink or a splash. Helmut had invented an ingenious device: a rod on which to hang fat-balls so she could sit inside and watch noisy sparrows and tits feeding in bad weather or through the winter months. She also had a red squirrel that visited her garden, gleaning the seeds dropped by the birds.

Jonathan's son Jason, Mum's grandson, had been commissioned by his grandmother to surround her garden with homemade fencing, since he had just started up his own business in the community. He used the wood from pines cut down from beside her plot, and turned them into fence panels. She was able to watch as he put in each panel.

This turned out to be a time of healing, physically for her, and spiritually for us both. As well as conversations over breakfast, our early mornings would include readings: Psalm 23, and Psalm 42 she enjoyed, and also Psalm 139. Sometimes I read to her from *Word for Today*, and bits of the Bible I was studying at the time. With sight in only one eye, she loved being read to, and listened to talking books from time to time.

I had kept and long treasured her copy of *Anne of Green Gables* which she had had as a girl and once read to us as children. It had belonged to my great grandmother, Mrs Bull, and been passed down through my grandmother to Mum. Remarkably, I had managed to carry it with us throughout our travels. I took this up to her on one of my visits, and began a new phase of interest, whereby her carers and I read to her not only *Anne of Green Gables* but half a library: all Laura Ingles Wilder's books, *Kidnapped* by R. L. Stevenson, several children's stories brought in by Kieron, another of her carers, and *Girl with a Pearl Earring* by Tracy Chevallier, being but a few. Reading to Mum became not only a bedtime routine which helped her drop off to sleep, but almost a full-time occupation, after the mundane medical and washing chores had been completed.

At one stage during a longer visit in July, I felt our relationship had stalled. She asked me to read from the daily notes put out by the Unitarian church which I knew did not believe in the Trinity, and which appeared to distort Bible quotes. I began to feel out of my depth, and in need of help. One afternoon, I asked Veronica if she could drive me over to Pluscarden Abbey to see the

Abbot, Father Hugh. I spent an hour-and-a-half with him, talking over my perplexities, my present role, and about being a poor pray-er. He told me how the Holy Spirit could build on the tiny bit of Holy Spirit in my mother. 'God sees your heart. He knows your sense of inadequacy. Your longing for your mother's salvation is a prayer. He knows it all. You are sowing seeds. You are a sower, but the growth work is His. Just by being there, being available ...the Holy Spirit will work.'

I gave Father Hugh a copy of my mother's autobiography *Flight into Freedom and Beyond*, and asked him whether he would ever have the time to come over to visit her. He said he would love to meet her. As I left the Abbey, I felt encouraged by his words and response. Veronica was waiting patiently outside in her car, having been for a long walk with Candy.

Mum was cross that I had been away for so long. Her obvious displeasure and jealousy that I had been out with Veronica for lunch and away all afternoon, surprised me. Then I remembered a similar jealous streak surfacing once before, during a visit she and Torrie made to us in Spain, after I had been out on a walk with Torrie. I realised then how much my mother wanted me all to herself. Fortunately, her mood changed quickly when I gave her my full attention.

By now, she was walking in small steps with the help of a Zimmer frame and was out of pain. The sunny weather pulled her out of the doldrums, and in just twelve days I had seen an enormous turn-around in her well-being. It was time to prepare her for my flight south again for a week, and I allowed a couple of days in advance for her acceptance of this, on the basis that I would be back again soon.

At home Peter was managing gallantly with housekeeping, dog-walking and our family requirements, all of which we had discussed by telephone. But by mid-July he felt I needed to come back home for at least a week or more in between visits, as three July birthdays of family members were in the offing.

During the time at home, midst the birthday celebrations, telephone calls to and from Scotland to Mum or her carers helped monitor her state of mind and health. On July 31st I was free to fly back. Jonathan was due to arrive home shortly in August to start the school term; Jason needed to finish his fence panels; more pine trees behind Mum's bedroom, darkening her room, were impeding telephone cables and needed lopping by the community's resident German tree surgeon.

Mum had suffered a fall and was in very low spirits when I returned. The accident had brought on another back spasm, and she was just climbing back to normality after her morphine hibernation. She was still in great pain and expressed how discouraged she felt at constant pill-swallowing. However, she perked up at my arrival and told me she had decided she would 'get up tomorrow'. She needed a lift in her spirits, or a 'carrot' as we often called it – a fillip to brighten her limited horizon and smarten up for. I could tell her that her grandson, Andrew, was preparing to drop in to see her. Our son had mentioned he wished to visit his grandmother and possibly interview her on film. He hoped to combine this visit with a short media training he planned to take in Edinburgh. Mum was pleased at the prospect of meeting a grandchild whom she had only rarely seen since he was small.

The private and incognito visit from Father Hugh needed some careful planning too. I did not mention it to Mum until I had confirmed an afternoon with her many carers when I could be on duty alone. By now, I could handle Henry the Hoist in order to move her into the sitting room after her siesta. She could only manage about an hour sitting up in the recliner, so their time together would only be brief. I suppose I hoped this occasion might bring her one step nearer to God's truth.

Father Hugh had told me in a recent letter that three other communities were now praying for Mum's (and her world family's) rescue from 'this parody into God's truth for mankind.' It was both a comfort and a joy that this burden was shared, and I was grateful that he had made that possible, and was proving such a strong ally.

The next step was to prepare Mum for their meeting. I reminded her that I had gone over with Veronica to visit Pluscarden, and had met Father Hugh. 'While we talked, he said he would like to meet you. He's read your autobiography and knows your story. He says your book prompts several questions he'd be glad for you to help him answer,' I ventured.

'Oh yes, I've been there to Pluscarden several times. I'd like to meet him. Do invite him,' was her reply.

From then on, she referred to him as 'The Rev' and kept asking me when he was coming. A day later, he threaded his way through the community warren of caravans and bungalows to her house. Fortunately, he was wearing 'civvies' as I'd suggested his flowing white Benedictine robe might cause a stir in the community. Mum looked beautiful that afternoon, thanks to her Austrian carer, Elisabeth's, ministrations in the morning – hair curled, make-up on, pearls and dangly earrings. Elisabeth had a knack of bringing the best out of Mum.

I was nervous but Mum was radiant and rose to the occasion. She and the Abbot had a relaxed hour together over tea when he told her about the history of Pluscarden and its mother abbey Prinknash, (pronounced prinnage, like spinach) and about another abbey he wanted to develop north of Oban. He talked of one of the brothers, Mungo, now in his eighties who was dying. 'So am I!' proclaimed Mum. He had read her autobiography and praised her piece on forgiveness in the *And Beyond* part.

'Very important,' said Mum. 'Forgiveness is very important. She (pointing to me) and I have had some wonderful talks together, of healing and forgiveness during this time,' she confided to him. A couple of times they laughed together while I was making tea, and I offered up a silent 'thank You' that Mum and he could enjoy their time together.

As he departed, he said he would like to come again, which Mum encouraged him to do. Then I took Father Hugh out through Mum's garden and up to a look-out where he could view the river estuary. As he looked down the slope to the road, he remarked that this would be a good secret way to come up from the road without being seen. He also invited me to go over to the abbey for another visit while I was still there. I told him there was a lot of sorting out to do of Mum's possessions, and a visit might need to be the next time I was up with her.

I breathed a sigh of relief after Father Hugh's departure. It had been a small miracle in itself that we were not interrupted in any way during his visit. My next news from him was that he had been promoted to become the Catholic Bishop of Aberdeen.

Mum's secretary, Rosie, and I had already been hard at work upstairs, sorting through countless gifts from admirers all over the world, memorabilia, thousands of photos, and a huge number of tapes from *Reader's Digest*, as well as books. There were electrical goods, umbrellas and clothes Mum had bought by mail order. Decisions needed to be made, and during the next days, Rosie did a superb job of disposing of box upon box of forgotten treasures, books and clothes to the local Red Cross and Highland Hospice charity shops, as well as through the community's boutique. Anything of value we kept back to be displayed in a sale within the community, planned for after her demise. Mum had been enthusiastic about the idea that these items might raise much-needed funds in aid of the seniors living in the Foundation, of which there were already several, all well known to her.

This exercise turned up several letters and papers amongst which I found my grandparents' birth certificates, Mum's and Dad's marriage certificate, her birth certificate, old passports, and her Will. The latter needed up-dating with correct addresses of her eight children. I divided the photos into separate envelopes containing snapshots appropriate to each family, and posted them off to them. Others, unidentifiable but obviously from the Jessop family's days in Alexandria, I took home in the hope that Torrie could enlighten me.

My thoughts were turning towards home again by now. Jonathan was due back any day, and the number of Mum's carers was soon to dwindle due to various courses which they had booked to attend in September. I could not leave until I knew that Mum's care was covered adequately.

Alison Collins and I were washing up in Mum's kitchen one day, discussing these arrangements. She asked, 'Would Penny be able to come over and take care of your mother, do you think?' Penny was living in New Zealand, but had lived, with her own family, in Forres for a while and knew the area well. She also knew Alison as they had worked together in a local senior residents' home at that time. I had talked with her on the telephone recently, and knew she was having an interview as receptionist for an estate agency, so I demurred on her behalf.

In the middle of that night, I awoke with the clearest thought that we should at least put the idea to her, so I called New Zealand that day. When I put the idea to her, her reply was, 'I'm at a crossroads, Jen, and not sure what I should be doing next. I'll give it some thought.' The fact that Jonathan could pay her fare over, and that she would be employed by him as an official carer helped, and she rang back later to say she would arrive in the second half of September. This was a marvellous solution to the forthcoming drop in the number of Mum's carers.

Andrew's visit to meet his grandmother on his way to Edinburgh was imminent, and he was due to stay a night in Veronica's B&B. He is a vegetarian, so I took her a macaroni cheese the day before he arrived, and had also made one for Mum. 'Always make sure to put enough milk in it,' she'd reminded me.

I was due to leave the following day with Andrew. Karin and I collected him from Inverness, and Alison Collins had cooked a roast chicken for him for our lunch (he was a chickenarian), and had made a chocolate cake for afternoon tea with Granny. He was unwell with a heavy cold, so his time with her was somewhat briefer than envisaged as he needed to sleep for two hours. After tea, I whisked him off to Veronica's for a good walk with Candy at high tide on the beach, and back through the village, before enjoying macaroni cheese and fresh-picked raspberries with Veronica from her garden.

Veronica's proverbial green fingers, and her garden, were the source of much that was now in Mum's garden. Andrew was inspired by her guided tour of it, and I flew back next day with a number of plants for him to add to his own garden in Brixton. In the meantime, Helmut had volunteered once more to transport us, and brought Andrew over from Veronica's to say his farewell to Granny. Again, as I kissed her, I was assailed by the thought this might be our last sight of her.

There were several occasions, while being with Mum, when her helplessness and frailty had me in tears. Sometimes her face looked so sad. It had taken almost a lifetime to become her daughter once more, and she had genuinely loved having me with her. Now I must let her go again, and each time was more difficult and heart-rending. The one comforting thought was that Penny would be there before too long. I just hoped she would arrive in time.

What would we have done without Helmut during those months? Now he chatted happily with Andrew all the way to Inverness Station to pick up the Edinburgh train; and then we drove on to the airport for my homeward flight. Helmut was very fond of my mother, and told me she would continue, even in death, to be his spirit-guide.

I rang Mum next day to tell her about Penny's decision to join her. 'How wonderful!' she exclaimed. Now she had another carrot to look forward to. She was also about to celebrate her 89th birthday, having told me adamantly that she would live until ninety. Before I left, we had talked of how she wished the community to commemorate her birthday, but that she would probably do so quietly in her own home rather than in the community centre. I had told her that we had arranged for Torrie to be staying with us so we could all toast her on 26th August, and would call her on her special day. We phoned her at breakfast that day, as Mum was getting dressed. She sounded in good form; she always rose to a special occasion.

The DVD set to music which Barbara Coates had made that summer of 'Eileen in her Rose Garden' belied Mum's cheerful voice and disposition at this time. When I showed it to Torrie and my cousin Jo Jessop, who came over for the day to visit her aunt, they were both shocked by her appearance – hunched in her wheelchair and painfully thin. They said they wished they hadn't seen the film. Seeing her through their eyes showed me how quickly she had deteriorated in a short space of time. I became more anxious about whether she would still be alive when Penny arrived.

Φ

For a long time I had harboured anxiety about where Mum would end up in the after-life. As I saw her life dwindling away this question became acute. There was one person I knew who might understand what lay at the root of my anxiety. He was priest and author Reverend Peter Lawrence. He lived near us at Canford, and had given a talk in our church hall recently. He understood spiritual warfare. He had told us in his talk that the spiritual plane is more real than the temporal world we live in daily. As it was my uncertainty of Mum's spiritual destiny on entering eternity that loomed large in my mind, I turned to Peter Lawrence to explain my fears. I knew instinctively that he would understand.

After listening carefully to all I could tell him about my mother, he scribbled down on a piece of paper a remarkable prayer, and handed it to me. 'You can use this when you are with your mother,' he advised. It read:

In the name of Jesus of Nazareth, I bind all demons in Mum. I place the cross between Mum and me and every member of the family so that all ungodly things will be absorbed in the cross while all godly things will continue to flow through.

I place the cross between Mum's spirit and all demons in her that they will no longer blind her eyes to the truth, that she may see Jesus and believe in Him alone before she dies. Amen.

A unique prayer, and a huge challenge to grasp. My understanding of Christ's cross had not stretched to how it might function in a relationship, or of the power it could generate in the realms of the human spirit. Oswald Chambers expresses this so much better than I could by his words:

The Cross did not happen to Jesus. He came on purpose for it... The Cross is the centre of Time and Eternity, the answer to the enigmas of both... The centre of salvation is the Cross of Jesus, and the reason it is so easy to obtain is because it cost God so much. The Cross is the point where God and sinful man merge with a crash and the way to life is opened – but the crash is on the heart of God. [1]

Thinking more deeply on the meaning of Peter Lawrence's prayer, I began to see it as a tool I could put to use in my mother's presence. The words Jesus uttered out of his pain on the cross came into my mind: 'Father, forgive them for they *know not what they do.*'

I knew already that the demons of darkness are out to divide and destroy, to gain full power over us. On the other hand, out of this power in the Cross, Jesus had also spoken to Mum: 'Father, forgive Eileen for she knows not what she did.' I had also found a place where I could stand and say: 'Father, forgive me for I knew not how I hurt her, and others, with my closed heart and judging words.'

But — and it seemed an impossible 'but' to overcome – could I honestly see the forgiveness of Jesus on the cross covering the pain, division, deprivation to family life caused by Peter and Sheena Caddy in order to achieve their secret agenda? No, I could not! But at the foot of his cross, seeing what Jesus' sacrifice had done for the whole of humanity, I realized that the unfathomable dimension of God's love could and did include even *their* wickedness. I was challenged to accept that fact. I had to trust Him in this, despite the fact that the Caddys had never themselves known the full significance of that incredibly gracious act, when Christ's life was given up for theirs too. After all is said and done, only God Himself can sort out every single one of us as either sheep or goats when we reach eternity.

I was yet to watch the genius, simplicity and timing of this amazing God of ours reveal themselves in the final phase of Mum's life in a way I could never have dreamed possible — through the loving heart and spirit of our youngest sister, Penny.

Mother of the Daughter

Birthed by you
I came for nourishment
Held close, secure – but
You could not feed me.

A toddler, yet torn from you
I grew without you
Lost from your touch –
No cradle of warmth.

As adolescent, red tape cut,
I came to seek my loss.
No maternal bonding
Yet a recognition of blood
In manner undenied.

As young adult I brought you
My mate choice, my life choice,
Craving acceptance,
Expectant, proud – yet cut by censure,
Censure of youth, all warning, no joy.

I came to you with the fruit of our passion –
The next generation – to succour, to teach,
To show them that love through past lost could endure,
But deep in your kingdom, too protected to reach
There was no time or energy for them.

I come to you in maturity
To capture life's last moments.
In softening need I hold you close,
The pain – oh so poignant –
The daughter now the mother
To the mother of the daughter.

PJNG (Aug. 2001)

29

Going Home

I look forward to leaving my old cocoon behind and letting the butterfly, the spirit, fly free. I don't feel there is anything to be afraid of. Spiritually I feel I am prepared to move on with no feeling of fear, only of joy and gratitude. I am indeed very, very blessed.
Flight into Freedom and Beyond — Eileen Caddy

IN the 1980s, Penny and her husband Pete and their four children had lived two years either in the Findhorn Foundation, or later in Forres six miles away. Penny wanted to be near Mum. Their time there had not been a success. At a time when Penny most needed a mother, she soon discovered Mum had little time to devote to her or the children because she was usually too busy with her alternative family. However, she did help the family put down a deposit for a house in Drumduan Gardens, Forres. Disappointingly, though, their natural blood relationship had little chance to bond.

The children went to Forres Academy where Tammy, the eldest, picked up a Scots accent. Penny worked in a retirement home in Forres and her husband Pete had a job as a milkman. Then he and Penny separated. He left his family, went off to Elgin in deep depression, tried unsuccessfully to commit suicide, and eventually disappeared altogether. Following these traumas, Penny decided to join sister Mary Liz in New Zealand, taking her two younger children with her and leaving the two eldest to pursue university and a chef's course in the U.K.

Come mid-September in 2006, Penny's arrival at our mother's bedside heralded a new phase in both their lives. It was a getting-to-know-you time, and a steep learning curve for Penny. She brought all her skills of intelligence, energy, spiritual sensitivity and practicality to bear in her new task as carer, though at first with much trepidation about how she would cope with the mother she hardly knew.

She began to find her way around the community, get to know Mum's other carers, her many visitors, the daily and nightly routines, and the all-important medication times and requirements. Being a thoughtful and caring person, she was able to slip into her new role fairly quickly. Her sense of humour and ready laugh brought lightness wherever she went. She kept a detailed diary of those months, and her notes have provided a helpful source for writing about Mum's final chapter.

Here are a few of her initial impressions, written on 30th September, a few days after her arrival:

Feel strangely in limbo – the eternal bag lady in transit – N.F.A. (no fixed abode). Neither fish nor fowl within a community structure of Eco money, Earthshare veggie packs, an Eco village of Eco-friendly built houses run with a Living Machine (sewage and grey water filtering system servicing it). Vegetarian meals at lunch and some evenings for which one has to purchase a blue meal ticket for £3 and write one's name up at the kitchen hatch before 10 a.m. if one anticipates 'taking lunch'!

The Phoenix, an on-site shop/store, is crammed full of arty crafty stuff, smothering incense and healing crystals, books, publications of every variety of self-help improvement/life philosophies, cards, games, jewellery, clothing, ethnic this and thats; New Age music, wind chimes, musical instruments; food (organic, of course!). Everything from nuts and seeds to pulses, honeys, jams, pastes, diabetic cakes, GI-free anything and everything – organic drinks, fresh breads (dependable, solid and good for the bowel), veggies and fruit with lots of spots, bugs, blemishes and nature spirits in them! Sugar-free cakes and biscuits.

There is an apothecary section for every type of herbal essence, medication, natural vitamin or supplement, oils, teas, detox and purification – even make-up – all served by intense and well-meaning folk with many layers of earth-coloured natural-fibre clothes, long straggly greying hair and strong garlic breath!

This description of the on-site shop, the Phoenix, describes something of the strange vibrations which resonated in the community, emanating from the 'alternative' lifestyles of those living there, and their requirements from their local 'super store'. Interestingly, neither Penny nor I sensed anything weird within the wooden walls of Mum's chalet, where life continued along fairly normal lines, amidst the clutter of crystals, photos, ethereal pictures on every wall, and other gifts filling her window-sills and every available nook, in spite of our earlier clear-up.

The next three months were busy for Penny. She did not relish entering the cold and gusty days of a Scottish autumn and winter after the equable climes of New Zealand. One compensation, however, was that she was freed over a couple of weekends to travel to Edinburgh to see her two grandsons and daughter Tammy, and also have them come to stay twice in the bungalow which had been designated to be her home near Mum. Others of Penny's family came to visit and stay with her too. On a coach trip from Forres to Edinburgh five years earlier she had written the poem which appears before this chapter, expressing the strange role-reversal she was even then beginning to experience.

Each day became precious as she watched Mum become ever more frail and often confused from antibiotics. Pen kept in close touch with us by telephone and email. As Christmas approached, the almost daily bulletin of Mum's health was increasingly disturbing. By the end of November, her doctor had said she might have two weeks or two months left to live. It was time to pay her another visit, and give Penny the sisterly support for which she felt in need. Her days were intense, emotionally and physically, and the night-care had become disrupted. By now, she or one of the other carers slept on a mattress on the sitting room floor, next to Mum's bedroom.

I flew up to Inverness on December 4th clutching a small Christmas tree and tree lights, with a miniature set of Nativity figures in my suitcase. The hope was that Helmut could use them decorating Mum's bedroom to bring a touch of Christmas spirit into the dark, cold days of winter. Resourceful man that he is, he also found a huge star to light up her window, and strung coloured lights from wall-to-wall on her sitting room ceiling. We all wanted her final days to be filled with light and joy.

Penny wanted to show me a recent letter which grandson Steve Combe had written to Eileen at the end of November. He had always known Mum as 'my distant Grandmother' or 'Granny in Scotland', and even when working in Scotland himself, had only visited her once. This letter was to make amends and tell her how much he loved her and treasured his brief times with her. Now in New Zealand with his family, he reached out to his grandmother with these words of encouragement:

There are times in your life that I can never understand what you went through. You made some decisions in circumstances that I would never wish for anyone. But the fruits of your love, courage, creativeness and passion now surround you. You have such a strong heart. I can only imagine how dearly God cherishes you.

It is my prayer (well not only mine – it was just given me by the Holy Spirit) that your soul be truly reconciled with God. I pray that your strong inner will surrenders to His grace and accepts the gift of Jesus Christ to lead you to the Father.

As an ex-soldier now, the concept of 'surrender' is a tough one for me. But I feel you have been a spirit-led prayer warrior all your life, and God wants to have you surrender to his decrees. I pray that you find a new Joy and Peace in Him that you have known so well.

Both Penny and I could identify with and echo those same longings for our mother.

Much of that brief visit was spent either chatting with

Mum about old times, or visiting new friends and making telephone calls to others, including Mum's 'adopted daughter' Linda in Australia, and Father Hugh at the abbey. Another piece of news came from the New Zealand branch of the family during those few days: the birth of Abigail Shackleton, Mum's ninth great grandchild – news which she could receive with rejoicing and pride. We also had time to do shopping for some basic needs for Penny's sparsely equipped holiday kitchen. As far as Mum was concerned, everything that could be done for her dignity, comfort and care was in place. When on Friday, December 8th it was time to leave her once more, I was trustingly content that she was in safe hands with Penny in charge, and knew that all would be well.

As I took off in the plane from Inverness to Luton, I wrote:

I can still see her, lying peacefully against a mound of pillows, 'I'm in a warm place' (her words) in her green reclining chair – her white hair brushed and fluffed up, her one seeing brown eye open, thoughtful or amused by turns, the left eye now opaque with blindness. How I love her – 'Always have and always will,' I told her this morning. She wore a deep pink blouse and her cream cashmere cardigan with the pink roses embroidered over the breast. Her smooth skin was the beige colour of her foundation cream. Her rose-pink lipstick matched the pink flowers of her cardigan. As I recounted some of my family's animal stories, she smiled and laughed. I held her hand in both mine – mine were always cold and she warmed them in hers as she had often done.

When it was time to leave, I kissed her – this time with a sense of peace and joy – not that awful sadness I'd had in the past so many times when I left her, thinking I wouldn't see her again. No. This was quite different. Penny was there and would give her all she needed in love, tenderness and blessing. She had Helmut's Christmas lights, the birds feeding and knocking fatballs against her window, and the garden to gaze out upon. She was most assuredly in a 'warm place.'

Three days later, Penny rang with the latest news –

Anana, Craig's daughter, had been in to play her harp for Mum the day before, and Mum wore her royal blue blouse for the occasion. She drank in the harp's gentle soul-music. But Mum was no longer taking her medication, eating or drinking much now. Pen said she had been sitting beside her on the Monday morning, trying to spoon some jelly into her mouth, and Mum had said to her, 'I'm going home. It's time to go home.' Pen replied, 'That's wonderful, darling,' and watched as she slept her way into a coma.

She writes her own account of 'my last special moments with Mum':

In those wee hours, just after 4 a.m. when I felt Mum slipping away, I kept talking quietly and praying inwardly as I listened to her breathing. There was a moment watching her closed eyes when it was right to encourage her steps forward. 'The Lord Jesus loves you and is waiting for you...do you see Him? Go to Him, Mum. Accept Him!'

Smiling, I made the sign of the cross on her forehead and said: 'I claim you for Him in the name of Jesus Christ!' thinking inwardly... whether you like it or not! Great sense of peace and relief. I felt the pressure of her hand relax... and thanked God for the privilege of being there, asking Him to take her weary self from her withered body.

It was as simple as that. As Penny told me Mum's and her own last words, a sense of joyous relief swept through me as I considered the way the good Lord had provided Pen to minister to our Mum in this final chapter of her 'many lives' (as she often referred to her own eighty-nine years), and the gentleness of His method of ushering our mother into His hands.

Mum was comatose over the next two days. Jonathan came in to hold her hand for a time. Penny remained there for sixteen hours, praying for Mum's soul as it moved into eternity and her little body wound down. I could not but wonder whether, within the dark depths of that coma, a final last-ditch conflict was being fought out between Mum's demons against God's all-powerful 'heavenly hosts', to claim her soul. Was this preparing her to meet her Maker with His compassionate forgiveness and loving 'welcome home' for which she had been waiting? She had told me recently she would 'enter the Light'. I had suggested that 'underneath were the everlasting arms' of the Person. I could only hope and pray that by now she had not only reached the light but also found the reality of my own, and my family's, deepest yearnings for her.

Profoundly weary by now, Penny relinquished her long vigil to Kieron who had come on duty, and she staggered to her bungalow to get some sleep. Kieron's summons came some hours later. Mum's breathing had changed and she should come. Penny ran to Cornerstone and was there as Mum gasped her final breath. It was in the early morning of December 13th.

Joyfully, together they prepared the body to be laid in the coffin Mum had asked Craig to make. By now it had been polished and the lid made and was no longer the chip-board shell Mum had shown me in Craig's house some time before. She was indeed practical to the last!

My last visit to Findhorn came three days later for the funeral. At the Inverness Crematorium as many of the family as were able to attend at such short notice had gathered, in spite of Mum's instructions in her Living Will that no family need be present.

The community mini-bus, called 'Sir George' (in memory of Sir George Trevelyan), was the hearse, and arrived with the few most loyal community members and friends accompanying the coffin – Craig, Robin, John Willoner, Rosie and Durten with some of her carers - all personally invited by Jonathan.

The twenty-minute service, or The Ceremony of the Release of Eileen's Body (printed on the funeral sheet and illustrated by grand-daughter Caitlin for 'Angel Granny Eileen'), was celebrated by Ken Hills, an old friend of Eileen's and a retired Anglican priest. It was a mixture of Celtic prayer-song to guitar music, one of Mum's meditations embodied in a short address by Craig, and my memories of Mum's first-family's up-bringing and how she had taught us our Christian faith, especially through those dark far-off days in London during the war. These were linked with parts of her 'Love Songs to God' from Psalms 149, 119 and 23, mentioned by her in the ... *And Beyond* section of the 2002 edition of her autobiography. As I spoke, a curiously sinking feeling crept over me. Was I talking into a vacuum, speaking a foreign language to this gathering of devoted, so-called 'enlightened' people? Then I looked up and saw our family ranged in the front seats, and felt encouraged.

The final prayer of committal by celebrant Ken Hills sent Mum's soul winging into the cosmos, in true new age fashion. We were left to imagine Mum's soul orbiting earth like a tiny star out in space. In a letter of thanks written later to Ken Hills, I took exception to this final committing of my mother to the universe. In reply he explained that he had chosen this language so the community members would understand.

Mum had asked that her death should be a joyous celebration, and when we all returned to Jonathan's home in the Foundation a generous tea-party had been laid on by the community's Sparkle Team (home care) with an array of home-made scones, jam and cakes. Mum would have approved of the cheerful party which ensued, amidst mixed feelings of joyous relief, tinged with sadness, at the manner of her final passing.

Jonathan, who had so ably held together the administration of Mum's medical and personal requirements over a couple of years, wanted to use this occasion to thank his remarkable team for all their loving devotion. A tribute of heart-felt gratitude was paid to each one by name: to Mum's devoted nurse Alison and her several care-givers, secretary Rosie and doctor Cornelia. If such words could bless, we hoped they felt their benediction. Mum's immediate family certainly had appreciated the ministrations of all these folk who had poured out their time in personal and medical care: gardening, cooking, endless bouquets of flowers, house-keeping, the fairly frequent 'drop-everything-and-run' emergency when Mum had a back spasm, and more — all performed with loving adulation and good grace for our mother by what Suzanne called 'our Mother's expanded global family.'

For all those years, beyond the bringing up of her first and second families, she had been the founder, spiritual mother and friend to the community for far longer than she had been *our* mother.

Later that same evening, ten of Mum's immediate family sat around the large table in Jonathan's kitchen, discussing the day's events. Neither Mary Liz in New Zealand, nor Suzanne in Canada had been able to attend Mum's farewell, but a fax had come through from Suzanne which Jonathan suggested Richard should read to us all. She entitled it 'My Mother', and it expressed some of the family's memories and the happiness of our family life before Peter Caddy had stepped into it. In her words:

You leave me sad, glad, and oh! so grateful for a happy childhood.

You were a truly <u>wonderful</u> mother and a fun friend to have. Always there, even though most of our lives have been lived continents apart.

When we re-met after 17 long years, time just vanished and we immediately re-connected and enjoyed each other all the more. You taught me (us) so many good lessons – how to love, even when we were scrapping as children, especially Rick and I who were very close and seemed to find something to squabble over daily – you would say, 'Children, do you love each other?' which made us stop and think.

You taught us to share. I remember spending my weekly sixpence pocket money on a Mars Bar, and when I got home you asked if I'd like to cut it up and share it with the family…

You taught me honesty and gave me a good conscience. We were food-rationed after the war – only two bananas a month. I ate one without permission, so had to come clean with the fact I was guilty of being the banana bandit – and I remember you just smiled.

You also taught me to cook – Yeh!! Aged four, standing on a chair over the AGA cooking scrambled eggs and fried bread for our ever-growing family. And then the happy hours let loose in the scullery with flour, sugar, margarine and currants to make Rock Cakes. Most of the ingredients were all over the table, on the floor and all over me, but what a thrill it was for me to serve my precious baking to Mum and Dad.

You showed us how to appreciate God's natural beauty which surrounded us in our Kingstackley garden: all those nineteen fruit trees and their spring blossoms; the wee snowdrops, violets, lilies of the valley (your favourite), the primroses, lupins, roses and delphiniums, let alone the amazing vegetable garden. And our dear old gardener, Mr Pigeon, whom we loved because he could rattle his teeth! Of course, Rick and I would ask him to do that as often as we dared. Happy and fun memories!

One of the greatest gifts you and Dad gave me, however, was when I asked if I could have a real baby, no more dolls. A few months later, Penny was born, so I knew she was a gift for me, and she has remained that ever since. God bless you, Pen!

Now, full circle, Pen came to care for you and was there when you left this world. How can I ever thank her, and all the many, many extraordinary care-givers you have had over the past while. Living so far away, but knowing you were so well loved and cared for has been a great comfort to me and my family here in Canada…

Even though I cannot be there to say goodbye, I know you are here in my heart and spirit and will continue to give me joy and that wonderful Irish twinkle you have passed on to us all.

I love you, love you, love you, Mum.

Your ever loving daughter, Sue.

This was the only written tribute to our mother by any of her close family at the time, and I have given it in full because Sue expressed for all of us some of the many things we felt.

Two more days were spent helping Alison Collins clearing out all the medical side of Mum's last months. Penny sorted out a few mementoes for each member of the family, including clothes and jewellery to be sent off to our sisters in Canada and New Zealand as well as to family members in the U.K. The residue of her possessions, at her own request, were sold within the community at a big Sunday Brunch Sale in aid of the Findhorn Elders' Fund.

My journey home two days later was marked by a trip with Jonathan and his partner Alison via the crematorium in Inverness to collect Mum's ashes. The lady in the office remarked on what a lovely coffin Mum had. As he returned to the car, Jonathan handed me the ashes and we drove to the airport with me clutching Mum's earthly remains on my lap in their cardboard box. This was my final farewell. Her wishes were that her ashes should be 'scattered around an oak tree planted in St Barbe Baker's wood. Give it plenty of space to grow into a mighty oak reaching to the heavens...' and that she would like 'a stone with a small plaque on it with my name, date of birth 1917 and date of my death, nothing more. Simplicity is my hallmark as God has always reminded us. So keep it simple.' Jonathan, Caitlin, Veronica, with Karin Pibernik, were among those able to perform this task some days later.

Various obituaries for Eileen Caddy appeared over the next days in the national and Scottish newspapers – some factual, some obviously written up a long while before her death, some 'quite inventive' remarked my cousin Peter Sinclair; and some more complimentary.

Only after a lapse of more than five years have I been able to write of that time.

30

Desert Flowers

Remember ye not the former things, neither consider the things of old. Behold, I will do a new thing; now it shall spring forth; ... I will make a way in the wilderness, and rivers in the desert.
Isaiah 43:18-19 (KJV)
The secret things belong to the Lord our God, but the things revealed belong to us and our children forever...
Deuteronomy 29:29 (KJV)

AS the eldest of the five of Mum's first family, I carried an unnecessary burden for years, convinced it was my responsibility to draw our mother away from all her soul-suffering, mental agony, the lies and indoctrination and denial in her life, to where all the pain could be absolved and forgiven by Jesus' own sacrifice through His crucifixion – the same Jesus I had heard her speak of in mocking tones some months before.

Yet, when it had come to Mum's last moments on earth, I was a fascinated bystander, watching the simple and remarkable steps God provided as He took her on the final stage of her earthly journey through the gentle ministrations of our youngest sister Penny. I could feel only great joy and incredulity at how Mum's demise had come about in answer to, or perhaps despite, all my aspirations and pleadings. I marvelled at the ingenuity and simplicity shown by a bountiful heavenly Father so mercifully.

After her death, many kind and moving letters and cards of sympathy poured in from friends. Varied tributes to Mum, and critiques of her work written in the tabloids, lent buoyancy for a short time. In particular, I hoped the comforting words of one kind friend would be true for Mum in the heavenly realms, and for us in time: 'May

Christ our Judge bring her to His perfect will, and keep you all in His everlasting care.'

I had always been certain of her love, and had loved her in the face of all difficulties of non-communication and even opposition. In those last months with her, I had done no more than one's heart longed to do, but had failed to fulfil my self-appointed responsibility of bringing her any nearer to a friendship with Christ. Equally, I had failed to see that this should be God's work and not mine.

Now I felt utterly bereft, not only of the mother I had loved all those years, in and out of absentia, but of all in which I had believed. The once-strong bonds of faith began to shred and fray like a threadbare carpet. I questioned everything I had known, been taught at home and school about God. I lost touch with Him and became a spiritual nomad in an emotional desert with no signposts. It was as though part of my psyche, or perhaps my soul, had gone to the grave with her. Certainly, the raison d'être for my faith had evaporated, and left a vacuum inside. Winter had come; the rose garden of our last summer together had withered and gone. How long would such desolation last?

In *A Grief Observed*, written by C.S.Lewis after he had lost his beloved wife, he commented:

...don't come talking to me about the consolations of religion or I shall suspect that you don't understand...We are under the harrow and can't escape. Reality, looked at steadily, is unbearable.[1]

I could echo those thoughts to the word. I had felt no grief as such when her tired body had freed her gallant spirit. For her, it was such a longed-for and merciful release. She had always been somewhere all our lives, waiting for us to return to her. Now that one vital feature was missing in our mental and emotional landscape.

Losing Mum had bowled over all my ideals like a lot of skittles. I began to make faulty judgements of people, and wrong choices. My spirit wandered, failing to find any spiritual comfort or encouragement in the wisdom of words.

Even our marriage began to founder. Words alone became meaningless and affection proved comfortless. Any seeds of love from my husband or family fell on a stony heart.

Yet throughout this inner turmoil, my husband Peter was the person who stood by me faithfully as my best friend. He remained my rock: solid, detached and sensible. We had decided at the beginning of our lives together that we would be honest with one another about all our ups and downs. Difficult and mortifying as this now became, the anchor had held fast at times in the rough seas of our past, and did so in our present relationship.

Thankfully, I did not forsake the daily habit of a morning quiet-time, Bible reading and journaling my thoughts. These remained a tenuous lifeline, even though often they were times of wrestling with doubts and lack of trust – both of God and people.

There seem to be stretches in an individual's life when an invisible hand compels us to keep plodding on though the pilgrimage holds no joys, no excitement, no 'carrots' to look forward to, and with only despair in the heart. There is nothing more to give of one's depleted strength, except to put one foot in front of the other... just one step more, and minute steps at that... I had come to this stage twice before — aged thirteen, after our mother left us, and again in my teens when suicide seemed an attractive solution. This became a repeat performance.

Where then was the hope I had proclaimed often to others—hope whispering of the possibility of a fresh beginning? I thought I had loved my God, but had no feeling for Him any more. What was it St Paul had written in his letter to the Roman disciples of the Way?

Moreover, we know that to those who love God, who are called according to his plan, everything that happens fits into a pattern for good. (Romans 8:28 J.B.Phillips)

I had lost the love. I had lost the plan. I only knew that the death of a loved one causes profound physical, mental, and spiritual pain. At that particular time it appeared to me that Paul's conviction fell flat on its face, along with most of my knowledge of Christianity to date.

Φ

Now, years later, I can view that loss in a kinder light. 'He restoreth my soul.' My faith in God's goodness has been re-constructed, bit by bit, through hours of meditating, walking the dog alone in all weathers, and with time's healing balm. Elisabeth Elliot once wrote: *God has never promised to solve our problems. He has not promised to answer our questions… He has promised to go with us.*

I discovered He had always been there, and as promised, had come with me. I began to appreciate a divine thread running through our family's lives. I even began to look forward, towards a future.

Soon after Richard set foot in South Africa and had begun farming in the Great Karroo, in one of his rare epistles he wrote of his wonder at springtime there. Each year, out of the parched, cracked and dusty terrain, the spring rains sought out dormant seeds and brought about a vast re-generation, clothing the barren wastes and kopjes (hills and plateaux) with an unending carpet of colourful wild flowers. My later visits to the Karroo were only during dry, desert-like times, but I stored away Rick's vivid description in my memory.

Years later, at the southernmost tip of Spain, Punta Tarifa, we travelled through the similarly spectacular 'Painted Fields' of springtime with their vistas of blue, pink and yellow, sweeping down towards the nearby breezy beach on the Atlantic where the rollers had become a magnet for international windsurfers.

One morning recently, while staying with Richard and Helen at their peaceful country home, The Old Cowshed, (often regarded by us as more like a retreat), there unfurled in my imagination a wonderful tapestry. Through the warp and woof of our five lives, the divine silver and golden threads had been woven by the Master Weaver, using the prayerful entreaties and even obedience of our parents, joined together with those of a thousand friends who knew and cared about us. I could see the threads shining through the fabric of each life, woven by a loving hand to form a unique and glorious pattern of love and constancy for each one of us.

When Richard was a teenager, apprenticed to a pig farmer in Suffolk, a South African veterinary surgeon called Mali Smuts, visited the farm. She was the great niece of Field Marshal Jan Smuts of Boer War fame, who had become Prime Minister of his country. Mali was not only a clever vet, but also a woman of faith who listened to the 'still small voice' in her heart, and daily sought God's direction for her life. She saw Richard, the farm hand, as a pig-farmer-in-the-making, and threw down a gauntlet – would he consider going out to South Africa where farming friends of hers in the Great Karroo wanted to start up a pig unit, using wild pigs which had been worrying their sheep? Thanks to her vision and encouragement, my brother rose to this challenge to try out his skills, and not only succeeded in the task, but later met and married Helen in his newly adopted country. After some years of farming and raising a family, they found their way back to England to educate their two children, and eventually bought their listed cowshed in Herefordshire.

Peter and I had been invited there for a weekend. During this short sojourn, Richard had taken me into his workshop in the barn — where every screw, nail and tool had its place, labelled lovingly during hours of solitary labour in this 'glory hole'. His model airplanes, mostly in process of being repaired, hung or perched upside down, and on the central table a vice held a chair belonging to a South African neighbour. The chair was under reconstruction and being glued together. In his workplace I saw a perfect model of order, cleanliness and care—evidence of the Carpenter's hands at work, using Rick's enormous potential for practical DIY. His joy and pride in presenting this, his own precious space for others to see, shone out of every pore.

We took advantage of a windless day to spend a happy hour flying two of his model aircraft out in the fields—an activity reminiscent of long-ago afternoons spent on Epsom Downs with the model-plane enthusiast, our Dad. Needless to report, on this occasion both planes nose-dived, in time honoured fashion, and were returned to the barn for further repairs.

I realised, once again, how Helen's love for our once shy, tongue-tied brother had drawn out abilities Rick never dreamed he had. In a thousand practical and ingenious ways she had used her own talents and intelligence to create a beautiful home with surrounding, colourful walled gardens where once had stood a farm-yard and dung-filled cow byre and barns. Together they had worked hard to create an ever-welcoming home and a productive and valuable estate. Richard had become a popular 'mine host' running his own bed-and-breakfast business for fourteen years, and was now finding difficulty in retiring because his guests always sought to return.

The family tableau then scrolled over the Atlantic to Toronto, Canada, where our lovely sister Suzanne had used her Cordon Bleu diploma and artistic culinary flair to build a flourishing catering business, while bringing up her two boys. Her huge heart, ready smile, wicked sense of humour, and great love for people often met their human needs while serving up fine and imaginative meals 'in the elegance of your own home,' as her first business card had promised. Her talents had not only made her many friends, but also given her entry to the top echelons of Toronto's business and arts worlds.

Then the canvas stretched further round the globe to New Zealand, where our beloved fourth sister, Mary Liz, now lived. She had been a vulnerable and sensitive six-year-old when mother left us, and had taken the emotional battering hardest of us all. She had eventually put down roots in New Zealand with her first Kiwi husband, whom she had met while working in London, and their small son. After many twists and turns in her life which included divorce, re-marriage to her second husband Bruce, and the birth of their daughter, she and Bruce had found a rock-like faith. Liz's warmth, sensitivity and compassion for others, born out of a deeply wounded soul, had given her rare insights and understanding which she put to good use with senior citizens, both Pakeha (white) and Maori; then as a teacher, caring for children with special needs in local schools. She is also the much loved step-grandmother of husband Bruce's ever-growing family, as well as grandmother to her own two sons' families, one in New Zealand and the other in northern Spain.

Our youngest bright star of a sister, Penny — only two years old when Mum left us — had gone out to join Mary Liz in New Zealand after the trauma and sorrow of a disappearing husband which up-turned her marriage and left her with four young children to raise and nurture. She, too, put down Antipodean roots, re-found her faith, and combined this inner strength with her gifted intelligence to face major difficulties in her life. As an excellent communicator, she continued from there to stabilise members of her beloved family – Michael now in Spain near his cousin Clive, Nicholas in New Zealand, Cathi in Scotland and Tammy, her eldest, in England, all with families. Much to everyone's delight, she eventually married Dave, Bruce's best friend, whom she had known in New Zealand over the previous twenty years.

We, who had been the focus of countless prayers, were surely a living proof that 'Love conquers all.' Throughout our five varied lives, each of us has benefited from the weaving of the strands of Mercy, Love and Provision mentioned by St Augustine (*d.* 605) who wrote: *Trust the past to the mercy of God; the present to His love; and the future to His providence.* They have been the strong bonding threads which have completed the ever-changing, kaleidoscopic patterns of rich, vivid colours, the shadowy patches of dark and light, which have knitted us closely together as a family in a tableau of people and countries over the years, to form the tapestry that makes up our history. I've mentioned them before, so forgive the repetition of these words of Benjamin Malachi Franklin which are so apt:

Not 'til the loom is silent
  and the shuttles cease to fly,
Shall God unroll the canvas
  and explain the reason why
The dark threads are as needed
  in the Weaver's skilful hand
As the threads of gold and silver
  in the pattern He has planned.

Those threads are the absolute proof of theologian Canon B. H. Streeter's belief, that 'God has a purpose and a plan – not only for the world but for every individual in it and for the smallest details in the life of the individual.'[2]

In this crazy and transient world, and hectic technological age, it is worth holding on to the anchors of past wisdom. One such was expressed by King David some three thousand years ago, in which he proclaimed: 'The Lord is *good*, his *mercy* is everlasting; and his *truth* endureth to *all generations*.' (Ps 100 – italics mine). I believe I can speak honestly for each one of our family when I say with certainty that such goodness, mercy and truth have echoed down the aeons since to us in our generation, in spite of all the damaging or ugly experiences life may have thrown at us.

Finally, should you have reached this far in our story, you may remember how, in chapter 19, I was warned off any further research by the shock of gazing down into that dark abyss of lost souls. Soon afterwards, one sweltering afternoon in Spain, when I habitually hibernated from the blazing outdoors, I opened the Bible at chapter 40 in Isaiah and began reading it aloud. The wise old prophet brought to life the loving, eternal and all-mighty Being of our God in a remarkable way, as he showed how futile were the hand-made idols manufactured for pagan consumers of the time. The climax of his prophecy was particularly inspirational, both then as I read the words, and as they still stand every time I read them now:

Why do you...complain, 'My way is hidden from the Lord; my course is disregarded by my God?' Do you not know? Have you not heard? The Lord is the everlasting God, the Creator of the ends of the earth. He will not grow tired or weary, and his understanding no one can fathom. He gives strength to the weary and increases the power of the weak. Even youths grow tired and weary, and young men stumble and fall; but those who hope in the Lord *will renew their strength. They will* mount up on wings *like eagles; they will run and not grow weary, they will walk and not be faint.*

Deo volente, may we each of us 'walk and not grow faint' while offering up heartfelt gratitude for the abundance of amazing experiences – tough often, but always life-changing – for the opportunities offered and taken, and the wealth of blessings showered down on us by an infinitely loving, Kingly hand. And may our faith, courage and strength be continually renewed, as we 'mount up on wings like eagles' at every challenge, until each of us is finally called home.

THE END

NOTES

NOTES

Chapter 1 Bread-and-dripping Years
1. *High Flight* – poem by John Magee
2. *Escape to Live* – by Wing Commander Edward Howell (Longmans, 1947)

Chapter 2 Challenges Ahead
1. *Overcoming Homosexuality* – by William R. Kimball (Christian Equippers International 1986)
2. Edward Howell, *op. cit.*

Chapter 3 Of Sugar-plums, Cotton-fields, and Home Sweet Home
1. *What's So Amazing About Grace?* – by Philip Yancey (Zondervan) – pp.132, 133

Chapter 5 Hoodwinked!
1. *Flight into Freedom* – by Eileen Caddy (Element Books in association with Findhorn Press, 1988) – p.25

Chapter 6 Hi-jacked!
1. *Flight into Freedom* Eileen Caddy p.26
2. *Ibid.*, p.26

Chapter 7 The Spider's Parlour
1. Eileen Caddy, *op. cit.*, p.26
2. *Ibid.*, p.26
3. *Ibid.*, p.26

Chapter 8 Soul-Snatchers
1. Eileen Caddy, *op. cit.*, p.26

Chapter 9 The Voice, The Choice and a Web of Lies
1. *Around Historic Somerset and Avon* – Colin Wintle (Midas Books 1978)
2. *Somerset* – Ralph Whitlock (Batsford)
3. Eileen Caddy, *op. cit.*, p.28
4. *Ibid.*, p.29
5. *Ibid.*, p.29
6. *Ibid.*, p.31
7. *Ibid.*, p.32
8. *Ibid.*, p.35
9. *Ibid.*, p.36
10. *Ibid.*, pp.38, 39
11. *Ibid.*, p.38

Chapter 10 You'll Be Sorry When I'm Gone
1. *In Perfect Timing: Memoirs of a Man for the New Millennium* – by Peter Caddy (Findhorn Press, 1995)

Chapter 14 We Meet Again
1. Eileen Caddy – *op. cit.*, p.148

Chapter 17 The Dynamic of Forgiveness
1. *The Hiding Place* – by Corrie ten Boom (Hodder & Stoughton, 1976)
2. Philip Yancey – *op. cit.*, pp.96 and 98

Chapter 18 All Change!
1. *The Challenging Counterfeit* – by Raphael Gasson (Logos Books, N.J., 1966)

Chapter 19 A Solitary Journey
1. *Flight into Freedom and Beyond* – by Eileen Caddy (Findhorn Press, 2002) p.36
2. Raphael Gasson, *op. cit.*, p.29
3. *The Beautiful Side of Evil* – by Johanna Michaelsen (Harvest House Publishers, 1982) p.154

Chapter 20 Birth of a False Prophet?
1. *The Magic of Findhorn* – by Paul Hawken (Harper & Row, USA, 1975) p.60
2. Eileen Caddy, *op. cit.*, pp.30 and 31
3. Raphael Gasson, *op. cit.*
4. Eileen Caddy, *op. cit.*, p.36
5. Raphael Gasson, *op. cit.*, p.52
6. Eileen Caddy, *op. cit.*, p.53
7. *Ibid.*, p.53
8. *Flight into Freedom and Beyond* – by Eileen Caddy, p.76
9. *New Age Lies to Women* – (Living Truth Publishers 1989, Austin Texas) p.106
10. *The Revelation of John* Vol. 2 – by William Barclay (The Saint Andrew Press, Edinburgh, 1959) p.146

Chapter 21 A Wolf in Sheep's Clothing
1. Paul Hawken, *op. cit.*
2. *The Gnostics* – by Tobias Churton (Channel 4 Productions, June 1999)
3. Paul Hawken, *op. cit.* p.24
4. *The Kingdom of the Cults* – by W. R. Martin (Bethany Fellowship Inc., Minneapolis, USA, 1977)
5. Paul Hawken, *op. cit.*, p.48
6. *Ibid.*, p.46–47
7. *Ibid.*, p.50
8. *Ibid.*, p.51
9. *Ibid.*, p. 59
10. *Ibid.*, p.51
11. *New Age versus The Gospel* – by David Marshall (Autumn House 1993) p.88
12. *Ibid.*, p.89

Chap. 22 Against Thy Divine Majesty
1. *Hidden Dangers of the Rainbow* – by Constance E. Cumbey (Huntington House Inc., Lafayette, LA, 1983)
2. *Inside the New Age Nightmare* – by Randall N. Baer (Huntington House Inc., Lafayette LA, 1989)
3. Johanna Michaelsen, *op. cit.*
4. Peter Caddy, *op. cit.*, p.113
5. *Encyclopaedia of Occultism and Parapsychology* – (2nd edition, Leslie Shepard, 1986)
6. Peter Caddy, *op. cit.*, p.113
7. *Flight into Freedom and Beyond* – by Eileen Caddy, p.40
8. *Ibid.*, p.40
9. *Ibid.*, p.42
10. Peter Caddy, *op. cit.*, p.119
11. Note: It was only after my parents' divorce in 1956 that Peter and Eileen were married in a registry office in Glasgow, Scotland. This was for legal reasons as they were about to apply for jobs as a couple in the hotel industry.

Chapter 23 A Bucketful of Frogs
1. Constance E. Cumbey, *op. cit.*
2. David Marshall, *op.cit.*
3. *The View over Atlantis* – by John Michell (Thames and Hudson, 1983)

Chapter 24 Fresh Insights
1. *Harry Potter and the Bible – The Menace behind the Magick* – by Richard Abanes (Horizon Books 2001)
2. Peter Caddy, *op. cit.*, p.30
3. Note: Jim Jones, founder of the People's Temple, was the worst of these when he led 909 US citizens in a mass suicide from cyanide poisoning in Jonestown, Guyana, in November 1978.
4. *People of the Lie – The Hope for Healing Human Evil* – by M. Scott Peck (Arrow Books Ltd, London, 1990)

Chapter 26 Celebration!
1. Note: 'Putting down a hangi' (pronounced hungi) – traditional method of cooking in the Umu (earth oven) of the Maori people of Aotearoa (NZ) by their ancestors until the present day.

Chapter 27 Further Steps along the Path
1. *The Grandmother* from *Enoch Arden* by Alfred, Lord Tennyson (Edward Moxon & Co., 1864) p.118

Chapter 28 A Long Summer of Bitter-sweet Content
1. *My Utmost for His Highest* – by Oswald Chambers (Dodd, Mead & Co., New York)

Chapter 30 Desert Flowers
1. *A Grief Observed* — by C.S.Lewis (Faber & Faber) © CS Lewis Pte Ltd 1961
2. *The God Who Speaks* — by B.H.Streeter (Macmillan)